D0709408

ANDRZEJ BRZESKI

STRUCTURAL CHANGE AND
ECONOMIC POLICY IN ISRAEL

A Publication of the Economic Growth Center, Yale University

STRUCTURAL CHANGE AND

ECONOMIC POLICY IN ISRAEL

BY HOWARD PACK

New Haven and London, Yale University Press, 1971

Copyright © 1971 by Yale University.
All rights reserved. This book may not be reproduced, in whole or in part, in any form (except by reviewers for the public press), without written permission from the publishers.
Library of Congress catalog card number: 75–140536
International standard book number: 0–300–01415–5
Set in Times Roman type,
and printed in the United States of America by
The Colonial Press Inc., Clinton, Mass.
Distributed in Great Britain, Europe, and Africa by Yale University Press, Ltd., London; in Canada by McGill-Queen's University Press, Montreal; in Mexico by Centro Interamericano de Libros Académicos, Mexico City; in Central and South America by Kaiman & Polon, Inc., New York City; in Australasia by Australia and New Zealand Book Co., Pty., Ltd., Artarmon, New South Wales; in India by UBS Publishers' Distributors Pvt., Ltd., Delhi; in Japan by John Weatherhill, Inc., Tokyo.

For Robert Szereszewski
1936–1967

Contents

Foreword

This volume is one in a series of studies supported by the Economic Growth Center, an activity of the Yale Department of Economics since 1961. The Center is a research organization with worldwide activities and interests. Its research interests are defined in terms of both method of approach and subject matter. In terms of method, the Center sponsors studies which are designed to test significant general hypotheses concerning the problem of economic growth and which draw on quantitative information from national economic accounts and other sources. In terms of subject matter, the Center's research interests include theoretical analysis of economic structure and growth, quantitative analysis of a national economy as an integral whole, comparative cross-sectional studies using data from a number of countries, and efforts to improve the techniques of national economic measurement. The research program includes field investigation of recent economic growth in twenty-five developing countries of Asia, Africa, and Latin America.

The Center administers, jointly with the Department of Economics, the Yale training program in International and Foreign Economic Administration. It presents a regular series of seminar and workshop meetings and includes among its publications both book-length studies and journal reprints by staff members, the latter circulated as Center Papers.

Gustav Ranis, Director

Preface

This is one of a series of country studies undertaken at the Economic Growth Center at Yale. Their aim is to describe and analyze the growth process in a number of underdeveloped countries. The nature of each study has been substantially conditioned by the extent and quality of earlier work on the country, and this book is no exception. Because of the existence of a considerable amount of high-quality work on Israel, I have been able to concentrate on two interrelated features of Israel's growth which were of particular interest to me, namely, changes in the sectoral and intrasectoral structure of the economy and the degree to which these were influenced by government policies. To obtain a complete account of Israel's development several other studies should be consulted. In particular, Don Patinkin, *The Israel Economy, The First Decade,* and Nadav Halevi and Ruth Klinov-Malul, *The Economic Development of Israel* both provide a considerable amount of data and analysis which have been excluded from the present study. Inevitably, some duplication has occurred, e.g. in some parts of the analysis of macroeconomic policy, but this is necessary to present a complete development of the themes pursued in this volume. Two books of A. L. Gaathon on productivity growth in Israel, *Capital Stock, Employment and Output in Israel, 1950–59* and his forthcoming *Economic Productivity in Israel, 1950–65* explore in much greater detail a number of the topics presented in Chapter 2 of the present volume, though inevitably with somewhat differing emphases. Dr. Gaathon has been extremely kind in providing the data which underlie most of my own productivity calculations. Were it not for his recent work on capital stock estimation and his earlier development of input-output tables for 1936 and 1951, most economic research on Israel, this work included, would exhibit a considerably different complexion.

The present study covers the years from 1950 through 1967. I have intentionally cut off the analysis at the end of 1967 because of the major changes wrought by the Six Day War, including a higher level of army reserve activity, an acceleration of the development of some industries producing primarily military goods, balance of payments problems generated mainly by military hardware purchases—all of which make for a major structural break. These of course were characteristics of the economy throughout the period considered, but they were of a steady type which allowed account to be taken of them by the various economic actors: the sheer size and duration of the changes since June 1967 have dwarfed all earlier magnitudes. Even during the 1956 Suez crisis, most of the effects had been dissipated within six months. However, I think that much of the analysis which is provided—for example, about the effects of limited market size and the sources of the balance of payments problems—is still relevant, although the relative importance of these factors in determining overall patterns has diminished as the importance of national defense has increased.

In writing this study I have incurred numerous debts. During a year's leave in Israel I benefited substantially from contact with the members of the staff of the Falk Institute for Economic Research in Israel. Don Patinkin, its director, was particularly helpful in a number of ways. Suzanne Freund of the Falk staff provided a helpful, quick introduction to Israeli statistical sources. Joseph Baruh and Mordecai Fraenkel of the Bank of Israel and Maurice Meir of the Central Bureau of Statistics furnished crucial data at a number of points.

Extensive, very useful comments on an earlier version of the manuscript were provided by Michael Bruno, Simon Kuznets, Richard Nelson, Hugh Patrick, and Gustav Ranis. I have had numerous helpful conversations with Charles Frank and Stephen Resnick. Susan Eggers provided resourceful research assistance throughout the duration of the study. Extended discussions with my wife Janet and her criticism of various drafts have had more than a marginal impact on the final version. While I absolve all of the aforementioned from any responsibility for errors of fact or interpretation in the final product, I am not quite sure this dispensation should extend to her.

This book is dedicated to Robert Szereszewski who was killed during the first hours of the Six Day War. Before his death he was engaged in a study of economic development in pre-1948 Palestine that would undoubtedly have yielded major insight into an important area of knowledge since much of the groundwork for Israel's future development was provided in the prestatehood period. The intense sense of loss his death evoked in his friends is unmistakable: part is attributable to the incongruity between his youth and high spirits and his sudden death; part, to those who knew his biography, to the loss of a friend whose very being constituted a denial of the meaner forces of life and strengthened their own optimism.

H.P.

Philadelphia
October 1970

1

Some Preliminary Observations

In the last two decades the attention of economists has gradually shifted from questions concerning the causes and control of fluctuations in aggregate demand to explanation of the success or failure of productive capacity to grow. In the developed countries the earlier concern with Keynesian problems has been supplanted by theoretical analyses of the growth mechanism and quantitative investigations of its actual sources. Most of these inquiries have been conducted within a neoclassical framework: full employment of resources,[1] profit- and utility-maximizing behavior, and pure competition are assumed; prices thus reflect social costs. Such models have provided a considerable amount of insight into the growth process of advanced nations. However, relatively few countries have experienced sustained growth in per capita income, and what might be called a "nongrowth" literature has consequently arisen to explain this failure. The economic and institutional characteristics that account for growth in advanced economies are found to be absent in the underdeveloped: saving is too low, hence capital accumulation is slow; the labor force lacks skills alleged to be a prerequisite to the adoption of a productive technology; technical change in agriculture is absent or scarce, preventing a restructuring of the labor force toward more productive industrial uses; the large-scale intrusion of government into the market, as well as existing institutional arrangements, result in prices that are poor indicators of social priorities.

Although a substantial theoretical literature exists on these and other development questions, there has not been a commensurate increase in empirical studies evaluating the validity and usefulness of these insights. Of the many countries of the less developed world, Israel provides an unusually good candidate for such a study. While

1. As a result of factor price flexibility and smooth production isoquants.

1

it has grown rapidly, it faces the same "non-neoclassical" problems as other small, open, underdeveloped economies—from the difficulties of realizing economies of scale to the distortions attributable to planned, large-scale import substitution programs. In addition, extensive government management of the economy provides a number of examples of the difficulties and limits that even a relatively skilled administration may encounter in attempts to accelerate development.

Nevertheless, it is sometimes suggested that Israel is not a proper object of study as a development model, since its current per capita income and its rate of growth, educational levels, and consumption patterns are those of an advanced country and since it has been the recipient of unusually large inflows of both labor and capital. These reservations seem to us to be only partially warranted. First, although per capita income, rate of growth, and other indicators of development are currently similar to those of developed countries,[2] this was not true at the beginning of the period studied: per capita income, for example, was then about I£360, which at a reasonable approximation to an equilibrium exchange rate, I£1.2 per dollar, would be $300. Thus, along with Japan and perhaps one or two other nations such as Taiwan, Israel is one of the few countries outside of Europe and the English-speaking countries of North America and Oceania to have developed successfully. It thus provides one of the few tests of many hypotheses about the growth process which have been derived from cross-section rather than time-series data. Moreover, the compression and rapidity of growth permit a detailed analysis of structural changes which in more slowly growing countries would be possible only over many decades.

Second, although it is tempting to attribute the sustained growth to heavy foreign capital inflows and a skilled labor force, this in itself is interesting, for if these constitute both the necessary and sufficient conditions for rapid development, the problems of economic policy makers are significantly reduced. Inflation, distorted price structures, the inability to exploit economies of scale, poor land quality, and the myriad other obstacles to development that an economy faces would be unimportant relative to the two prime

2. Although, to be sure, of the poorer ones.

factors of capital and labor; these obstacles might condition the structure of the growth but only impose marginally important quantitative limits on the overall rate of growth rather than preclude any development at all. If this were the case, however, it would be difficult to explain the relatively low income levels and growth rates of a number of Latin American countries, most notably Argentina, which have exhibited both high investment ratios and a skilled labor force.[3]

The growth of specific productive factors may thus be viewed as a necessary condition for aggregate growth. Unfortunately, the sufficient conditions are often difficult to identify and usually intractable to economic analysis; yet it is precisely these conditions that are often of greatest interest. While much of this study is devoted to analyzing the sources of growth and the constraints imposed by the obstacles mentioned above, inevitably the impact of the factors that may make Israel a special case—the capital inflows and the high educational level—are touched upon. Ideally, I would have wanted to present an analysis of how the development obstacles were confronted in a manner different from any that would have been possible without the availability of special factors. This hypothetical type of reasoning is very difficult to carry far.[4] For the next six chapters, then, special factors will be in the background, referred to where appropriate, but not considered systematically. Recognizing, however, that these factors must be considered, in the last chapter of the book I attempt a more systematic examination of their impact and attempt to attribute the sufficient conditions of growth to features of the nation other than the familiar ones of education and capital inflow.

NONECONOMIC FACTORS

The scope of this book is the economic growth of Israel since 1948.

3. More generally, a number of countries, particularly those producing oil for the world market, have a virtually costless (to themselves) source of foreign exchange, whose effect may be compared to that of foreign aid in its potential for augmenting capital. Moreover, these funds may also provide for the importation of skilled foreigners, who may, for a time, substitute for a skilled domestic labor force.

4. For a discussion of the problems involved in evaluating the impact of the high level of education, see Chap. 2.

It does not consider the political, military, or social framework,[5] unless these are relevant to the economic issues under discussion. This neglect may introduce a systematic understatement of both the problems and the achievements of the country, especially since it is difficult to analyze and quantify these effects. For example, the inability to trade with most countries in the immediate area and the need to obtain imports from fairly distant sources raised import costs of a number of important raw and semifabricated materials to a level much higher than they normally would have been. Import substitution was then encouraged in branches in which a country the size of Israel should not have been involved. Exports, on the other hand, had to be producible at lower prices than would have been true had transport costs to buyers been lower. Although the resultant cost structure was not the only factor in making the domestic market more attractive than foreign markets, it certainly was a contributing one. As a result, the range of domestic production was much too large given the size of the country and the importance of economies of scale in many branches. Undoubtedly, some of this diversification was attributable to a concern about self-sufficiency in case of war or a deterioration of the political situation, both of which could interrupt the flow of trade. Moreover, as in many other less developed countries, there was also some desire for greater autarky per se, which would have resulted in import substitution, though to a lesser extent, even had these other factors not been present.

However one accounts for the considerable diversification in domestic production, the pursuance of this "balanced growth" path and the concomitant difficulty in realizing either scale economies or the benefits of specialization undoubtedly reduced the income level that might otherwise have been realized from the available primary factors.

Many other areas can be cited in which the political-military situation had important feedback effects on economic development. Among the most significant was the absorption by the armed forces

5. Of the many books available on these topics, two of the best are S. N. Eisenstadt, *Israeli Society* (New York: Basic Books, 1968), and Nadav Safran, *The United States and Israel* (Cambridge, Mass.: Harvard University Press, 1963). An incisive, more popular study is Terence Prittie, *Israel: Miracle in the Desert* (New York: Praeger, 1967).

of a large number of men with considerable organizational and leadership ability, while the private industrial sector often exhibited a rather obvious shortage of men possessing these qualities. From another viewpoint, many agricultural settlements that had poor prospects for economic viability were nevertheless begun for security reasons.

These noneconomic factors must be remembered in some of the following chapters, especially those on productivity and the development of individual productive sectors. While I shall attempt to point them out where relevant, it is probable that their relevance has occasionally slipped by me.

BACKGROUND

The analysis will begin with 1950, a year and a half after the founding of the country in May 1948. Considerable economic development had occurred before 1948, and a fairly competent administrative structure existed. The British, who since 1918 had ruled Palestine under a mandate from the League of Nations, had permitted both the Jewish and non-Jewish populations substantial autonomy; the institutions developed by the Jewish sector, particularly the Jewish Agency and the Histadrut,[6] had provided for its officers substantial experience in the governing of a modern state. Thus, when Israel achieved independence, it did not experience the trauma over the absence of leadership that has often occurred in colonies in which the indigenous population was granted very limited autonomy.[7]

The sectoral structure of the economy before 1947 had been dualistic; the Jewish sector[8] accounting for most of industry and

6. The Jewish Agency was responsible for immigration and other external relations of the Jewish community in Palestine. The Histadrut is the only trade union in the country. Not only does most of the labor force belong to it, but many also are employed by it in Histadrut enterprises. A careful analysis of the economic role of the Histadrut is presented by Haim Barkai in "The Public, Histadrut and Private Sectors in the Israeli Economy," in the Falk Project, *Sixth Report, 1961–63* (Jerusalem: Falk Project, 1964).

7. For the institutional background, see Eisenstadt, *Israeli Society,* chaps. 1–5, 9.

8. The Jewish sector refers to the part of the economy owned by and mainly employing Jews.

6 Structural Change and Economic Policy in Israel

modern services, the Arab sector being mainly agricultural.[9] In 1947 slightly over one-quarter of the Jewish labor force was engaged in industry and another 60 percent was in construction and services. Thus only about 13 percent of the labor force was employed in agriculture, compared to perhaps 60 percent in the Arab sector.[10] Since the non-Jewish labor force was about twice the size of the Jewish one, the entire economy was mainly agricultural and economy-wide per capita income levels were fairly low, although substantial differences existed between the two sectors. Between 1939 and 1945 sustained growth in per capita income had occurred in response to rapidly increasing demand, attributable to the requirements of the British armed forces and to the protection afforded by the cutoff of European supplies.[11] Much of this increase was concentrated in manufacturing, although noncitrus agricultural output in the Jewish sector grew at a rapid rate. The experiences in industrial production gained during this period were undoubtedly of great value in helping the economy to meet the augmented output requirements of the post-independence mass immigration. Moreover, much of the productive capacity built during the war was not fully utilized after 1945 and thus provided an important immediate source of increased output when immigration began in 1948.

Thus on the eve of independence the economy of Palestine, although exhibiting a fairly low per capita income, had two features that increased its adaptability and provided a basis for further growth, namely, a substantial industrial sector that had recently undergone considerable growth and an experienced group of administrators. On the other hand, with the exodus of a substantial percentage of Palestinian Arabs during the 1948 war and the unwillingness of the surrounding countries to engage in trade, the

9. For a survey of the pre-1948 economy see Nadav Halevi and Ruth Klinov-Malul, *The Economic Development of Israel* (New York: Praeger, 1968), chap. 2. Detailed estimates of national product for 1922–47, along with a clear explanation of the procedures employed, may be found in Robert Szereszewski, *Essays on the Structure of the Jewish Economy in Palestine and Israel* (Jerusalem: Falk Institute, 1968).

10. Halevi and Klinov-Malul, *Economic Development of Israel*, pp. 23–26.

11. Ephraim Kleiman, "The Structure of Israel Manufacturing Industries 1952–62," mimeographed (Jerusalem: Falk Propect, 1964).

problem of insuring sufficient food supplies assumed immediate importance.

The transition to independence was far from tranquil; a sustained war, which had begun in the late part of 1947, was in progress and simultaneously an enormous immigration began. After the conclusion of the war in the early months of 1949, the rehabilitation of damaged physical assets, as well as the absorption of immigrants, were the main economic motifs. Although the productive facilities inherited from the mandatory period provided a base for further growth, the doubling of the population (and the labor force) by mid-1952, a rapid rise in the capital stock, and a drastic reallocation of these new resources toward agriculture, all tended to dwarf the importance of the received economic structure. It was not until 1952 or 1953, when a decline in immigration occurred, that the economy began to function normally.

The productive absorption of the 700,000 immigrants who entered the new nation between 1948 and 1951, as well as those (much fewer in number) coming in later years, was to be a dominant concern of the nation. The difficulties in such absorption are suggested by the following.

Israel suffered from another major economic disadvantage. In the first three and a half years of her existence, roughly 700,000 immigrants flooded in from all over the world, speaking no common language and usually no Hebrew. Of the non-Europeans, few could be regarded initially as assets to the economy. A great proportion had spent their working lives in small business enterprises, enjoying a relatively low standard of living. Many were illiterate. The Europeans (half of the total number of immigrants) suffered from different disabilities. Many of them had spent years in German concentration camps, followed by frustrating months or even years in the Allied camps for displaced persons, and were only now emerging from the shadow of desperate fear, shocking ill treatment, and near starvation. The health of many of them had been ruined; a large number suffered from tuberculosis. It was perhaps easier for them than for the others to adjust to the new way of life in Israel, but it was just as hard at the outset to put them to productive work; psychologically, they were worse off, for the worst scars of persecution and suffering were mental and spiritual. All of the immigrants alike arrived destitute. To clothe them, feed them, and house them was an initial burden on the state.[12]

Clearly the problems encountered in successful absorption would transcend the purely economic; in a number of instances economic considerations were subordinated to the broader ones of social policy.

Some aspects of the immigrants' background relevant for their economic absorption have been examined extensively by Moshe Sicron, who found that their occupational structure "did not conform with Israel's economic structure and development needs. Abroad, immigrants were concentrated in the crafts and industry, particularly handicrafts, and in commerce, and in some instances also in clerical occupations. An insignificant number of immigrants received agricultural training before immigrating; and there was a lack of agricultural workers. Members of the liberal and technical professions were also in short supply. Thus a basic and farreaching change in the occupations of many of these immigrants was unavoidable. [In June 1954] between 50 and 70 percent of the new immigrants were working in different occupations from those they had held abroad (and the proportion would have been higher yet if specific groups within occupational categories had been taken into account)." [13]

Not only was the occupational structure of new immigrants "wrong," but their adaptability to a relatively modern society as measured by literacy rates was low for those from North Africa and the Middle East. Thus only 75 percent of males over fourteen years of age and 47 percent of females from these areas could both read and write in 1957.[14] The problem is well stated by Leonard Fein: "The Jews of Africa and Asia were not simply transplanted from Warsaw or Kiev, accidentally resident in Bagh-

---

12. Prittie, *Israel: Miracle in the Desert,* p. 41.

13. Moshe Sicron, *Immigration to Israel: 1948–1953* (Jerusalem: Falk Project, 1957), cited in Don Patinkin, *The Israel Economy, The First Decade* (Jerusalem: Falk Project, 1960). Also issued by CBS as Special Series Publication no. 60.

14. Patinkin, *Israel Economy: The First Decade,* Table 5. Moreover, it should be noted that these figures include those persons who had learned the skills after coming to the country.

dad or Tunis . . . they were of these places. Just as the European Jew had brought with him the culture of his birthplace . . . so also did the Easterner." [15]

The absorption problem was thus not only quantitative but also qualitative. The dimensions of the problem are suggested in Table 1.1, where we see that between 1948 and 1951 the proportion of

Table 1.1: Jewish Population by Continent of Birth, 1948–67

	1948	1951	1954	1957	1960	1964	1967
Israel	35.4	25.5	31.4	33.9	37.4	39.4	42.8
Asia	8.1	20.6	19.0	16.6	15.7	13.8	13.0
Africa	1.7	7.0	7.9	12.4	11.9	14.9	14.5
Europe-America	54.8	46.9	41.7	37.1	35.0	31.9	29.7

Source: Statistical Abstract of Israel, 1968, p. 42.

the population born in Asia or Africa increased from 9.8 to 27.6 percent. Since then the percentage of the population born in Asia and Africa has remained roughly at this level. In addition, over 10 percent of the total population has been composed of Arabs exhibiting, for the most part, a traditional rural background and outlook. Thus about 40 percent of the total population has been composed of groups whose attitudes and background are often not likely to make for easy adaptability to the dictates of a modern economy. It must be emphasized that this is a general characterization of the groups in question; there were many individuals among Asian and African Jews and the resident Arab population who were thoroughly modernized. Moreover, the absence of modernity among the larger group must not be taken in a pejorative sense. It is simply a datum that conditions the economic possibilities of the society.

In summary, the recent trauma through which many of the European immigrants had passed, combined with the lack of relevant skills and, perhaps, adaptability of a large percentage of immigrants, were important features of the initial economic landscape. In most of this study aggregates such as the labor force and employment constitute the variables analyzed. The use of aggregates always suppresses much of the underlying richness of

15. Leonard J. Fein, *Israel: Politics and People,* rev. ed. (Boston: Little Brown, 1968), p. 52.

economic processes for the sake of analytic manageability. The loss in information is particularly important when we ignore the characteristics of the Israeli labor force just discussed: this undoubtedly results in a picture that greatly understates the development achievement in Israel. However, to consider fully the impact of these factors would require another monograph. Nevertheless, it is well to remember that an explicit systematic analysis of the neglected factors would make the successful development performance even more impressive.

OBJECTIVES OF ECONOMIC POLICY

A substantial part of this book attempts to describe and assess the government's policies in overcoming the above problems. Official guidance of the economy was so pervasive that it provides the unifying theme of the development process; an understanding of the government's role helps to explain both the direction of the economy's evolution and many of its structural characteristics. The dimensions of government influence will be indicated in later chapters. Here we briefly consider the reasons for the assumption of this major role.[16]

The doubling of the population between 1948 and 1952 from 700,000 to 1,400,000 and the need to integrate the new members into the society, while providing for their basic needs, inevitably required government intervention in numerous spheres; the sheer size of the programs and the implied coordination of needs simply could not have been provided by the private sector. The provision of housing, food, and employment became immediate concerns of the government. Simultaneously, the inflow of foreign funds, which were used in these years mainly to provide for such needs, was largely channeled through the government; this remained the pattern in later years after immigration had declined.

The key role of the government in immigration and its financing continued the pattern established in the prestate period under the British mandate. The British policy was laissez faire, and the institutions set up by the Jewish sector in Palestine spent large sums on social services not provided by the mandatory government, as

16. Cf. Safran, *United States and Israel,* pp. 168–70.

well as on land purchase and agricultural settlement.[17] This policy was viewed as a means toward increasing the absorptive capacity for further immigration and improving the living standards of the population already resident. As there was considerable overlap between the leaders of these mandatory institutions and the post-statehood government, the similarity in problems was likely to evoke a similar response.

Apart from the immediate problem of immigrant absorption, the magnitude and urgency of which had decreased by 1954 or 1955, government intervention was to be expected on other grounds. The relative paucity of natural resources[18] and the con-comitant absence of any obvious direction in which industrialization might proceed, combined with a skepticism of the ability of a free market to provide adequate signals for the allocation of resources, would suggest to many administrators that public authorities assume a catalytic role in identifying potential economic projects and fostering their development once they are undertaken.[19]

A final basis for government intervention may be found in the need to coordinate military with economic needs in face of continuing hostility from nearby countries. Although it is difficult to evaluate the quantitative significance of the military's impingement on economic decisions, it is nevertheless clear that some decisions were strongly influenced by military requirements.

Given the many needs of the country, into what policy objectives were these crystallized? From repeated pronouncements of government officials and directives to planning staffs,[20] three major goals are identifiable: the provision of adequate employment, a reduction in the import surplus, and the redistribution of the population away from the central coastal plain toward the less densely settled areas in the north (the Galilee) and south (the Negev). These objectives have always been the stated aims of

---

17. Halevi and Klinov-Malul, *Economic Development of Israel,* p. 38. Chapter 2 of this book provides a detailed discussion of economic policy in the mandatory period.

18. Among the few significant resources are suitable soil for growth of citrus products and deposits of minerals in the Dead Sea.

19. This does not imply that the government undertook ownership; usually it did not.

20. Admittedly, early plans were not taken very seriously in terms of implementation; rather they indicated desirable goals.

economic policy, although, as shall be seen throughout this study, the actual policies may often have emphasized only one of the objectives at any given time.

These objectives represent "stylized" goals, because an important aim (implicitly) was the increase of both national product and productivity. If it is assumed, however, that the authorities felt that, at some reasonably close future point in time, the unavailability of foreign exchange, and hence of raw and fabricated materials not produced domestically, would act as a constraint on the growth of net product, then the output target may be subsumed under the balance of payments goal. Indeed, in the early 1950s the imminent shortage of foreign exchange was of great concern to policy makers.[21] Even after the early 1950s, however, it does appear that most investment influenced by government was undertaken on the assumption (often proved incorrect) that it would have a positive effect on the balance of payments.

Another reason for considering the above-named objectives as stylized is the presence of important subgoals that may have conditioned the extent to which policy makers were willing to move toward complete realization of their primary aims. Thus an important component in Zionist ideology, one with which most of the country's leaders were in complete sympathy, was the need to establish a normal economic structure, in contrast to the one in the Diaspora which was heavily weighted toward the urban service sector. In particular there was an intensive desire to establish a substantial agricultural sector; the achievement of this goal may, to some extent, have conflicted with others, for example, reducing the import surplus in an efficient manner. Similarly, retention of the inherited institutional structure was undoubtedly another, if more flexible, objective that may have made the attainment of other goals more difficult. For example, the refusal of the government to alter the unwillingness of Kibbutzim (collective farms) to employ hired labor led to undesirably high capital intensity and a resulting

21. After 1954, and until 1963 or 1964, the possibility that a shortage of foreign exchange would limit output growth was much lower than in the previous period. However, the possible decline of one or another type of unilateral transfer suggested continual diligence in trying to reduce the trade deficit. For a detailed chronological survey of different periods in Israel's development, see Halevi and Klinov-Malul, *Economic Development of Israel*, chap. 1.

decrease in employment opportunities within this subsector of agriculture. Yet, in view of the social contribution of the Kibbutzim, it is impossible to weigh easily the employment loss against the noneconomic contribution of this social group. In the following chapters we shall try to indicate such noneconomic subgoals, where relevant, in evaluating government policy within the more narrow economic focus of the three major goals.

We now turn to a discussion of each of the major policy objectives.

Employment

Between 1948 and 1966 the population of Israel tripled and the increase in the labor force was of a similar order, a compound rate of growth of 8.1 percent per annum. The difficulty of generating a sufficient number of jobs to absorb all of the new labor force members was similar to that in the urban sector of many underdeveloped countries, in which both the high rate of natural increase and the substantial rural-urban migration increase the urban labor force at a rapid rate, perhaps 5 to 6 percent per year.[22] As a result of the mass immigration between 1948 and 1950 and the resulting dislocation, the unemployment rate reached 11.2 by 1950, with perhaps an additional 5 percent of the labor force employed part time and seeking more work.[23] High rates of open unemployment (rates over 7 percent) existed until 1958 (Table 1.2). In addition, disguised unemployment appears to have characterized the service sector during the years prior to 1955.[24] Between 1958 and

22. Richard Nelson has pointed out, in another context, that the growth of the labor force relative to the existing capital stock may raise the latter's marginal productivity, thus inducing further investment, which will then lead to additional employment. These conclusions depend upon assumptions about substitution possibilities in the production function, as well as factor market competition. As the latter assumption was widely violated in Israel, we do not follow Nelson's lead, although it is of considerable interest. See Richard Nelson, "Full Employment Policy and Economic Growth," *American Economic Review* 56 (Dec. 1966): 1178–1192.

23. This estimate is based on the actual underemployment rates for 1956 obtained from the Labour Force Surveys, underemployment in 1956 being 3.6 percent. We assume that it would have been at least one-third higher in 1950, and even this is probably an underestimate. See Central Bureau of Statistics, *Labour Force Surveys* (June 1956), Table 31.

24. See Gur Ofer, *The Service Industries in a Developing Economy: Israel as a Case Study* (New York: Praeger, 1967), p. 137.

Table 1.2: Unemployment as a Percentage of the Labor Force, 1949–67

Year	A	B
1949	9.5	13.9
1950	6.9	11.2
1951	6.1	8.1
1952	7.2	8.8
1953	11.3	11.5
1954	8.9	9.2
1955	7.4	
1956	7.8	
1957	6.9	
1958	5.7	
1959	5.5	
1960	4.6	
1961	3.6	
1962	3.7	
1963	3.6	
1964	3.3	
1965	3.6	
1966	7.4	
1967	10.4	

Note: Column A gives unemployment figures for those outside temporary immigrants, camps, as the residents of these were not allowed to actively seek work. Column B includes the potential labor force resident in immigrant camps.

Sources: 1949–65: Nadav Halevi and Ruth Klinov-Malul, *The Economic Development of Israel* (New York: Praeger, 1968), Table 14.
1965–67: *Statistical Abstract of Israel*, 1968, p. 248.

1961 unemployment rates declined to less than 4 percent and remained at this level through 1965. A recession in 1966–67 again moved unemployment rates toward the 10 percent level.

The task facing policy makers was to absorb the unemployed and to provide for the anticipated growth in the labor force. The rate of job creation depended to a large extent on government decisions; with the overall rate of capital accumulation determined jointly by foreign capital inflows and fiscal policy, the employment-generating effect depended upon the sectoral allocation of investment (whether to branches of high or low capital intensity) and upon relative factor prices, both of which were decisively affected by government policy.

Balance of payments

From its beginning, Israel's balance of payments on current account has been unfavorable, the import surplus (exclusive of tariffs and subsidies) totaling over 20 percent of gross national product (in current prices) during the early years of statehood until 1956, declining steadily from 1956 until 1960, and then rising between 1960 and 1964.[25] See Table 1.3. Each year a

25. During the serious recession of 1966–67 there was a sharp decline in the importance of the import surplus, but this seems not to reflect any basic changes in the economy's structure. See the discussion in Chap. 7. The data on the import surplus in Table 1.3 in current prices provide two measures, one inclusive and one exclusive of taxes on imports and subsidies on exports. The latter measure is useful as the import surplus is not changed by alterations in the tariff-subsidy structure. However, insofar as tariffs and subsidies are substitutes for devaluation, the import surplus inclusive of these provides one measure of the real value of the resources made available to the economy.

Table 1.3: Import Surplus as a Percentage of GNP, 1950–67
(current prices)

Year			Year		
1950	22.9[a]	25.8[b]	1959	13.4[a]	18.4[b]
1951	18.6	21.4	1960	12.9	17.1
1952	23.8	27.2	1961	13.8	18.5
1953	22.2	26.6	1962	20.2	26.2
1954	19.4	23.8	1963	17.2	22.0
1955	23.0	28.6	1964	18.8	23.8
1956	24.8	30.6	1965	14.2	19.0
1957	19.7	26.4	1966	10.6	14.7
1958	16.9	21.3	1967	9.7	12.7

(1955 prices)

Year		Year	
1950	58.2[b]	1959	21.8[b]
1951	46.0	1960	21.7
1952	35.5	1961	26.5
1953	35.2	1962	27.1
1954	30.2	1963	23.7
1955	27.7	1964	26.0
1956	29.7	1965	22.6
1957	25.1	1966	19.6
1958	26.3	1967	18.2

[a] Excludes subsidies on exports and taxes on imports.
[b] Includes subsidies on exports and taxes on imports.

Source: *Israel's National Income and Expenditure* (Jerusalem, CBS, 1963), p. 48. *Statistical Abstract of Israel, 1968*, pp. 138–41.

significant portion of the current account deficit has been covered by unilateral transfers; thus by itself the deficit in no sense mortgaged the future. It has been recognized, however, that with the diminution of these inflows over time, continued development of the country requires the progressive elimination of the deficit; otherwise, given the severe resource constraints and the resulting need to import substantial amounts of raw and semifinished materials, foreign exchange shortages will eventually limit the rate of growth. In response to the deficit, government policy emphasized the importance of establishing firms whose products would provide potential exports or substitutes for current imports. However, there was only a limited attempt to use the macroeconomic instruments of policy to foster an improvement in the trade balance. A substantial portion of the following chapters provides a detailed account of the efforts to reduce the trade deficit and its impact upon the economy.

Population dispersal

When independence was achieved in 1948, almost the entire population of Israel was located in the northern part of the country, particularly concentrated around Tel Aviv and Haifa. The southern area, the Negev, contained two-thirds of the total land area but only .9 percent of total population.[26] A program of dispersal was thus begun to settle new immigrants in the southern region, as well as in underpopulated districts in the Jerusalem hills and the Galilee. So-called development towns were established in these areas and received priority in housing construction and social overhead facilities. Immigrants were assigned to these towns upon arrival in the country and could not move to other areas until a specified number of years after their arrival. By the end of 1954, 4.1 percent of a vastly increased population resided in the Negev; by the end of 1957 [27] the figure had risen to 6.9 percent. Further, these percentages do not include residents in development areas in other parts of the country.

   On purely economic grounds the dispersal program may not have been justified. The cost of augmenting the existing social overhead facilities in the major population centers would almost

26. *Statistical Abstract of Israel, 1965,* p. 27.
27. *Statistical Abstract of Israel, 1961,* p. 32.

ANDRZEJ BRZESKI

certainly have been lower than erecting a completely new capacity in the outlying areas. Similarly, locating new factories and farms away from the majority of plants and population, and far from the port of Haifa, led to increased transportation costs for both inputs and outputs. These negative aspects of the development policy were known beforehand, but they were ignored on social, political, and military grounds.

Although we have listed dispersal along with employment generation and balance of payments improvement as the major economic goals, it is unlikely that it was viewed as being of equal importance with the two latter objectives. Indeed, much of the available evidence indicates, as we shall see, that dispersal was subordinated to other objectives if conflicts arose. From 1958 or so onward, however, more equal dispersal of both population and economic activity became an increasingly important desideratum in economic decisions.[28]

28. See Chap. 6 for further details.

2

Factor Inputs, Output Growth, and Productivity

Gross national product grew quite rapidly between 1950 and 1965, at an annual rate (compounded) of almost 11 percent. Since we intend to consider productivity in this chapter, we omit the post-1965 years from our analysis because this was a period of considerable Keynesian unemployment of both labor and capital. This growth was made possible by the enormous increase in the quantity of primary inputs, especially labor and capital, as well as by a factor, which for lack of a better name, will be called *technical change*. The sources of the growth of capital will be discussed in Chapter 7, in the context of macroeconomic policies, and will thus be viewed as a datum in this chapter, which focuses on growth of the labor supply and technical change.

GROWTH OF THE LABOR SUPPLY

Between 1950 and 1965 the civilian labor force grew from about 450,000 to 912,000, this growth being the product of a large increase in population and an almost constant labor force participation rate.[1] (Table 2.1) Population is to a large extent exogenous to the economic system (although it may exhibit some response to changes in income levels and other economic variables).[2] Similarly, the participation rate is mainly explained by noneconomic demographic and social variables such as the distribution of the popu-

1. Defined by the Central Bureau of Statistics as the ratio of labor force members to the potential employable population, which is taken to equal the population fourteen years of age and older.
2. An extensive description and analysis of population growth is presented in Halevi and Klinov-Malul, *Economic Development of Israel*, chap. 4.

18

Table 2.1: The Civilian Labor Force, 1949–67
(thousands)

		Compound rates of growth	
1949	343	1949–53	15.0
1950	450	1954–58	3.5
1951	545	1958–65	3.9
1952	584	1954–67	3.3
1953	599		
1954	608		
1955	619		
1956	646		
1957	690		
1958	698		
1959	714		
1960	736		
1961	774		
1962	818		
1963	840		
1964	884		
1965	912		
1966	943		
1967	927		

Sources: 1949–65: Halevi and Klinov-Malul, *Economic Development of Israel*, Table 14.
1966–67: Bank of Israel, *Annual Report, 1967*, p. 224.

lation by age, sex, and country of origin. However, it appears to be somewhat responsive to changes in the availability of job opportunities and the general level of prosperity.

The growth of population is important not only as a source of labor input, but also as a factor determining many of the structural characteristics of the economy, for example, the possibility of engaging in large-scale production and the relative importance of sectors such as construction and agriculture, in both of which the growth of demand is to a considerable extent linked to population growth.

The total population (Jews and non-Jews) grew from about 810,000 at the beginning of independence (May 1948) to 2,707,700 at the end of 1967.[3] Table 2.2 indicates the sources of increase of population. Immigration accounted for 63 percent of the increase in the Jewish population between May 1948 and the

3. *Statistical Abstract of Israel 1968*, p. 17.

Table 2.2: Sources of Increase of the Population, 1948–67
(thousands)

	Population at beginning of period	Natural increase	Migration balance	Total increase	(3)/(4)
	(1)	(2)	(3)	(4)	(5)
Jews					
May 1948–51	649.6	88.4	666.4	754.8	.88
1952–54	1404.4	101.4	20.2	121.6	.17
1955–57	1526.0	100.7	136.1	236.8	.58
1958–60	1762.8	101.5	46.9	148.4	.32
1961–64	1911.2	134.2	193.8	328.0	.60
1965–67	2239.2	108.9	35.5	144.4	.25
12/31/67	2383.6				
Non-Jews					
1950–67	160.0	160.1	−.6	139.3	
12/31/67[a]	324.1				

[a] Excludes the population of East Jerusalem, the area annexed during the Six Day War of 1967.

Source: Statistical Abstract of Israel, 1968, p. 18.

end of 1967,[4] while natural increase accounted entirely for the growth in non-Jewish population. An important characteristic of the population in terms of its impact upon the labor force is the relatively high rate of dependents (children up to fourteen years of age) in the total population: about 35 percent. This is attributable to the high birth rates of Jews from Asia and Africa and of the Arabs, and the relatively high percentage of Jewish women in child-bearing ages (twenty to forty-four) as a result of the unusual age distribution of immigrants.[5]

The ratio of the labor force to total population (about 35 percent), is somewhat lower than observed in Europe and North America and on a par with that in South America and Africa.[6] It does not appear that Israeli age-specific rates are lower than in European countries for which reliable participation rates exist by age group. Even the relatively low participation rates of women of Asian-African birth are not lower than those in such European

4. This understates the contribution of immigration, since it excludes the natural increase attributable to immigrants.
5. This percentage has declined steadily since 1951. See Halevi and Klinov-Malul, Economic Development of Israel, p. 59.
6. Halevi and Klinov-Malul, Economic Development of Israel, Table 25.

countries as Norway and Italy.[7] Thus it appears that most of the lower overall participation rates (relative to Europe and South America) is attributable to the high percentage of population in the under-fourteen age group.

LABOR FORCE QUALITY

So far, we have considered only the determinants of the numbers in the labor force. However, Israel has been widely considered an atypical underdeveloped economy because of the unusual quality of the labor force, both in terms of its motivation and its educational level. While the former is nonmeasurable, one may attempt to quantify the second.[8]

The quality of the labor force may, as a first approximation, be represented by the educational achievements of its members. Richard Easterlin has shown that Israel's population in 1948 had about the same percentage of college graduates but a higher percentage of high school graduates than the United States (Table 2.3). On the other hand, several indices of education that I have

Table 2.3: Percent of High School and College Graduates,
Israel and the United States, 1948

		Completed higher education	*Completed secondary education (only)*
Israel:	Male	9.8	28.7
	Female	4.4	27.4
United States:	Male	7.3	17.6
	Female	5.2	22.6

Sources: Richard E. Easterlin, "Israel's Development: Past Accomplishments and Future Problems," *Quarterly Journal of Economics* 75 (Feb. 1961): 71.

U.S. secondary school completion percentages: U.S. Bureau of the Census, *Census of the United States: 1950. Population*, vol. 2, Part 1, Tables 114, 44, 115, 38.

7. Data for most countries can be found in International Labor Office, *Yearbook of Labor Statistics*, Geneva, 1967. Data for Israel can be found in various issues of CBS *Labor Force Surveys* and issues of the *Statistical Abstract of Israel*. The introduction to the *Labor Force Surveys* also provides thorough analyses of the factors affecting participation rates. Chapter 5 of Halevi and Klinov-Malul, *Economic Development of Israel*, also contains a discussion of participation rates. The most complete analysis is to be found in Avner Hovne, *The Labor Force in Israel* (Jerusalem: Falk Project, 1961). A detailed examination of the characteristics of the Arab labor force is provided in Yoram Ben Porath, *The Arab Labor Force in Israel* (Jerusalem: Falk Project, 1966).

8. For a discussion of the probable influence of motivation, see Chap. 8.

calculated indicate that the average educational achievement of the entire population remained constant during the decade from 1950–61. Table 2.4 contains data on average years of education

Table 2.4: Average Years of Education, Population 25 Years and Over, by Sex and Continent of Origin, 1950, 1955, and 1961

	Israel born		*Asian-African born*		*European-American born*	
	Male	*Female*	*Male*	*Female*	*Male*	*Female*
1950	9.7	7.6	5.7	2.5	9.6	8.7
1955	9.9	8.5	5.8	2.7	9.5	8.7
1961	10.1	9.4	6.0	3.2	9.5	8.8

Source: Calculated from unpublished data of the Population and Housing Census, by extrapolating backward from 1961 data.

for each major population group by continent of origin. Although in all groups the average years of education remained about constant or increased, an index for the entire population indicates that the overall average has remained constant as a result of the increasing proportion of the population of African or Asian background.[9] Rather than simply present the average years of education embodied in the aggregate labor force, I have, in addition, used data on income by years of education to derive indices of the movement of labor force quality between 1950 and 1961, a measure that allows for the differential productivity of various educational levels. I have assumed that 50 percent of income differentials between groups of different educational levels were due to differences in education.[10] These results are shown in index number form in Table 2.5. The index reflects both the effects of the labor force participation rate by educational class as well as the income differentials.[11] This index indicates that the formal education dimension of quality declined slightly over the decade.

9. These data have been utilized by Joseph Baruh in an interesting study on educational capital in Israel. See Joseph Baruh, "Changes in the Quality of Labor Input in Israel, 1950–1961," Bank of Israel, *Bulletin,* no. 25. By a slightly different route he reaches the same conclusion.

10. Using 25 or 75 percent did not change the nature of the results. The method, of course, is that suggested by Edward Denison, *The Sources of Economic Growth in the United States and the Alternatives before Us* (New York: Committee for Economic Development, 1962).

11. Given the marked violation of the competitive assumptions about factor markets, the calculation is at best very rough. A simple index of average years of education of labor force members yields a similar profile.

Table 2.5: Index of Years of Education of Labor Force
Weighted by Income Differentials, 1950–61
(base 1950 = 100)

1950	100.0
1951	99.1
1952	99.0
1953	98.9
1954	98.8
1955	98.5
1956	98.2
1957	98.1
1958	98.1
1959	98.1
1960	98.0
1961	98.0

Source: Population and Housing Census 1961 (Israel), unpublished data, and various issues of *Labor Force Surveys.* Income data from Ruth Klinov-Malul, *The Profitability of Investment in Education in Israel* (Jerusalem: Falk Institute for Economic Research in Israel, 1966), chap. 2.

It is still true, however, that the *absolute* level of education is high. Evaluating the impact on the economy's development of this initial group of highly educated people as well as subsequent additions, whether through immigration or domestic education, poses an extraordinarily difficult analytic task. Existing approaches to the relationship between economic development and education may be divided into two broad groups: (1) calculations of rates of return on investment in education and (2) educational planning models usually embodying fixed proportions assumptions.[12] The former calculates the contribution of formal education (or on-the-job training) to increased productivity, presumably reflected in differential earnings, and compares this figure to the cost, both implicit and explicit, of obtaining the training. The latter assumes that workers of different education (or skill) levels are used in fixed proportions in producing each type of good; given a planned final bill of goods, the implied labor skill distribution can be found and resources can be devoted to the education system to allow

12. For a survey of various approaches, see William G. Bowen, "Assessing the Economic Contribution of Education: an Appraisal of Alternative Approaches," *Higher Education. Report of the Committee under the Chairmanship of Lord Robbins, 1961–1963* (London: HMSO, 1963).

these skill levels to be achieved. Neither of these approaches is of use in the problem at hand. While rates of return for particular types of education are suggestive in evaluating the value of additional training, this is so only when the additional training has a marginal impact on the overall quality of the labor force; the calculation of the value to society of training 100 civil engineers or industrial managers in the United States is feasible, as they will not significantly change the basic structure of the economy—the same would not be true for, say, the Congo, which was left with few high school graduates upon Belgium's withdrawal in 1960. In the latter case, the increased potential for undertaking and coordinating new projects would alter the entire constellation of economic possibilities for the country. In an analogous manner it seems to me to be impossible to identify the marginal productivity of the entire group of highly educated people present in 1948. Their contribution was coordination and implementation of, among others, immigration, foreign aid, investment allocation, and social services. Without these activities the productivity of the entire economy would have been altered; even had the form of the economy-wide production function been the same, its level would have been much lower.

A similar problem exists in using the planning approach: while it may be fruitful in analyzing additional education requirements, it is impossible to point in retrospect to specific sectors that have high education inputs and to suggest that only they would not have grown as rapidly had less educated manpower been available. Surely the impact of a substantially lower educational level would have been a slower growth of all sectors.

Thus, while the high educational level was undoubtedly an important factor in the growth process, its quantitative importance is perhaps impossible to assess, although we shall suggest one measure below.

We have seen that the use of formal education as a criterion suggests there was no significant decline in "quality" of the labor force after 1950. Partly, this reflects the diminution in quality that had already taken place during 1948 and 1949 as relatively poorly educated immigrants entered the labor force. Even allowing for this, the result seems implausible and is attributable to the conventional quality measure used. During the years 1950 to 1952 the labor supply increased by almost 30 percent (Table 2.1). Many of the newly employed were performing jobs in which they had no prior experience and in areas that were often far removed from their previous occupation.[13] They were often either unskilled or possessed skills not suitable for Israel's economy.[14] For the most part they had been artisans or had worked in the service sector; once they arrived in Israel they were channeled, in disproportionate numbers, to agriculture and modern manufacturing. Further, a substantial percentage came from the countries of North Africa and the Middle East, and thus had had little previous contact with a modern economy; this resulted in poor employee discipline, high absenteeism, and so forth. Thus the new labor force members probably were considerably less productive when initially employed, relative to those members with previous experience, although it is plausible to assume that their rate of productivity growth may have been greater than, and their productivity level may have eventually approached, that of veterans. The quantitative importance of this phenomenon depends on the relative importance of new members in the total labor force growth and the differential levels and rates of growth in productivity. If we consider the rapid growth of the labor force between 1950 and 1953, it would seem that the "quality," given the above factors, must have declined during part of this period. However, after 1954, with the labor force growing more slowly, with more experienced immigrants presumably approaching the productivity levels of veterans, it is likely that movements in the quality-adjusted labor force would have been in the same direction as that in the nominal labor force.

Although these factors are extremely difficult to quantify, it is plausible that the average duration of residence in the country is a useful proxy for changes in skills acquired on the job and for general changes in attitudes. Further, the duration of residence is also correlated with a knowledge of Hebrew. An increasing knowledge of Hebrew probably made workers more adaptable, as well as resulted in increased geographic and job mobility.

13. Table 20 in Halevi and Klinov-Malul, *Economic Development of Israel*, shows that, through 1954, 59 percent of immigrants had jobs in Israel that differed from those they held abroad.

14. See Sicron, *Immigration to Israel: 1948–1953* and Ofer, *Service Industries in a Developing Economy*, chap. 5.

The average duration of residence of the labor force is the average number of years members of the labor force have spent in Israel. However, it is probable that duration of residence has diminishing returns in economic productivity and that after some point no further gains result from an additional year of residence. As a simple approximation to this concept a calculation has been made, which assumes equal gains in productivity during each of the first ten years with no further gains after ten years.[15] The calculation has been done for the entire population, rather than for the labor force itself: it is likely that the labor force underwent similar movements.

The results of this calculation, presented in Table 2.6, show that

Table 2.6: Index of Duration of Residence in Israel, 1949–65
(base: 1949 = 100)

1949	100
1950	80
1951	72
1952	75
1953	82
1954	89
1955	95
1956	101
1957	103
1958	109
1959	118
1960	125
1961	129
1962	128
1963	128
1964	127
1965	130

the average duration of residence fell considerably between 1949 and 1951 but started upward in 1952 and continued until 1956, when it came almost to a standstill. This reflects the resumption of large-scale immigration in 1956 and 1957, after the relatively low immigration of the 1952–55 period. The index increases more rapidly in 1958–60 but again slows down in the early 1960s as a

15. It is assumed that those in the country before independence did not benefit from further residence. If diminishing returns to residence were explicitly allowed for by, say, an exponential function, the variations in the index would be even more dramatic.

result of renewed large-scale immigration. Thus the duration of residence was increasing throughout the period following 1952, probably resulting in increasing labor efficiency, but of an unknown magnitude. It is important to note that after 1953 the yearly growth of the labor force was usually small in percentage terms, so that even the addition of new immigrants whose productivity was considerably below the average of those already in the labor force did not lower the overall quality, given the continually growing experience of the latter.

A comparison of incomes, by duration of residence, may provide some information on the productivity implications of the residence indices. Careful work has been done on such income differentials by Giora Hanoch of the Falk Institute,[16] using data from the family expenditure and savings surveys. Table 2.7 shows indices

Table 2.7: Employment Income of Heads of Household
after Adjustment for Age and Education Differences
(base: 1932–38 = 100)

	Immigrants from Asia-Africa	Immigrants from Europe-America
Total veterans 1947 and before	100	99
Total new immigrants after 1948	64	79
Period of immigration		
Before 1931	110	109
1932–38	100	100
1939–47	88	91
1948–49	74	83
1950–51	67	79
1952–57	44	59

Source: Giora Hanoch, "Income Differentials in Israel," *Fifth Report*, 1959–1961 (Jerusalem: Falk Project for Economic Research in Israel, 1961), p. 100.

of income for heads of households, by continent of origin and period of immigration, adjusted for levels of education and age. Since the influence of these two factors has been eliminated from the analysis, there is evidence that increased duration of residence does result in higher earnings, and we may assume that this is at least partially attributable to productivity differentials. Part of the difference may be explained, however, by differences in occu-

16. See Giora Hanoch, "Income Differentials in Israel," *Fifth Report* (Jerusalem: Falk Project, 1961).

pational structure for which it was not possible to adjust, since occupational data were not available for 1957–58. However, data for other years indicate that occupation does play a significant role in determining income differentials; this was probably the cause of the disparity between the pre-1931 and 1932–38 group, as well as the large divergence between the European-American and Asian-African groups arriving in 1950–51 or 1952–57.

Although Table 2.7 presents some evidence indicating the possible importance of increasing productivity due to the duration of residence, we must await more information on the narrowing of differentials over time before we can safely estimate its quantitative significance;[17] if, for example, the differential between the 1948–49 and 1952–57 groups does not decline over time, then the observed differential must be caused by factors other than the length of residence. Similarly, the above assumes competitive pricing of different types of labor. Insofar as this is not true, new evidence generated by an increasingly competitive economy may provide further information on the general hypothesis.

Several nonquantifiable features of the immigration process should be noted. Well over half of the immigrants came from Asian or African countries in which health standards were low. The upgrading of the general health levels, in particular the elimination of such debilitating diseases as bilharzia, must have led to increasing productivity. Another important factor is the training in basic skills and vocational education received by a considerable percentage of the male immigrants who entered the armed forces. These, of course, are not reflected in formal education data but are clearly of significance, since the magnitude of such training relative to formal education was extraordinarily high.

TECHNICAL CHANGE

As we have seen, Israel's labor supply grew at a very rapid rate as a result of immigration. Capital accumulation, financed mainly by foreign aid, proceeded even more quickly. Factor growth does not necessarily lead to increasing output per capita, nor to

17. There is some evidence that the unadjusted income differential does not decrease over time, but as of yet there are no data that allow the calculation of adjusted income differentials. Ibid., p. 73.

increasing output per unit of combined input. Growth in this latter sense may be taken as one measure of the level of development of an economy and its capacity for fruitfully utilizing increasing inputs, especially foreign aid. Moreover, without increasing productivity, economic development faces great difficulties and is likely to come to a halt.

Table 2.8 presents gross domestic product (GDP) data (in

Table 2.8: Gross Domestic Product, 1950–67
(1955 prices)

	Millions of I£	*Percentage change from preceding year*	*Compound rates of growth*	
1950	1,160		1950–53	10.6
1951	1,514	30.0	1954–58	9.6
1952	1,598	5.5	1958–65	9.9
1953	1,577	−1.3	1954–65	9.8
1954	1,884	19.5	1954–67	8.5
1955	2,141	13.6		
1956	2,330	8.8		
1957	2,534	8.8		
1958	2,719	7.3		
1959	3,066	12.8		
1960	3,255	6.2		
1961	3,605	10.7		
1962	3,972	10.2		
1963	4,400	10.8		
1964	4,849	10.2		
1965	5,245	8.2		
1966	5,298	1.0		
1967	5,465	3.2		

Source: Statistical Abstract of Israel, 1968, pp. 140–41.

1955 prices) for 1950–67, along with compound rates of growth for several subperiods. The period through 1965 may be divided into two segments with significantly different characteristics, 1950–53, and 1954–65. During the earlier years, movements in overall output were erratic; GDP increased by 30.0 percent from 1950 to 1951, by 5.5 percent in the next year, and then declined slightly from 1952 to 1953.[18] Beginning with 1954, growth proceeded at a

18. The observed gyrations might, in fact, be statistical artifacts. However, Harold Lubell, who was responsible for the estimates for 1950–54, indicates that he believes them to be reliable. Further, the estimates from

sustained high rate until 1965. During 1966 and 1967 GDP grew only slightly as a result of a recession, partly induced by government policy (Chapter 7).

Among the reasons for the erratic behavior in the early years are the substantial organizational problems involved in absorbing the huge immigration of the 1948–51 period, shortages of imported raw materials due to the lack of foreign exchange,[19] and the introduction in 1952 of the "New Economic Policy," which resulted in decreased aggregate demand as the government sharply reduced its deficit and the rate of growth of the money supply. The last-mentioned factor was probably a significant determinant of the decline in GDP in 1953.

The unusual nature of these years may also be seen from elementary productivity calculations. Using the geometric measure of productivity change,[20] the following are the year-to-year movements in total factor productivity for the total private economy,[21] on the assumption that the elasticity of output with respect to capital was one-third:

$$1950\text{–}51 = 7.2 \text{ percent}$$
$$1951\text{–}52 = -6.9 \text{ percent}$$
$$1952\text{–}53 = -7.1 \text{ percent}$$
$$1953\text{–}54 = 14.8 \text{ percent}$$

Presumably, the large positive residuals in 1950–51 and 1953–54 reflect increases in capacity utilization and, in addition, in the latter year, a normalization following the initial deflationary impact

the expenditure side move in about the same manner as the independently estimated value added shares. Even if there are some errors, they certainly could not account for the major year-to-year movements. See Harold Lubell, *Israel's National Expenditure, 1950–1954* (Jerusalem: Falk Project, 1958), especially pp. 9–11.

19. In some years this lack of foreign exchange led to idle capacity, manifesting itself in small increases in output, despite large additions to capacity.

20. See Evsey D. Domar, "On the Measurement of Technological Change," *Economic Journal* 71 (Dec. 1961): 709–729, for a discussion of this measure.

21. Gross national product minus income generated by the government and private nonprofit institutions. The adjusted GNP series, as well as capital stock data were kindly provided by A. L. Gaathon. As we mentioned in the preface, the reader interested in a more extensive analysis of Israel's productivity growth might well consult his *Economic Productivity in Israel, 1950–65* (New York: Praeger, 1970).

of the New Economic Policy. In contrast to this early period, productivity rose steadily after 1954. Therefore, we shall concentrate on the years 1954–65 in studying the overall growth of the economy, these being indicative of the more permanent, rather than the transitional, features of the economy. However, in focusing on the post-1954 years, there is a danger of oversimplifying and understating the difficulties faced by Israel in moving toward a path of sustained economic progress.[22]

Between 1950 and 1954 employment in the private sector increased by 25 percent, while the fixed capital stock rose by 90 percent. If 1949 were used as the base, the comparable employment figure would be in the neighborhood of 60 percent. Despite these substantial increases in factor availability and the implied difficulties of coordinating the activities employing them, total factor productivity remained about constant or declined only slightly;[23] moreover, as seen earlier, during at least part of the period it appears probable that a correct adjustment would indicate a decline in the quality of the labor force.[24] The failure of productivity to decline drastically in the face of the enormous difficulty inherent in factor absorption, particularly of so many low skilled, essentially nonmodernized workers, presents an extraordinary performance, one that may be lost sight of in analyzing the following normal period. This achievement is one measure of the importance of the initial group of highly educated persons, as the coordination of the multitude of factors permitting this success is unimaginable without them. While the market mechanism may provide an effective allocator of resources in a more slowly growing economy, in pre-1954 Israel the size and mutual dependence of new undertakings made some form of nonmarket coordination mandatory.[25]

22. See also Chap. 1.
23. The actual result depending on assumed factor elasticity. With an assumed capital elasticity of .5, total productivity remains constant.
24. However, there may have been some increase in capacity utilization that would increase the effective capital input.
25. To be sure in some spheres such as foreign exchange allocation, more reliance on the market mechanism would have been helpful. Even here, demand based on current conditions might in some cases have led to some undesirable allocation effects. For an approach to the question of the coordination of decisions, see Hollis B. Chenery, "The Interdependence of Investment Decisions," in Moses Abramovitz et al., *The Allocation of Economic Resources* (Stanford, Calif.: Stanford University Press, 1959).

In turning now to trends in the post-1954 period, one finds relatively steady growth of total factor productivity. However, important parts of the foundation for this growth, particularly the initial absorption of unskilled immigrants, had been built in the preceding period.

Two methods are available for analyzing the sources of output growth. An index of weighted inputs may be calculated.[26] The percentage of total output growth attributable to the primary factors can then be ascertained. Alternatively, a production function that will provide similar information may be estimated directly. In Israel, the latter method is preferable because of the likelihood that factor shares do not represent output elasticities, an important assumption of the geometric index method; in particular, the wage share is almost certainly above, and therefore the profit share below, competitive levels because of the existence of a politically strong trade union movement. This source of bias probably decreased during the late 1950s and 1960s.[27]

The following analysis of productivity concentrates on the private economy, that is, the entire economy excluding the activities of government and private nonprofit institutions, these having, by definition, zero productivity change, since their output is measured by their input.

Given the erratic movements of product in the years 1950–53, we omitted these from the analysis; 1954 was assumed to be the first year in which patterns of activity were normal. Two equations were estimated for the total private economy for 1954–65.

$$Q = Ae^{\lambda t}K^{\alpha}L^{1-\alpha} \qquad (2.1)$$
$$Q = AK^{\alpha}L^{\beta} \qquad (2.2)$$

where Q is the net output in 1955 prices, K is capital, net of dis-

---

26. The weights used may be per unit factor remuneration or factor shares: the former constitutes an arithmetic index, the latter a geometric index. A discussion of their respective merits is given in Domar, "On Measurement of Technological Change." A. L. Gaathon in a pioneering study analyzed productivity growth using the latter method. See A. L. Gaathon, *Capital Stock, Employment and Output in Israel, 1950–1959* (Jerusalem: Bank of Israel, 1961).

27. See also Michael Bruno, "Estimation of Factor Contribution to Growth under Structural Disequilibrium," *International Economic Review* 9 (Feb. 1968): 49–62.

cards, in 1955 prices,[28] and L is the size of the employed labor force. Two capital variables were used, one equal to the value of capital at the beginning of each year, and the second, the value at the beginning of the preceding year. The use of the first implies an average lag of six months before new capital becomes productive, whereas the lagged variable implies an eighteen-month gestation period.

The first equation is a simple Cobb-Douglas function with a trend term representing disembodied technical change. The second equation represents a Cobb-Douglas form, without coefficients being constrained to unity; that is, allowing the possibility of increasing returns to scale.[29] The results are presented in Table 2.9.

Table 2.9: Production Functions for Total Private Economy, 1954–65

(1) $\log (Q/L) = -\ .0139 + .0269t + .6022 \log (K/L)$ $R^2 = .9962$
   $\qquad\qquad\quad\ (.6023)\quad (.0235)\quad\ (.3864)$

(1′) $\log (Q/L) = -\ .0177 + .0241t + .6483 \log (K_{t-1}/L)$ $R^2 = .9970$
   $\qquad\qquad\quad\ (.4110)\quad (.0173)\quad\ (.2827)$

(2) $\log Q \quad\ = -1.6348 + .2649 \log L + .9202 \log K$ $R^2 = .9986$
   $\qquad\qquad (1.1808)\quad (.3951)\qquad\quad (.1615)$

(2′) $\log Q \quad = -1.8956 + .3901 \log L + .8663 \log K_{t-1}$ $R^2 = .9987$
   $\qquad\qquad\ (.9515)\quad (.3147)\qquad\quad (.1273)$

For the production functions with disembodied technical change, the equations with either capital variable yield similar results, in-

28. Although excess capacity existed throughout the period, there is no utilization data. Using a capital measure unadjusted for utilization implies a constant percentage of underutilization, an assumption that is probably not unreasonable for this period. However, Gaathon in an unpublished study suggests that utilization may have been increasing. If this is accurate, then the technical change term is overstated. For a discussion of the problem presented by idle factors in estimating production functions, see Robert M. Solow, "Technical Progress, Capital Formation and Economic Growth," *American Economic Review* 52 (May 1962): 76–86. The procedure used by Solow, namely, the use of the labor unemployment rate to arrive at a simultaneous estimate of potential output and the production function cannot be used in our case because unemployment was not due to demand factors, but was structural, involving both rigid wages and skill deficiencies among the unemployed. On these points see also Chap. 7.

29. In an unpublished paper Michael Bruno has estimated these, as well as a number of other production functions for 1952–61. Because of the difference in years covered and the different measures of the variables, the results are not comparable.

dicating an elasticity of output with respect to capital of about .6. In both cases the associated rate of technical change is about .025 per year. However, because of the substantial multicollinearity in the independent variables, only one of the coefficients in the equation is significant at the 5 percent level. In the equations that allow for increasing returns, only the capital coefficient is significant, so that it is impossible to test meaningfully for increasing returns.[30]

Given the low significance levels of these estimates, we turn to geometric productivity measures as an alternative, using as factor shares the weights found in the 1958 input-output study.[31] The annual compound rate of growth of productivity for 1954–65 is 4.7 percent, which is almost double the 2.5 percent derived from the regressions. The difference results from the low capital elasticity of .33, implied by the observed factor shares, whereas the estimated production function indicates that the elasticity is about .6. The geometric productivity measure almost certainly yields too high a residual, since the weight attached to the fastest growing factor, capital, is undoubtedly lower than it should have been.[32]

These two productivity measures, 2.5 and 4.7, may be compared with those calculated by Domar et al., who found the following residuals for the period 1948–60: 1.4 for the United States, .7 for the United Kingdom, and 3.8 for Japan, all calculated

---

30. Because of the multicollinearity of the independent variables and the high coefficient of determination, there was no attempt to estimate an embodied technical change model, since this procedure utilizes changes in the size of R^2 as the criterion for determining the embodiment rate. Further, two recent contributions have shown that it may not be possible to obtain meaningful estimates of the rate of embodiment. See Eitan Berglas, "Investment and Technological Change," *Journal of Political Economy* 73 (Apr. 1965): 173–80; Dale Jorgenson, "The Embodiment Hypothesis," *Journal of Political Economy* 74 (Feb. 1966): 1–17. Moreover, the basic assumption of the embodiment hypotheses, namely, that there is a given rate of improvement in efficiency in each year's investment, is particularly questionable in an economy such as Israel's, in which little attention to design (until recently) was given in the construction branches. On the other hand, imported machinery may reflect improvements insofar as they occur in the exporting country.

31. These weights are one-third for capital and two-thirds for labor for the total private economy. Data from the input-output table are used, rather than those from the national accounts because they appear to be more accurate.

32. See above, p. 32.

for the private economy, while the residual for the entire economy in Canada was 1.2 for 1949–59 and 3.6 in Germany for 1950–59.[33] Although the residuals were calculated using the arithmetic index, while ours is a geometric index, the results are roughly comparable.

It is interesting that Japan and Germany, the fastest growing countries, had the highest rates of technical change. Both started from a low economic base after World War II, with relatively small capital stocks and relatively highly trained labor. This is, of course, similar to Israel's pattern. Also similar was the extremely rapid growth of their capital stock. Contributing to a high growth rate in these countries may well have been the new techniques embodied in the rapidly growing capital stock and the added flexibility to allocate the new capital stock to rapidly growing industries, as well as to adjust relative factor proportions to existing factor supplies.[34]

However, the size of the residual may not be an adequate indicator of the efficiency of an economy, as the share of growth accounted for by even a large residual may be relatively low. Both the absolute size of the residual and its relative importance in explaining total growth are useful measures. A high rate of growth accompanied by a substantial residual presumably indicates a considerable amount of organizational ability, that is, success in absorbing a large quantity of factors and utilizing them in a productive manner. Even if the share of the residual in total growth is higher in a more slowly growing economy than in Israel, it may not be true that the former is more efficient, since it might not have been able to coordinate the absorption of a large influx of resources: if its aggregate growth rate had been as high, the importance of the residual would have been lower than in Israel.

Consider now the relative performance of Israel and the previously mentioned countries. If the rate of technical change in Israel is assumed to be 2.5 percent per annum (using estimated

33. Evsey Domar, et al., "Economic Growth and Productivity in the United States, Canada, United Kingdom, Germany and Japan in the Postwar Period," *Review of Economics and Statistics* 46 (Feb. 1964): 33–40.

34. For a good discussion of the impact of a rapid growth in capital stock on aggregate growth, see Richard R. Nelson, "Aggregate Production Functions and Medium Range Growth Projections," *American Economic Review* 54 (Sept. 1964): 575–606. His discussion of the importance of high capital growth in permitting disembodied technical change to be realized is particularly relevant.

elasticities), then 23 percent of output growth is accounted for by the residual. If the 4.7 percent rate is used (based upon observed factor shares), 43 percent of output growth is accounted for by the residual. These may be compared with 50 percent for Germany, 46 percent for Japan, 47 percent for the United States, and 30 percent for Canada.[35] If we use a capital elasticity for Israel of .40, well below the estimated .60, but 20 percent above that recorded in the input-output table, the residual is 3.9 percent per annum, which is 36 percent of total output growth, lower than the comparable figures for the other countries, except Canada. However, Japan and Germany, the two countries with high absolute growth rates, were essentially modern industrial countries returning for part of the period to prewar levels, and it is not surprising to find their performance to be better than Israel's. Nevertheless, Israel's productivity performance, if not quite at the level of the most industrially advanced countries, is still close enough to them to suggest that at least in this dimension it has a relatively advanced economy. This impression is further strengthened by comparisons involving some of the richer, more industrialized economies of Latin America. In this context a recent study of the residual in five Latin American countries[36] by Bruton is also of interest. Using a geometric productivity index, he found that the residual was close to zero in these countries for much of the period since 1940.[37]

In summary, to the extent that the residual measures productivity performance, Israel appears to be closer to the developed countries' side of the spectrum. In terms of the relative importance of the residual, it requires somewhat more material resources to achieve a given rate of growth than countries with a sustained record of growth, while exhibiting considerably greater productivity growth than other semi-industrialized nations. As will be suggested in the following chapters, the slightly lower productivity growth, relative to advanced nations, may in part be attributable to the inability to realize economies of scale.

At a number of places we have indicated that factor markets

---

35. However, at least part of the slow growth of U.S. total factor productivity may be the result of overly tight aggregate demand policies.

36. Argentina, Brazil, Chile, Colombia, and Mexico.

37. Henry Bruton, "Productivity Growth in Latin America," *American Economic Review* 57 (Dec. 1967): 1099–1116.

were not competitive; thus it was inaccurate to utilize observed factor shares as the factor output elasticities in computing the residual. The use of an estimated production function eliminates these problems, provided that the specification is correct. One fact which suggests that the Cobb-Douglas form used above may not be an accurate representation of the underlying technical relations is the decreasing share of wages in national income, although this could occur even with a Cobb-Douglas if there were a changing degree of noncompetitive factor pricing.

An alternative explanation is the existence of a production function with an elasticity of factor substitution of greater than unity. As one test of this hypothesis I estimated a constant elasticity of substitution (CES) production function for 1954–65.[38] The results indicated implausibly high elasticities of substitution, close to 2. Michael Bruno has suggested an interesting alternative specification of the production function, which, combined with an equation specifying the relation between the real wage and marginal productivity, yields a good explanation of many of the relevant aspects of the Israeli economy.[39] His production function is

$$Q = Ae^{\lambda t}K^{\alpha}L^{1-\alpha} - mL \tag{2.3}$$

where m is a fixed structural parameter. Equation 2.3, along with an equation allowing for the possibility that the real wage is not equated to the marginal product, has a number of properties that are relevant in explaining the observed growth process in Israel. In particular, (1) the model embodies an explicit mechanism capable of explaining changing factor shares, and (2) technical progress is not neutral, but with an elasticity of substitution of less than unity, it begins as capital saving, moving toward neutrality as the capital-labor ratio and/or t increases.[40] The latter property is very reasonable, given the probability that new immi-

---

38. See Kenneth Arrow, et al., "Capital-Labor Substitution and Economic Efficiency," *Review of Economics and Statistics* 43 (Aug. 1961): 225–250. We estimated the production function directly from output, capital, and labor, using a nonlinear estimation procedure rather than an implied production function from wage data.

39. Bruno, "Estimation of Factor Contribution to Growth under Structural Disequilibrium," pp. 49–62. Bruno's equations are estimated for 1953–64 and his results are thus not directly comparable to ours.

40. For this to hold, m must be positive, as it is in the estimates. Ibid., pp. 52, 57.

grants became more productive during their early years in the country, with the phenomenon becoming quantitatively less important as time passed.[41]

When Equation 2.3 is used to estimate the importance of technical change in explaining output growth, the results are quite similar to our earlier results.[42] Bruno estimates that for 1953–64 the residual explained from one-quarter to one-third of the growth of GDP in the total private economy and about one-sixth of the growth in manufacturing, while our estimates for 1954–65 are one-quarter and one-fifth.

The estimates of productivity growth presented so far suggest that the elasticity of substitution is, at the most, unitary,[43] Bruno's function indicating elasticity less than one, although approaching unity as output increases. However, given the relatively high multicollinearity of capital and labor, these estimated functions do not rule out alternative specifications, as the R^2 for almost any reasonable function is likely to be well over .99. While, as mentioned earlier, a straightforward estimate of the constant elasticity of substitution function yields an implausibly high elasticity of substitution, what are the implications if it is in fact greater than unity? [44]

Richard Nelson has shown that the growth of output can be approximated by the following expression:

$$\frac{Q'}{Q} = \frac{A'}{A} + (1 - \alpha)\frac{L'}{L} + \alpha\,\frac{K'}{K} + \frac{1}{2}\alpha(1 - \alpha)\frac{\sigma - 1}{\sigma}\left(\frac{K'}{K} - \frac{L'}{L}\right)^2$$

where A'/A is disembodied technical progress and σ is the elasticity of substitution, α is the output elasticity of capital, and the prime indicates a change in the variable. The explanation of output growth given by the first three terms on the right-hand side correspond to the Cobb-Douglas case with A'/A estimated as a residual, in the manner followed earlier. However, if $\sigma > 1$, and $K'/K > L'/L$, then the residual is overestimated and, correspond-

41. See above, pp. 25–28.
42. This is not surprising insofar as Equation 2.3 asymptotically approaches a Cobb-Douglas as m becomes smaller.
43. The geometric index implicitly assumes a Cobb-Douglas function.
44. The following analysis draws upon my longer study, "The Contribution of Education to Growth," *Economic Growth Center Discussion Paper* no. 5.

ingly, part of the output growth can be attributed to the ease with which the economy substitutes capital for labor. Assume that $\sigma = 1.2$, considerably less than its estimated value and that $\propto = .6$. Between 1954 and 1965 the growth of the capital-labor ratio was 6.5 percent per annum. Thus the impact of the high elasticity of substitution would have been to increase the growth rate by 1 percent per annum, or roughly 40 percent of the total residual when the latter is estimated using .6 as the capital elasticity. A σ of 1.4 almost eliminates the conventional residual; a high elasticity of substitution, which slows the onset of decreasing returns to the faster growing factor, replaces the residual as a source of growth. Does this simply represent the substitution of a mechanical concept for the more embarrassing one of ignorance? I think not.

The production function of a country that mainly imports its equipment, as well as production concepts such as the optimal relation between buildings and equipment, depends on its ability to search for, and decide among, alternative foreign production processes. The relevant production isoquant for the importing country then consists of points from a number of countries, probably including several from some of these countries. Thus the state of knowledge existing in the importing country does not represent its technical frontier. Rather, the latter now consists of a set of foreign techniques. Presumably, the greater the number of foreign techniques capable of being investigated and the greater the ability actually to adapt them for domestic purposes, the higher will be the potential elasticity of substitution that the economy faces. If the ability to examine alternative foreign techniques is a function of the domestic level of education, and this seems to be quite plausible, then education enters the growth process by allowing greater flexibility in factor proportions—in a sense an increase in absorptive capacity. Assuming that educational level has been of importance in Israel, this process would constitute one plausible way in which the mechanics of its impact may be envisioned, its quantitative impact depending upon the actual increase in the elasticity of substitution then made possible.[45]

Given our inability to discriminate sharply among alternate

45. This is one dimension of the different constellation of economic opportunities that would exist because of the presence of a highly educated group. See above, pp. 23–24.

versions of the production function, these possibilities suggested by a greater than unitary elasticity are of considerable interest, but must remain speculative until more conclusive evidence is generated.

SECTORAL PRODUCTIVITY

Estimates of the residual for each of the sectors have been calculated and are presented below. The implications of different rates of technical change will then be analyzed, with a view toward separating the residual for the entire private economy into two parts: one attributable to changes in resource allocation among sectors in which factors have different productivities and the other to the growth of the residual within sectors. The four major sectors that constitute the private economy are agriculture, manufacturing and mining, transportation and other branches, which includes public utilities, construction, finance, and trade. Further disaggregation would certainly be desirable but is not feasible because of the limitations of the data.

Agriculture

The net output in agriculture grew at a rate of 12.6 percent per

Table 2.10: Compound Rates of Growth of Agricultural Inputs and Output

	Net output	*Employment*	*Capital stock (excluding irrigation facilities)*	*Cropped area*	*Water*
1950–54	15.6	6.8	10.5	9.5	18.7
1954–58	12.5	4.9	10.9	2.6	10.9
1958–62	9.7	1.1	8.7	0.6	3.0
1950–64	12.6	3.5	9.3	3.5	8.4
1954–64	11.4	2.2	8.9	5.3	4.5

Sources: Capital and output: A. L. Gaathon, unpublished data.

Employment 1950–55: A. L. Gaathon, unpublished data. Employment 1955 and after: Bank of Israel, *Annual Reports.*

Cropped area: *Statistical Abstract of Israel, 1964,* p. 374; *1965,* p. 364; *1966,* p. 392.

Water: *Statistical Abstract of Israel, 1966,* p. 346.

annum between 1950 and 1964.[46] Until 1955, there was a pronounced two-year cycle of output, reflecting annual fluctuations in rainfall. Since 1955, with the exception of 1959–60, this cycle has disappeared, partly as a result of the increasing importance of irrigation.

The compound annual rates of growth of labor, capital, land, and water are shown in Table 2.10. Most inputs had similar time patterns, increasing most rapidly between 1950 and 1954 and, except for capital, growing more slowly after 1954.

The residuals, by period, considering only labor and capital inputs, are:[47, 48]

$$
\begin{aligned}
1950\text{–}54 &= 7.2 \text{ percent} \\
1954\text{–}58 &= 5.0 \text{ percent} \\
1958\text{–}62 &= 5.3 \text{ percent} \\
1950\text{–}64 &= 6.6 \text{ percent} \\
1954\text{–}64 &= 6.3 \text{ percent}
\end{aligned}
$$

This calculation has assumed that land and water were not resource constraints, while in fact it is clear that both had marginal products greater than zero and their availability varied over the period. To ascertain the impact of these factors, along with capital and labor, would require the use of an estimated production function because farmers' expenditures on land and water would be incorrect estimates of the output elasticities, since both factors were subsidized. However, the time series exhibit considerable multicollinearity, and therefore a precise estimation of the required elasticities is precluded.

How biased are the estimates of the residual? Since 1958 the

46. Estimates of the residual for an earlier set of years, along with attempts to estimate the productivity growth for individual crops are presented in Yair Mundlak, *Long-Term Projections of Supply and Demand for Agricultural Products in Israel* (Jerusalem: Falk Project, 1964), pp. 50–55.

47. The relative shares in value added were 56.3 for labor and 43.7 for capital. These were obtained from the 1958 input-output study and are to be preferred to the national accounts estimates, as the latter do not include imputations for self-employed labor.

48. The analysis of productivity does not include 1965 because this year appears to have been characterized by considerable excess capacity. See Bank of Israel, *Annual Report, 1965,* chap. 2. Since one aim of the sectoral estimates is that of separating the total private economy residual into its components as indicated above, and this requires comparable years, our analysis for other branches is limited to the pre-1965 period.

amount of cropped area has changed very little; thus its contribution to increased production would be nil. Even in the 1954–58 period, the growth of land was slow, so that its omission could not seriously bias the results, unless its output elasticity were extremely high. On the other hand, the omission of water may lead to some upward bias in the residual during the 1950s, when water use rose by over 10 percent per annum.

Manufacturing

Compound annual rates of growth of output and inputs in manufacturing and mining are shown in Table 2.11. For the entire

Table 2.11: Compound Rates of Growth in Manufacturing and Mining
1954–64

	Output	Capital	Labor	Residual	
1954–64	12.8	12.1	6.2	5.1[a]	3.0[b]
1954–58	10.3	10.8	4.8	3.9	1.9
1959–64	14.5	12.5	7.5	5.7	4.0

[a] Calculated using observed factor shares as elasticities.
[b] Calculated using estimated factor elasticities.

1954–64 period, productivity grew at 5.1 percent per annum.[49] These data suggest an increase in the efficiency of the manufacturing sector over the period, as the absolute size of the residual rose; however, the percentage of the total output increase accounted for by the residual is 38 in 1954–58 and 39 in 1959–64.[50]

It is quite likely that the residual estimated using observed factor shares is biased upward. As discussed earlier, the manufacturing sector is highly unionized; given the nature of wage agreements, the wage share in manufacturing undoubtedly overstates the output elasticity of labor. To obtain a better estimate of the residual, an attempt was made at estimating a Cobb-Douglas function with disembodied technical change for the years 1954–64. The best equation out of a number of alternate specifications was[51]

49. The weights used in the calculation of the residual were .26 for capital and .74 for labor, obtained from the 1958 input-output table.
50. On the relative usefulness of absolute versus relative measures of the residual, see pp. 35–36 above.
51. The same equation using a lagged capital variable results in a higher capital elasticity, a lower coefficient of t, and a slightly poorer fit.

$$\log \left(\frac{Q}{L}\right) = \underset{(.7209)}{.1226} + \underset{(.0235)}{.02576t} + \underset{(.4464)}{.6037} \log \left(\frac{K}{L}\right) \quad R^2 = .9872.$$

(2.4)

Due to the high collinearity of the variables, the estimated coefficients are not significant at a high confidence level. If the elasticity of output with respect to capital were of the order suggested in the equation, the residual for 1954–58 would have been 1.9 and that for 1959–64 4.0 percent per annum. In this case not only does the absolute size of the residual increase over time, but so does its relative importance in explaining output growth. This confirms the intuition of many observers who suggest that manufacturing efficiency has been increasing.

Transportation

The output of the transportation sector grew at a (compound) annual rate of 11.3 percent per annum, between 1954 and 1964, while the growth rates of capital and labor in this sector were 12.5 and 4.2 percent, respectively. The implied residual, using a weight of 20.3 for capital, is 5.4 percent per annum.

Other private nondwelling branches

This sector is rather heterogeneous and includes construction, public utilities, and private services such as finance and insurance. Output in these sectors increased at a compound average annual rate of 9.9 percent during the 1954–64 decade. Capital increased at the even faster rate of 11.7 percent and labor at 3.5 percent. Using a weight of .48 for capital,[52] we find that the residual is 2.5 percent per annum or one-quarter of the total growth in output.

We attempt now to utilize the above productivity measures to analyze the extent to which intersectoral shifts of capital and labor have affected overall productivity.

Assume, for the moment, that the observed shares of capital and labor used in calculating the residual are the result of competitive price and factor markets; then the marginal product of capital and labor in each industry can be calculated as $MP_K = \alpha(Q/L)$ and $MP_L = (1 - \alpha)Q/L$, where α is capital's share of in-

---

52. Obtained from the 1958 input-output table.

come. Part of the increase in the productivity of the total private economy may be attributable to shifts of factors toward those sectors in which their marginal productivities are higher. The increase in output attributable to factor shifts can be shown to be equal to[53]

$$S = \alpha \sum \frac{MP_i^K}{MP_K} K^*_i + (1 - \alpha) \sum \frac{MP_i^L}{MP_L} L^*_i \qquad (2.5)$$

where α is the elasticity of output with respect to capital in the entire private economy, MP_i^K the marginal product of capital in industry i, K^*_i the percentage change in the ith branch's share of total capital over the period, and MP_K the economy-wide marginal product of capital.[54] Table 2.12 shows the change in each sector's

Table 2.12: Changes in Share of Primary Factors by Sector, 1954–64

	Agriculture	Manufacturing and mining	Transportation	Other branches
Change in share of capital (1954–64)	−15.2	12.5	7.1	10.3
Change in share of labor (1954–64)	−16.4	21.7	2.7	−5.3

share of capital and labor between 1954 and 1964. Both primary factors were allocated more than proportionally to manufacturing, in which the marginal products of capital and labor were both higher than in agriculture or transportation. Agriculture, however, was not obtaining its proportionate share of new factors.[55] "Other branches" also declined in its importance as an employer, which may suggest that part of the employment in this sector initially represented a "push" into the sector rather than a "pull" of employment opportunities, although given the diversity in the components of this sector, one must be careful in interpreting this thesis. Thus we see that industry's share of labor was increasing,

53. See Benton Massell, "A Disaggregated View of Technical Change," *Journal of Political Economy* 49 (Dec. 1961): 547–57.
54. The marginal product was calculated using the factor shares in the 1958 input-output table and the output-labor, output-capital ratios, calculated as the average of the values in 1954 and 1964.
55. The gain in manufacturing compared to agriculture occurred primarily in the period after 1959.

while that of agriculture and other branches was decreasing.[56] The total effect of the shifting of labor on the overall residual for the entire private economy is .14 out of a total residual of 5.1, about 3 percent.[57]

When we consider the marginal allocations of capital, all sectors gained at the expense of agriculture. If our data and assumptions are accurate, they imply that the reallocation of capital is responsible for a growth in productivity of .36 percent over the period or about 2.5 times as much as the labor reallocation.[58]

Thus, of the total private economy residual of 5.1 for 1954–64, 4.6 or 90 percent may be attributed to *within-sector* increases in productivity.[59] Given the level of aggregation, part of the residual may well be traceable to improved within-sector allocation of resources, as well as a pure residual. Despite the rough nature of our calculations, it appears that most of the growth in the residual is attributable to what has recently been called *X* efficiency,[60] which includes the effect of improved management, more effort by the labor force, and so forth, rather than resource reallocation among various branches. However, until detailed estimates that permit a finer industrial classification become available, this must remain a tentative hypothesis.

56. Although the transport sector's employment has risen as a percentage of the total, it is absolutely quite small.

57. The figure 5.1 is the residual for the private economy for 1954–64. See note 48.

58. Much of this depends on the high marginal productivity of capital in "other branches," which is open to some doubt, since it stems from a low output capital ratio and small errors in the capital estimate can lead to substantial errors in the marginal productivity estimate $\alpha(Q/K)$. If this were reduced by a quarter, a good part of the shift effect would be removed.

59. Had we used the output elasticities from estimated production functions in the calculation of marginal products, as well as in the calculation of the estimated rate of technical change, there would not have been much difference. This is mainly attributable to the fact that the percentage increase in the marginal product of capital, when estimated elasticities are used, was the same for the total private economy and manufacturing.

60. See Harvey Leibenstein, "Allocative Efficiency vs. 'X' Efficiency," *American Economic Review* 56 (June 1966): 392–415.

3

The Intersectoral Structure
of the Growth Process

In the previous chapter the sources of the growth of output were examined. We turn now to an analysis of the changing demand patterns that determined the particular sectoral growth patterns. Observed final demand vectors measured in an input-output framework reflect not only income elasticities but also shifts among products in response to changing relative prices resulting from altered supply conditions. Thus, when we use "demand" in this chapter, it is in the sense of measured ex post demands that are the result of the interaction of both supply and demand factors. The following discussion of demand factors is not meant to suggest that supply automatically adjusted to changes in demand as determined by income elasticities and export possibilities. Indeed, given the importance of the government in determining the allocation of capital, land, water, and to some extent, labor, sectoral output occasionally diverged from the direction of growth dictated by income elasticities and comparative advantage. Nevertheless, an examination of the evolution of observed final demand does aid us in understanding the growth patterns that occurred and provides a framework within which the impact of many of the basic determinants of the structure of the development process such as consumption elasticities, changes in technology, and government policies can be integrated. Input-output analysis permits us to trace the impact of changing final "demand" patterns on the transformation of the sectoral structure of production and employment, which is usually considered to be the core of the development process.

The intersectoral analysis that follows considers only the post-1951 period. However, the initial relative importance of the various sectors conditioned the ensuing growth process. In particular, the absence of any decrease—in fact, there was a slight increase—in the relative importance of the agricultural sector between 1951 and 1958 is attributable to the fact that, by 1951, the sector had reached a level approximately equal to that which could be expected given the observed share of agriculture in advanced economies. However, this does not mean that no transformation took place in the sectoral structure of production at any time during the development process. Rather, much of the transformation had already occurred in the three years preceding 1951.

In 1947 over half of the total (Arab and Jewish) labor force in Palestine was engaged in agriculture. At this time, there were 1,260,000 Arabs and 630,000 Jews.[1] About one-half of income originating in the entire economy was in agriculture.[2] After the United Nations vote establishing Israel, a substantial percentage of Arabs left that part of Palestine which became Israel. However, by 1951, when as a result of immigration the population in this area had increased to its 1947 level, only 17 percent of the total labor force was employed in agriculture. Nevertheless, this reduced labor force was capable of supplying most of the needs of the entire population. Simultaneously, income originating in this sector declined from 50 percent to about 12 percent (in current prices) of total value added.

The ability to feed the same size population with a third as many workers was made possible by the large amounts of capital devoted to the sector between 1948 and 1951, which significantly increased product per worker. Had there been no factor additions to other sectors, the share of agricultural product in total product would not have decreased as it did. In fact, however, other sectors were provided with enormously increased quantities of both labor and capital, which led to rapidly growing income in them and thus to the decline in the share of agriculture from 50 to 12 percent.

1. The estimated number of Arabs in the area that eventually became part of Israel was 763,000, arrived at by taking the Arab population residing in this area in 1944 and assuming a 3 percent rate of natural increase. See A. Hovne, *Labour Force in Israel,* Table 8.

2. In the Jewish sector these percentages were quite different. About 13 percent of the labor force was in agriculture; a slightly lower percentage of value added originated in this sector. See Halevi and Klinov-Malul, *Economic Development of Israel,* Chap. 2.

In terms of the changes in the labor force, the process may be viewed as follows. If the Arabs had remained in the country and agricultural productivity had increased as it did, a large percentage would have sought employment elsewhere. The immigrants entering the country after 1951 were, in a sense, the physical counterpart of this released labor. Their employment, mainly in nonagricultural branches, was permitted by the enhanced productivity in agriculture. Thus the country did undergo an agricultural revolution, both in the labor force employed and in agriculture's importance in income, although it was obviously of a different sort than the usual one and certainly more compressed. As a result, by 1951 the relative sizes of the agricultural and nonagricultural sectors were almost at the levels that would ultimately develop.

CHANGE IN THE STRUCTURE OF DEMAND AND ITS EFFECT

The following discussion analyzes the growth patterns that evolved from the 1951 base.[3] It attempts to ascertain the relative importance of changes in domestic demand, exports and imports and technological change[4] in the generation of output growth. In the paper just cited, no attempt is made to go back still further and to explain the observed growth of final demands or imports. The following chapters, however, move in the latter direction.

The particular variant of the input-output model used by Chenery, Shishido, and Watanabe is

$$X_i + M_i = Y_i + W_i \qquad i = 1 \ldots n \qquad (3.1)$$

where X_i is the gross domestic output of the ith industry; M_i is the imports of goods that had their origin abroad in the ith industry; W_i is the domestic intermediate use of the output of the ith industry; Y_i is the final use of the output of the ith industry. The rearranging of Equation 3.1, noting that $W_i = \Sigma_j X_{ij}$, and using the usual Leontief relations of the form, $X_{ij} = \bar{a}_{ij} X_j$, yields

3. The analysis follows that suggested by Hollis B. Chenery, Shuntaro Shishido, and Tsunehiko Watanabe: "The Pattern of Japanese Economic Growth, 1914–1954," *Econometrica* 30 (Jan. 1962): 98–139.

4. The concept of technological change used here involves changes in the size of the technical coefficients and is not directly related to the "residual" cited above in Chap. 2.

$$X_i - \sum_j \bar{a}_{ij} X_j = Y_i - M_i \qquad i = 1 \ldots n \qquad (3.2)$$

In the usual matrix notation, the solution to Equation 3.2 is

$$X = (I - \bar{A})^{-1}(Y - M) \qquad (3.3)$$

In Equation 3.2 the $\bar{a}_{ij}$ coefficients indicate the total amount of intermediate flows going from i to j, regardless of whether they are produced domestically or imported. Thus

$$\bar{a}_{ij} = \frac{X_{ij} + M_{ij}}{X_j}$$

where M_{ij} indicates imports having their origin in the ith industry abroad used in the jth domestic industry. Similarly, Y_i includes final imports of the ith good, as well as domestically produced final goods. M_i is thus equal to the total imports of good i, whether used to satisfy intermediate or final demand. In any year M_i is known ex post. Denoting $(I - \bar{A})^{-1}$ as R and separating Y into domestic final demands P and exports E, Equation 3.3 may be rewritten as

$$X = R(P + E - M)$$

If R remains constant between two periods, then changes in gross outputs could be explained as

$$\Delta X = R(\Delta P + \Delta E - \Delta M) \qquad (3.4)$$

However, to provide an explanation of changes in the relative size of sectoral gross outputs, the magnitudes in Equation 3.4 should be expressed in terms of their deviations from the average growth rate of domestic demands, $\lambda = \Sigma P_2 / \Sigma P_1$, where subscripts denote the period. We may then rewrite Equation 3.4 as

$$\delta X = R(\delta P + \delta E - \delta M) \qquad (3.5)$$

This expression, at least in an accounting sense, explains the changes in the relative importance of the gross output of each branch.

The right-hand side of Equation 3.5 does not provide a complete explanation of δX if changes have occurred over time in the coefficient matrix itself. In that case, the following expression constitutes a total explanation of δX:

$$\delta X = R(\delta P + \delta E - \delta M - \lambda T) \qquad (3.6)$$

where λT shows the changes in intermediate requirements as a result of differences in the coefficient matrix between two periods.[5]

There are input-output tables for Israel for 1951 and 1958, and final demand data according to input-output definitions are available for the period since 1958.[6] The table for 1951 was estimated by A. L. Gaathon in six-branch detail,[7] although considerable information, not specifically included in the table is also provided in his study. Thus, in analyzing the 1951 through 1958 period, we are limited to a six-sector study. For the period after 1958, 25-branch detail is available. The 1958 input-output table, aggregated to six sectors, is used for the 1951–58 analysis.[8]

The existence of the 1951 and 1958 tables determines the first set of years to be studied, and the availability of final demand by input-output definition through 1964 demarcates the second set of years. Fortunately, these dates are analytically relevant. At the beginning of the period 1951–58, the absorption of new immigrants was the primary task of the economy. During this period, as absorption was accomplished, emphasis shifted to providing increased consumption levels for the economy and to import substitution. By the end of this period, in fact, most economically feasible import substitution had been completed.[9]

The period 1958–64 was one in which import substitution was of less importance, but increasing exports of manufactured goods and expanding domestic demand resulted in significant changes in the sectoral structure of production. Each of these periods will be considered separately.

One basic data problem is that no appropriate price indices by

5. $T = (A_2 - A_1)X_1$. In Equation 3.6, R is the inverse matrix of period 2. If the inverse used is the first-period matrix (as in our analysis of 1958–64), T can be shown to equal $(A_1 - A_2)X_2$.

6. The 1951 table is to be found in A. L. Gaathon, *Survey of Israel's Economy, 1951* (Jerusalem: Central Bureau of Statistics and Falk Project for Economic Research, Israel, 1959); the 1958 table is in Michael Bruno, *Interdependence, Resource Use, and Structural Change in Israel* (Jerusalem: Bank of Israel, 1962).

7. Agriculture, manufacturing, construction, utilities, transportation, and services (including trade, finance, and government).

8. Although a 25-sector breakdown for 1951–58 would clearly be desirable, price indices at this detailed level cannot be obtained although most of the required output data are available.

9. While, in 1951, imports constituted 45 percent of GNP and 29 percent of total resources (GNP plus imports), by 1958 these ratios had declined to 25 and 18 respectively, all at 1955 prices.

input-output sectoral categories exist for the 1951–58 period. In lieu of these, our deflators are taken from the national accounts, although in modified form. They are obtained from items in the national accounts that correspond closely to the sectoral definitions in the input-output tables. The main source of error in this procedure stems from using only the price movements of final goods, although the prices at which intermediate and final goods are sold may differ. Therefore, the results of the analysis have been checked by sensitivity tests in which the price deflators are varied simultaneously. Although this results in some changes in the explanation of structural change, the main thrust of the discussion below remains valid.[10] Finally, both 1951 and 1958 imports have been revalued to reflect scarcity values better, since in both periods the official exchange rate was overvalued.[11]

It should be emphasized that the following analysis is mainly descriptive, with relatively little explanation of the underlying determinants of the observed changes. It is designed to illuminate the overall intersectoral background necessary for the intensive analysis of individual sectors in subsequent chapters. In particular the evolution of primary factor allocations by sector receives only brief attention, as do the relations between changes in the production structure, and comparative advantage.[12] The reason for these omissions is the impossibility of accounting for these aspects within a traditional economic framework; the structure of production as well as factor allocations was subject to considerable govern-

10. In addition to sensitivity tests, for the 1958–64 period the price indices obtained from the national accounts were compared to the actual price deflators contained in the input-output data of the Bank of Israel. The correspondence was quite good. In addition to the problems of price indices, a considerable number of data changes in the 1951 table were required to make them suitable for the present analysis. Improved data, which became available after Gaathon's study was completed, have been incorporated and certain inconsistencies removed. Imports had to be reallocated, so that they would appear by sector of origin abroad as well as by sector of destination in Israel. Most of these revisions were based upon data contained in Lubell, *Israel's National Expenditure,* especially chap. 3. This source contains a considerable amount of data on intersectoral flows that are not available in the national accounts data based on them.

11. The revaluation of 1958 imports is based on data to be found in Joseph Baruh, "Import Taxes and Export Subsidies in Israel, 1955–61," Bank of Israel, *Bulletin,* no. 18.

12. For a detailed attempt of this type, see Leif Johansen, *A Multisectoral Model of Economic Growth* (Amsterdam: North Holland, 1960).

ment influence, as well as market pressures. Indeed, a good part of the next three chapters is devoted to the description and explanation of these decisions.

1951–58

Between 1951 and 1958 gross output grew at considerably different rates in the six major sectors.[13] The ratios of gross output (in constant prices) in 1958 to those in 1951 for each sector are:

Agriculture	2.8
Manufacturing	2.6
Construction	1.1
Utilities	4.2
Transportation	2.1
Services	2.0

Agriculture, manufacturing, and utilities increased their shares in total gross production, while the relative importance of construction, transportation and services declined. The increased gross production in the former branches did not reflect an increased use of imports as they remained nearly constant during the period.[14] On the contrary, much of the expansion of gross production could be attributed to import substitution. While agriculture and manufacturing were the leading sectors in the growth process, both transportation and services, much of whose output is directly related to that of the two primary sectors, also grew rapidly. Similarly, the expansion of utilities reflected in part the increase in production requirements of agriculture and manufacturing. Too much significance should not be attached to the rapid growth rate in this sector, since base production was very small.

Agriculture

The results of applying Equations 3.4 and 3.5 to the data for 1951 and 1958 are shown in Tables 3.1 and 3.2. The amount by which

13. In *Essays on the Structure of the Jewish Economy in Palestine and Israel,* Szereszewski carried out an input-output analysis of the 1951–58 period and compared the results for this period with those for 1936–51. His work provides an alternative, though similar, approach to the analysis of structural change during this period.

14. Of increased imports of $143 million between 1951 and 1958, only $28 million were for commodity imports, although part of service imports, government, n.e.s., is composed of military hardware.

Table 3.1: Sources of Absolute Growth of Sectoral Output, 1951–58
(000's of 1958 I£)

	Domestic demand		Exports		Imports		Change in total requirements $(2) + (4) - (6)$	Observed total change in gross output
	Direct (1)	Total (2)	Direct (3)	Total (4)	Direct (5)	Total (6)	(7)	(8)
Agriculture	240,956	433,010	80,176	138,213	101,628	140,818	430,405	499,530
Manufacturing and mining	408,264	912,080	118,285	266,577	14,587	115,722	1,062,935	1,234,194
Construction	68,865	70,552	0	404	0	1,170	69,786	73,565
Utilities	11,636	56,779	0	13,167	0	12,141	57,805	86,349
Transportation	25,039	120,245	82,801	111,292	19,935	65,285	166,252	276,795
Services	267,968	480,339	46,352	117,106	242,106	339,207	267,238	688,767

Note: Direct change is the increase in the absolute level of final deliveries (or imports) originating in each sector; total includes the indirect requirements generated by the final demands of other sectors as well. This table corresponds to Equation 3.4.

Table 3.2: Sources of Deviations from Proportional Growth, 1951–58
(000's of 1958 I£)

	Domestic demand		Exports		Imports		Sum of total deviations (2) + (4) − (6)	Observed nonproportional change in gross output
	Direct deviation from proportional growth	Total effect of deviations from proportional growth	Direct deviation from proportional growth	Total effect of deviations from proportional growth	Direct deviation from proportional growth	Total effect of deviations from proportional growth		
	(1)	(2)	(3)	(4)	(5)	(6)	(7)	(8)
Agriculture	158,582	194,703	66,352	113,155	89,481	35,562	272,296	372,346
Manufacturing and mining	46,166	26,266	94,212	212,679	−311,849	−469,611	708,556	863,321
Construction	−163,955	−164,054	0	285	0	692	−164,461	−159,255
Utilities	6,106	19,729	0	10,642	0	−3,467	33,838	73,621
Transportation	−40,698	−49,629	70,645	92,591	13,976	27,018	15,944	101,386
Services	−9,138	−28,747	27,761	82,690	191,795	200,749	−146,806	367,281

Note: This table corresponds to Equation 3.5.

agricultural gross output exceeded proportional growth is seen to be attributable mainly to the growth of domestic final demand (primarily consumption), which itself reflects a combination of rapid population growth and rising per capita income. The impact of increasing exports on agricultural output was also substantial, and within this category oranges accounted for almost all of the nonproportional growth in direct exports. However, the indirect, and thus the total, impact of exports is probably overstated.[15] Although agricultural inputs were important in some manufacturing export branches, for example, food processing, much of the nonproportional growth in manufactured exports, for example, occurred in polished diamonds, which have no agricultural inputs.[16]

The impact of the changing import pattern had two distinct effects on agricultural output: (1) agricultural imports increased more than proportionally and thus offset part of the increased production requirements stemming from the growth of domestic demand;[17] and (2) the rapid process of import substitution in processed foods and textiles led to increased requirements for agricultural output. These countertrends resulted in a total import effect on agricultural output that was smaller than the direct effect alone.

Manufacturing

Table 3.2 shows that manufacturing output grew much more than proportionally. The dominant influence in this growth was extensive import substitution within the sector. While the gross supply requirements of manufactured goods were rising rapidly as a result of enormously increased domestic demands, imports of manufac-

---

15. The total effect of exports includes agricultural input requirements in exports of other sectors, as well as indirect requirements of agricultural exports.

16. This error results from the use of the 6 × 6 table. For this aggregation to be strictly valid, either all final demands would have to grow at a similar rate or the input structures would have to be similar. Neither of these holds for diamonds vis-à-vis the rest of the manufacturing sector. Although the aggregation error crops up at several points in the 1951–58 analysis, the general tenor of the results would not be changed much even if more detail were available. In particular, a detailed examination of imports by commodity group suggests that merchandise imports in most categories increased by substantially less than GNP and presumably by less than total uses in each category.

17. These imports were primarily in cereals and animal feeds.

tured goods remained about stable, so that the entire supply increase was met out of domestic production.

Table 3.1, which is based on absolute changes in the relevant magnitudes, rather than deviations from proportional growth, shows that of the total increase in manufacturing output of I£1.2 billion, about three-quarters is attributable to the increase in domestic demand, mainly for agricultural and manufactured goods and about one-fifth to increased exports. Of these increased requirements, only about 10 percent were offset by increased imports in all sectors.[18] Moreover, imports of manufactured goods themselves rose by only I£14.6 million (or about $8 million) in constant prices, despite the increase in manufacturing output of I£1.2 billion. During this period the share of domestic output in the total supply of manufactured goods increased from 53.6 to 74.2.

Returning to the sources of the increasing relative importance of manufacturing (Table 3.2), we find that the main determinant, accounting for over half of such growth, was the import substitution process. Moreover, most of the import effect occurred within manufacturing, as may be seen by comparing the direct and total effects (columns 5 and 6). Exports are the other main source of nonproportional growth, explaining a quarter. However, as in the discussion of the impact of exports on agricultural production, there is likely to be an upward bias, since the main source of the increased export requirements stem from agricultural and manufactured exports. A large portion of these were oranges and diamonds, which have less impact on the manufacturing sector than the average branch in these sectors.

The large deviation in transportation exports also probably exerted less feedback on manufacturing than appears in the calculation, since air and sea transportation have far different coefficients from the domestic transportation branches. The net nonproportional impact of changes in final domestic demands was slight (I£26 million out of a nonproportional change in gross output of I£863 million).

18. The main offset of increased imports was attributable to imports in agriculture and services. For example, increased imports of food reduce the required fertilizer output in manufacturing.

Construction

Given the negligible intersectoral purchases from construction, the main factor in its growth was the retarded growth rate of final demand, particularly for housing. This reflects the end of the mass immigration and the smoothing out over time of the construction programs that aimed at replacing temporary dwellings with more adequate ones. The slowdown in the building program also significantly reduced the pressures on the manufacturing sector and was at least partly responsible for the fall in the import coefficient in certain branches, especially stone and cement, between 1950 and 1958.[19] As construction has little feedback on sectors other than manufacturing, its slowdown had few further effects.

Utilities

The value of the output of utilities increased by I£86,349,000 (Table 3.1), the largest part of which was attributable to the more than proportional increases in domestic demands. The percentage of the explained gross output deviation in utilities is smaller than in the three previous sectors; this is a result of the increasing mechanization of the economy, which requires an enormous input of electricity both in manufacturing processes and in the rapidly expanding irrigation system.

Transportation

The transportation sector also appears to have undergone a substantial degree of change in its production coefficients; nonproportional changes in final demands explain only a small fraction of the more than proportional increase in gross output. It appears that the growth of domestic intermediate goods production in other sectors led to an increase in demand for transportation services. This was probably a result of the dispersal of industry to the south and north of the country.

Services

While the results for the sectors discussed above conform with other available evidence about the economy and lead to reasonable explanations of observed output patterns, the calculations for the

19. See below, Chap. 4.

service sector yield implausible results. As may be seen in either Table 3.1 or 3.2, very little of the increase in service output is explained by the changes in domestic demand, export, and imports. Nor is there evidence to suggest that changes in the service input coefficients occurred. It appears that there are substantial estimation errors in both the initial and terminal years. Both Gaathon and Bruno cite the weakness of the data, in particular the data on markups.[20] These errors are undoubtedly reflected more in the price margins on intermediate sales, and other intermediate service inputs such as legal and financial services, than in the estimate of final services such as entertainment or personal services. This conjecture is borne out by the very large differences in coefficients of service inputs into the other sectors:

	A	M	C	U	T	S
1951	.03	.03	.03	–	.02	.03
1958	.02	.08	.08	.10	.10	.18

These differences can also be seen in a summary measure, namely, the division of gross output between final and intermediate uses. According to the 1951 data, 86 percent of gross output in services went to final uses, whereas in 1958 the percentage was 61. It seems unlikely that changes of such magnitude could have occurred even though these data are not in constant prices. The implication of the underestimate of intermediate service uses is that the growth in gross output was less than that recorded and that the change in output which is to be explained is considerably smaller than the data in Tables 3.1 and 3.2 indicate. It should be noted that an error in the estimate of service intermediates does not affect the analysis of the other sectors, since the estimates of domestic final demands, imports, and exports in 1951 appear reasonably accurate.

As a result of import substitution, major changes occurred in the domestic input-output matrix in agriculture and manufacturing; indeed, the impact of import substitution is best seen by referring to the domestic coefficient matrices[21] presented in Table 3.3. Although

20. See Bruno, *Interdependence, Resource Use, and Structural Change,* pp. 212–13; Gaathon, *Survey of Israel's Economy, 1951,* chap. 26.

21. The typical coefficient in the input-output table used above is $\bar{a}_{ij} = (X_{ij} + M_{ij})/X_j$; the domestic coefficient matrix consists of the elements $a_{ij} = X_{ij}/X_j$. Even if $\bar{a}_{ij}$ remains constant, a_{ij} will change as the ratio of X_{ij} to M_{ij} changes.

Table 3.3: Input-Output Matrices for 1951 and 1958
(current prices)

1951

	Agriculture	Manu-facturing and mining	Construc-tion	Utilities	Transport and communi-cations	Services
	A	M	C	U	T	S
A	.2238	.0217	0	0	0	0
M	.0366	.1637	.3423	.0405	.0620	.0195
C	0	0	0	0	0	0
U	.0088	.0059	0	0	0	.0084
T	.0278	.0258	.0898	0	.0174	.0021
S	.0291	.0269	.0314	0	.0149	.0293

1958

	A	M	C	U	T	S
A	.1350	.0731	.0001	.0001	0	0
M	.1274	.2446	.3441	.0564	.1017	.0638
C	0	0	0	0	0	.0034
U	.0505	.0115	.0001	.1867	.0016	.0038
T	.0309	.0212	.0631	.0292	.0234	.1002
S	.0212	.0814	.0832	.1290	.0966	.1811

Sources: 1951: Computed from A. L. Gaathon, *Survey of Israel's Economy, 1951* (Jerusalem: Central Bureau of Statistics and Falk Project for Economic Research in Israel, 1959).

1958: Computed from Michael Bruno, *Interdependence, Resource Use, and Structural Change in Israel* (Jerusalem: Bank of Israel, 1962), pp. 37–38.

the matrices are not in constant prices, the major changes in coefficients are unlikely to be attributable to relative price movements. The main changes in coefficients are a_{aa}, a_{am}, a_{ma}, a_{mm}, a_{ms}, and a_{mt}.[22]

The increase in the coefficients of manufacturing sales to other branches was attributable to the considerable amount of import substitution in manufacturing and the enlarged range of products produced locally. Whereas, in 1951, insecticides, fertilizers, packing materials, and spare parts were imported by the agricultural

22. We omit changes in the transportation and utilities row, as they are not primarily attributable to import substitution, and those in the service row because of the uncertain nature of their reliability.

sector, by 1958 almost all were produced within Israel. In addition, the transport sector was able to obtain spare parts locally. Within the manufacturing branch there was a considerable deepening of production; in particular, chemicals, metals and metal products, and paper, which formerly were imported, were now produced within the country, albeit with imported raw materials.

The increase in a_{am} reflects the increasing growth of industrial crops, along with dairy farming. Whereas, in 1951, large amounts of cotton, sugar, and milk were imported for processing, by 1958 domestic production of these had increased enough to permit import substitution.

The decline of intra-agricultural sales was apparently due to the decrease in the amount of output used for seed purposes; 1951 was a year of considerable expansion of the number of farms, as well as recovery of many existing farms neglected during the war of independence, and seed requirements were extensive.

1958–64

During the years following 1958, the economy underwent significant changes. Unemployment slowly dropped and by 1961 had almost disappeared. Immigration, which had slowed down in 1958–60, rose sharply in 1961 and continued rising through 1964; thus demand for housing again became an important stimulus. The substantial changes that occurred in the sectoral structure of production are shown in Tables 3.4 and 3.5.[23] Agricultural gross output increased much more slowly than average domestic demand, while both manufacturing and construction rose more rapidly.

Agriculture

The slower growth of agriculture was to be expected, given the relatively low income elasticities of demand for its output and the difficulty encountered in exporting high cost products. It can be seen from Table 3.5 that the main source of the relative decline in gross output was the slow growth of domestic demand. The impact of this was partially offset by the import substitution that took place in the branch (mainly in industrial crops) and the rapid rise

23. Tables 3.4 and 3.5 are obtained from aggregating the 25-branch results.

Table 3.4: Sources of Absolute Growth of Sectoral Output, 1958–64
(000's of 1963 I£)

	Domestic demand		Exports		Imports		Change in total requirements $(2) + (4) - (6)$	Observed total change in gross output
	Direct (1)	Total (2)	Direct (3)	Total (4)	Direct (5)	Total (6)	(7)	(8)
Agriculture	170,005	552,319	73,205	195,395	78,065	169,364	578,350	509,674
Manufacturing and mining,	1,462,425	3,405,997	772,895	1,558,319	1,066,436	1,925,134	3,039,182	3,680,172
Construction	843,885	850,447	0	2,856	0	3,843	849,460	853,541
Utilities	56,155	164,434	0	49,925	0	60,376	153,983	81,419
Transportation	203,024	579,816	212,543	375,728	30,102	211,351	744,193	680,316
Services	986,255	1,875,031	373,811	816,114	611,095	1,098,024	1,593,121	1,805,166

Note: This table corresponds to Equation 3.4.

Table 3.5: Sources of Deviations from Proportional Growth, 1958–64
(000's of 1963 I£)

| | Domestic demand | | Exports | | Imports | | Sum of total deviations | Observed nonproportional change in gross output |
| | Direct deviation from proportional growth | Total effect of deviations from proportional growth | Direct deviation from proportional growth | Total effect of deviations from proportional growth | Direct deviation from proportional growth | Total effect of deviations from proportional growth | (2) + (4) − (6) | |
	(1)	(2)	(3)	(4)	(5)	(6)	(7)	(8)
Agriculture	−225,899	−341,365	−58,743	22,421	−138,546	−203,513	−115,431	−232,883
Manufacturing and mining	108,634	209,116	611,064	1,167,883	245,435	382,062	994,937	1,520,233
Construction	168,035	167,799	0	1,820	0	1,716	167,903	171,839
Utilities	33,073	10,960	0	24,767	0	−12,356	48,083	−32,487
Transportation	256	−231	70,500	164,178	−3,098	47,854	119,093	78,106
Services	−85,927	−67,281	254,930	519,866	334,922	490,398	−37,813	38,796

Note: This table corresponds to Equation 3.5.

in citrus exports. Rapidly growing exports of oranges and, in the industrial sector, of processed citrus products and cotton textiles, are responsible for most of the more than proportional export increase (see Table 3.5). Nevertheless, these increases in demand were overwhelmed by the slowing of the growth of domestic demand for both processed and unprocessed foods.

Manufacturing

The large deviation from proportional growth in manufacturing is almost totally attributable to the extraordinarily rapid growth of manufactured exports, whose average annual rate of increase in the 1958–61 period exceeded 28 percent, although it was smaller in the next three years. This expansion was more broadly based, that is, not as heavily dependent on polished diamonds, as had been true in the pre-1958 period. However, in contrast to the earlier period, the combined impact of import increases in all branches was a decrease in the required rate of growth of manufacturing output. Domestic absorption of manufactured output increased slightly faster than overall domestic demand, and the total effect of domestic demands led to a nonproportional increase of I£209 million, about 20 percent of the calculated nonproportional increment to gross output. However, while exports were the primary source of the rising relative importance of manufacturing, Table 3.4 shows that increases in domestic demand still accounted for twice as much as exports of the absolute increase in total demand for manufacturing. As in 1951–58, the sector still relied on the expanding domestic market for the bulk of its sales.

Other sectors

The relative gain in the construction sector represents, for the most part, the influence of the renewed immigration upon residential construction.

The gross output of utilities rose considerably less than it would have risen had the technical coefficients remained constant; the actual increase was I£81.4 million (Table 3.4), while that derived from adding the total demands was I£154 million. The implied decrease in intermediate uses of electricity is surprising, since it indicates a decreasing average use of electricity per unit of output. However, much of the change is probably attributable to the decrease in the amount of water used in irrigation relative to agricultural output,[24] and irrigation is by far the most intensive user of electricity in the economy.

The gross output in transportation increased more than proportionally. Most of this was attributable to the increase in export requirements from other branches, reflecting the rapid growth in manufacturing and citrus exports. The total nonproportional increase in requirements generated by the final demands exceeded the observed nonproportional increase in output. (See the last two columns in Table 3.5.) This difference is attributable to a decrease in the coefficients that occurred between 1958 and 1964.[25]

The output of the service sector increased slightly more than proportionally, while the explained deviation is slightly negative. The absolute differences are quite small and minor coefficient changes would have led to the observed differences.

IMPORTANCE OF FINAL DEMANDS

A convenient summary of the changes in the importance of the various final demands can be obtained by calculating the percentage of each sector's gross output that is attributable to each of the final demands.[26] These results are shown in Table 3.6 for 1951, 1958, and 1964 for agriculture and manufacturing, the sectors which underwent the greatest changes. Consumption is defined to include government purchases on current account.

Between 1951 and 1958 there was a shift in the ultimate source of demand for gross agricultural output from consumption to exports, the percentage of output going to consumption declining from 75 to 66 percent.[27] This reflects the rapid increase in citrus

24. Between 1958 and 1964, agricultural water use increased by only 15 percent, while gross output increased by 40 percent. Some of the decrease stems from somewhat more rain in 1964 than in 1958 but most probably accrued from the large improvement in the efficiency of water use during the period.

25. A preliminary input-output table for 1963 indicates that, for almost every branch, the coefficient for land transportation declined.

26. Gross output can be exhaustively allocated to each final demand by calculating: $X = RC$, $X = RI$, etc. Here R is the inverse of the domestic A matrix, not the matrix used in the preceding calculations, which included imports. For 1951, Gaathon's input-output table was used.

27. As the 1951 and 1958 data are not in comparable prices, some of the changes in these years may reflect price changes. However, sensitivity

Table 3.6: The Destination of Gross Output, 1951, 1958, and 1964

		Consumption	*Investment*	*Exports*
Agriculture:	1951	75.0	15.8	9.2
	1958	66.0	15.7	18.2
	1964	75.6	6.1	18.3
Manufacturing:	1951	62.0	32.8	5.2
	1958	63.2	22.3	14.5
	1964		76.4	23.6

Sources: 1951: Calculated from data contained in Gaathon, *Survey of Israel's Economy 1951*, p. 46.
1958: Bruno, *Interdependence, Resource Use, and Structural Change*, p. 82.
1964: Calculated from Bank of Israel, *Annual Report, 1964*, pp. 266, 236.

exports, rather than a slowdown in the growth of domestic demand for food. Investment requirements for agricultural output, mainly afforestation, irrigation, and livestock accumulation, remained about the same in both periods.[28] After 1958 there was a significant change in the demand structure: investment declining, and consumption increasing in relative importance. The decline in agricultural investment was mainly a result of the completion of the planned expansion of livestock and fruit orchards.[29]

Between 1951 and 1958 exports' absorption of manufacturing output rose relative to that of investment, consumption remaining about constant. This change is attributable in large measure to the decreased importance of the construction sector, which had accounted for two-thirds of output destined for investment in 1951, and the rapid growth of exports during the period.[30] The export orientation of the post-1958 years is clearly shown by the large

tests indicate that the errors introduced are not large, so that the pattern does reflect basic changes.

28. The industrial investment goods branches have virtually no need for agricultural inputs, wood being the only significant agricultural input and it is imported.

29. The 1964 data for agriculture are not on exactly the same basis as that for earlier years and may have small errors understating the importance of exports.

30. The declining impact of the construction component may be seen from the fact that production requirements in manufacturing necessary to satisfy construction demands constituted 25 percent of gross manufacturing output in 1951 but only 12 percent in 1958.

increase in the percentage of gross output destined for exports. In the years between 1958 and 1964, well over 30 percent of the incremental gross output in manufacturing in each year was devoted to exports, the percentage reaching 50 in some years.

THE STRUCTURE OF VALUE ADDED

Although the preceding has concentrated on the structure of gross output, it is of interest to examine the movements in value added by sector, since much of our empirical knowledge of the development process relates to movements in this measure.[31] Analysts of the Israeli economy have often noted that the sectoral distribution of value added in current prices has remained remarkably constant, while income per capita has more than doubled. In particular, the lack of a relative increase in the share of income originating in manufacturing has been cited as an anomalous feature of the growth process,[32] given the findings of Kuznets and others; several explanations have been offered for this phenomenon. However, these studies have either taken the current price data as indicators of movements in real value added or have simply used wages to deflate them. Current price data are, however, of little use if there are differential rates of inflation of wages and profits among sectors. The use of wages as the sole deflator is subject to several objections, for example, movements in wages may represent productivity increases rather than inflation; nonlabor returns and labor returns may have different rates of inflation. The more common method of deflating value added has been to deflate output and purchased intermediate inputs separately and to define the difference between

31. For example, both the time series and the cross-section analyses of Kuznets use value added, as does the work of Chenery. See Simon Kuznets, *Six Lectures on Economic Growth* (New York: Free Press of Glencoe, 1959); Hollis B. Chenery, "Patterns of Industrial Growth," *American Economic Review* 50 (Sept. 1960): 624–54. Value added originating in a sector does not necessarily follow gross output if, for example, there are shifts within a sector among branches with differing ratios of value added to gross output. Moreover, changes in the degree of vertical integration may cause shifts in gross output without a concomitant one in value added.

32. See Halevi and Klinov-Malul, *Economic Development of Israel,* chap. 6; Ephraim Kleiman, "The Place of Manufacturing in the Growth of the Israel Economy," *Journal of Development Studies* 3 (Apr. 1967): 226–48.

the two as a measure of real output.[33] However, in a recent article Paul A. David has shown that the double-deflation method is incorrect and has suggested another, which deflates value added by the final price index of the industry in which it originates.[34] David's procedure has been followed here and the results are shown in Table 3.7.

Table 3.7: Deflated Value Added by Sector as a Percentage
of Aggregate Value Added, 1952, 1958, and 1964

	1952	*1958*	*1964*
Agriculture	9.7	10.6	10.1
Manufacturing and mining	17.3	20.1	26.7
Construction	10.7	8.8 ⎫	11.2
Utilities	1.1	1.0 ⎭	
Transportation and communications	8.6	8.6	8.9
Services	52.6	50.9	43.1
Total	100.0	100.0	100.0

Note: Price deflators are those used in an earlier part of the chapter, calculated from final demand components of national accounts. For 1958–64 a similar calculation was made using price indices implicit in constant price input-output data of the Bank of Israel, and the results were similar to those for 1958–64, using the national accounts deflator. Value added is exclusive of the imputation for ownership of dwellings.

Sources: Statistical Abstract of Israel, 1968, pp. 160–61; CBS, *Israel's National Income and Expenditure,* p. 104.

The importance of manufacturing in terms of the percentage of value added originating in the sector increased over the 1951–64 period, most rapidly during the last six years; this was offset by a corresponding decrease in the share of services. The share of value added originating in agriculture increased between 1951 and 1958, and declined somewhat during the succeeding years. These move-

33. See R. Geary, "The Concept of Net Volume of Output, with Special Reference to Irish Data," *Journal of the Royal Statistical Society* 107, Part 2–4, 1944: 251–59.

34. Paul A. David, "Measuring Real Net Output: A Proposed Index," *Review of Economics and Statistics* 48 (Nov. 1966). David's procedure assumes a linear homogeneous production function for each industry and competition in both product and factor markets. However, even if monopoly or monopsony exist, the proposed deflator yields a correct measure if the degree of imperfection does not change.

ments in the percentage of income originating in each sector follow those of gross output discussed previously, and the determinants of the latter also explain the former. Thus attempts to reconcile a rapidly growing income per capita with the failure of manufacturing's share of value added to increase were unwarranted. Israel's evolution in this respect conforms to the Chenery-Kuznets findings that the relative importance of manufacturing increases as per capita income rises.

However, there is one result not in accord with the earlier investigations, namely, the decline in the relative importance of services and their high share even at the end of the period. The service sector (including transport and communications) comprised over half of the value added throughout the period in question and provides an interesting paradigm on the relationship between sectoral structure and macroeconomic balance.[35] As stated in Chapter 1, during the period since independence, Israel has run a substantial import surplus. How will the import surplus affect the sectoral composition of output? Let α_i denote the desired sectoral distribution of domestic absorption, D, determined by the various income elasticities of demand where i indicates the various sectors (agriculture, manufacturing, services) and $\Sigma\alpha_i = 1$; β_i and μ_i denote the sectoral origin of exports and imports, respectively. If trade were balanced, and if we assume that β_i and μ_i are roughly equal, the sectoral composition of domestic output would be determined by the α_i's. However, in the presence of an import surplus, the composition now depends on the sectoral composition of the import surplus and the service share of value added is likely to exceed α_s. This may be established as follows: let R be the ratio of service sector value added to that in manufacturing and agriculture (denoted by T); then

$$R = \frac{\alpha_s D + \beta_s E - \mu_s M}{\alpha_T D + \beta_T E - \mu_T M} \qquad (3.7)$$

If we assume that β_i is approximately equal to μ_i, R will exceed α_s/α_T if

---

35. The impact of a large import surplus on the sectoral structure of production in Israel is analyzed in detail in Ofer, *Service Industries in a Developing Economy.* The remainder of this section is an algebraic statement of Ofer's analysis.

$$\frac{\alpha_s D - \mu_s(\overline{M})}{\alpha_T D - \mu_T(\overline{M})} > \frac{\alpha_s}{\alpha_T} \qquad (3.8)$$

where $\overline{M} = M - E$, the import surplus, and Equation 3.8 simplifies to

$$\frac{\mu_T}{\mu_s} > \frac{\alpha_T}{\alpha_s} \qquad (3.9)$$

The inequality (3.9) is likely to hold, as both imports and exports consist mainly of goods, μ_T/μ_s being roughly 3, while α_T/α_s is close to 1. Thus, in the presence of an import surplus, the observed sectoral distribution of domestic production will not reflect the influence of income elasticities that usually provide the underlying basis for the observed evolution of sectoral structure. In Israel the declining relative importance of services partly reflected the decreasing importance of the import surplus (as a result of import substitution and export growth), rather than low income elasticities of demand.

FACTOR ALLOCATION AND PRODUCTIVITY

Until now our analysis has focused on the determinants of the evolution of the sectoral structure of production. We now relate this to the allocation of primary factors and the productivity discussion of the previous chapter.

In an economy in which a unitary exchange rate is set at a level resulting in a balanced current account, the sectoral allocation of resources will follow comparative advantage. However, the high disequilibrium exchange rate established in Israel led to government dominance of the allocation procedure. This occurred at two levels. At the macro level the continuing import surplus determined, to a large extent, the division of output between goods and services.[36] Then, within each of these broad sectors, the detailed allocation of resources was decisively influenced by decisions on investment financing and protection. Thus the allocation mechanism may be viewed roughly as consisting of public determination of the desirable configuration of output, with the sectoral production functions implicitly determining the requisite factor allocations

---

36. Services as used here includes construction. The allocation mechanism implicit in this section is presented in Chaps. 6 and 7.

rather than themselves being a major determinant of such allocation. Put slightly differently, with the sectoral distribution of output determined by public policy, sectoral total factor allocation will depend on differential productivity growth rates. The composition of this allocation between labor and capital will depend upon sectoral output-factor elasticities. However, for our purpose at this point, we concentrate on the implications of the different total factor productivity growth rates.

In Chapter 2 we saw that the residual in both agriculture and manufacturing was higher than that for "other private non-dwelling branches" which includes construction, public utilities and private services, when observed factor shares are used as output elasticities: it seems likely that the same relationship among residuals would hold if all output elasticities were generated by explicitly estimating production functions. These results are not surprising given the production characteristics inherent in construction and many private services. Moreover, the inclusion of government and private nonprofit institutions would be unlikely to raise the residual in services even if it were possible to obtain separate measures of input and output. The implication of these results is that "other branches" will require more total resources to maintain a given output growth rate than will agriculture and manufacturing. This, in fact, is what occurred.

Between 1951 and 1964 the approximately constant ratio of agriculture to total value added was maintained despite a substantial decline in the sector's share of total capital stock[37] although its share of the total labor force was maintained (Table 3.8). In fact, despite a fall in the share of both labor and capital in the 1958 to 1964 subperiod, the agricultural output share remained roughly constant. Between 1951 and 1964 the relative importance of manufacturing in value added increased by about 50 percent (Table 3.7), although its share of capital and labor increased by less than 25 percent. On the other hand, the decline in service sector value added from 52.6 to 43.1 percent of total value added was accom-

37. Fixed, including irrigation capital stock. The "service" sector capital stock does not include construction equipment, since the latter is only available as part of the manufacturing capital stock. Presumably, it is quite small in relative terms. Capital and labor data are given for 1951, although the value added data in Table 3.7 with which they will be compared are for 1952. This is due to the lack of comparable labor force data for 1952.

Table 3.8: Capital Stock and Labor Force by Sector, 1951, 1958, and 1964
(percentage distribution)

	Agri-culture	Irrigation	Manu-facturing and mining	Construc-tion	Electricity	Transport and communi-cations	Services
			Capital				
1951	29.9	10.4	22.6		5.6	18.7	12.8
1958	23.9	10.7	23.7		7.2	18.2	16.3
1964	19.2	9.4	25.8		6.3	19.0	20.3
			Labor				
1951	13.8		23.6ª	9.5		7.0	46.1
1958	17.6		21.7	9.8	2.0	6.8	42.1
1964	13.9		25.9	9.7	2.0	6.3	42.2

ª Includes workers in electricity generation.

Sources: Capital Stock: A. L. Gaathon, unpublished data.
Labor Force: 1951: Gur Ofer, *The Service Industries in a Developing Economy: Israel as a Case Study* (New York: Praeger, 1967), Table 4.6. 1958 and 1964: Bank of Israel, *Annual Report*, various issues.

panied by a large rise in the sector's share of capital and only a slight decline in its share of labor. Although data for construction and utilities are not separately available for all years, it appears that their share of resources corresponded roughly to movements in their share of value added.

These findings on primary factor allocation are interesting in light of a recent study by Fanny Ginor, in which it is pointed out that a country exhibiting an import surplus may enjoy a higher income level than if its current account were balanced.[38] Her argument assumes that the less developed countries suffer from a smaller relative productivity disadvantage in nontraded products (particularly services and construction) than in traded goods. As most of a country's import surplus will consist of goods, the ability to concentrate domestic resources in construction and services raises the capital importing country's income level relative to a balanced trade position. While this point has some force, it is clearly static in nature. As we have just seen, the maintenance of a

38. Fanny Ginor, "The Impact of Capital Imports on the Structure of Developing Countries," *Kyklos* 22, fasc. 1, 1969: 104–23.

large service sector in Israel required a substantial commitment of resources precisely as a result of low productivity growth in services. Had the same resources been allocated to the goods sector, the rate of growth of output would have been higher, although there would be an initial static loss of income.[39] Although the economy's production-possibilities schedule of goods for services may show a high marginal rate of transformation, outward shifts in the transformation curve are likely to be more rapid for goods, so that it will prove beneficial to switch production toward goods.

The Israeli development process provides another confirmation of some hypotheses about the evolution of the sectoral structure of production during the development process. The relative importance of agriculture (measured by its share in aggregate value added) first increased because of changes in the composition of the population; then, in accordance with expectations based upon income elasticities in other countries, it declined. The role of manufacturing continually increased, fueled initially by import substitution, then by export growth. Between 1951 and 1964, the share of manufacturing in value added increased by 50 percent. Contrary to findings in other countries, the service share declined, this phenomenon being attributable more to changes in the balance of payments situation than to underlying income elasticities.

39. As we saw in Section 3, however, a balanced domestic consumption bill requires concentration in services as long as an import surplus exists.

4

Import Substitution and Export Growth
in Manufacturing

It was shown in the last chapter that the growth of the manufacturing sector can best be understood if the years before and after 1958 are viewed separately. In the first period the increased *relative* importance of manufacturing in the total gross output of the country stemmed primarily from import substitution, while during the latter period the main source of relative growth was the rapid increase in industrial exports. Nevertheless, in both periods the main source of the increase of *total* demand was the rising level of domestic demand. For each period we shall describe the changes in the branch structure of the manufacturing sector and evaluate the social desirability of the observed evolution. It will be shown that this evolution had no obvious base in static comparative advantage, a factor that might have been expected to be of great importance in a very open economy, had a free market mechanism been operative. The differential growth of the various branches occurred in response to differences in private profitabilities, largely dictated by government policies, which will be discussed in considerable detail in Chapter 6.

1950–58

In 1950 and 1951 the manufacturing sector, indeed the entire economy, was dominated by the need to furnish basic provisions for the large and continuing influx of immigrants. Consumer demands for all manufactured goods were rapidly increasing, but no commensurate increase in domestic supply was forthcoming, since relatively few of the immigrants had as yet been absorbed into the domestic labor force. The principal reasons for this latter phenomenon were, among others, the lack of capital [1] with which to employ potential workers and the immigrants' unfamiliarity with industrial occupations. Moreover, a lack of housing made it difficult for jobseekers to move to areas in which work opportunities existed. The result of this increasing demand and the limited ability to expand domestic supply was a heavy dependence upon imports; thus in 1951 imports constituted 46 percent of the total supply of manufactured goods (domestic plus foreign), as compared to 25.8 percent in 1958.[2]

Table 4.1 shows the extensive dependence of most branches of

Table 4.1: Ratio of Imports to Total Available Supply, 1950, 1954, and 1958
(current prices)

	1950	1954	1958
Consumer goods			
Food processing	21.2[a]	_[b]	17.0
Woodworking	10.6	20.3	5.8
Clothing	2.3	1.8	1.2
Leather and footwear	33.5	24.0	.8
Intermediate goods			
Paper and printing	20.1	18.9	15.0
Chemicals	62.1	67.3	25.0
Textiles	19.9	13.9	13.0
Minerals	55.3	75.4	77.0
Investment goods			
Machinery (including household equipment)	71.4	84.9	57.8
Electrical appliances	45.9	24.7	43.4
Stone and cement	15.9	3.4	2.6
Metals	45.2	40.8	31.1

[a] 1951 ratio.
[b] Data not available.

Sources: 1950 and 1954: Harold Lubell, *Israel's National Expenditure, 1950–1954* (Jerusalem: Falk Project, 1958), p. 47.

1951, food processing: A. L. Gaathon, *Survey of Israel's Economy, 1951* (Jerusalem: Central Bureau of Statistics and Falk Project for Economic Research, Israel, 1959), p. 126.

1958: Michael Bruno, *Interdependence, Resource Use, and Structural Change in Israel* (Jerusalem: Bank of Israel, 1962), pp. 37, 39.

1. Given the fixed minimum wages set by the Histadrut, increasing employment could only be generated by larger amounts of capital. See below, Chap. 7.

2. Both in 1955 prices.

manufacturing on imports to supplement domestic output.[3] The import ratio was usually higher for those branches whose output consisted mainly of intermediate products and investment goods, while consumer goods[4] industries showed lower import ratios.

The greater self-sufficiency in consumer goods reflected the development of the economy in the years preceding 1948. Low tariffs maintained by the British before World War II had precluded the establishment of any significant amount of local manufacturing, except for food processing and some types of building materials and clothing. However, during World War II the difficulty of assuring continuing supplies from abroad resulted in the British army's becoming a large customer of local industry. The demand for large quantities of both food and clothing led to an extensive enlargement of capacity, much of which lay idle after the war, so that even the subsequent mass immigration required little increase in the import ratio. In woodworking, although most production was destined for consumption, a substantial fraction constituted an input to the construction industry; it was the high import ratio in the construction materials component that led to a relatively high ratio for the branch as a whole in 1950 and 1954.[5]

The general picture given by Table 4.1 is that between 1950 and 1954 limited import substitution took place; the rapid expansion in production was sufficient to meet a large part of the growing demands but was not large enough to permit a relative decrease in the reliance on imports. Some substitution did occur, however,

3. The numbers in Table 4.1 show the ratio of imports originating in branch *i* abroad to the total supply of good *i* available domestically. These ratios are in current prices, as sectoral price deflators are not available for domestic production. An additional source of bias may stem from the failure to evaluate imports at their effective rate of exchange, i.e., inclusive of duties, for 1958, as this would reflect scarcity values. However, there are no data on effective exchange rates for 1950 or 1954. For those branches in which the effective rate increased, the figures in Table 4.1 overstate the extent of import substitution. Despite these qualifications we believe these ratios are accurate enough to provide good approximations of actual movements. Of course small changes in the import coefficients may be due to these biases and must be interpreted in the light of other information.

4. Food processing, clothing, woodworking, and leather products are designated consumer industries. Printing, which in our breakdown is combined with paper, cannot be independently assessed, although it is believed the import component in the combined branch was due mainly to high imports of paper that persisted until a major mill was set up in the mid-1950s.

5. See Lubell, *Israel's National Expenditure, 1950–1954*, p. 47.

particularly in textiles, leather and footwear, electrical appliances, and stone and cement. The substitution in the last-named branch reflected the rapid augmenting of production capacity specifically designed to decrease dependence on imported building materials.[6] The substitution in leather reflected increased domestic tanning capacity, while that in textiles was encouraged by the development of domestic cotton production. Thus most of the import substitution in the 1950–58 period occurred after 1954, although part of this was probably the result of investment that took place before 1954.

In the consumption branches, large declines in import ratios after 1954 occurred in leather and woodworking. In the former the trend set in the preceding years continued, while in woodworking considerable processing capacity was built, sufficient to meet domestic demand and to permit wood products to become an important export item. There was relatively little scope for further substitution in the remaining consumption branches, clothing and food; in the former, imports were already insignificant, and in the latter, imports consisted mainly of processed food products for which the basic commodities could not be grown locally (or only with difficulty), for example, sugar, cocoa, and coffee. Despite the relatively small decline in the import ratio in the food industry, the industry is so large that a small percentage change in the coefficient implies a large absolute change in domestic output. The absolute amount of import substitution, defined as the difference between actual imports of good i in 1958 minus the expected level had the 1951 import ratio remained unchanged and the 1958 total supply been required, is shown in Table 4.2.[7] This measure is more useful for some purposes than changes in the import ratio, as it suggests the orders of magnitude of total primary resources that were allocated to achieve the recorded level of import substitution.[8] For example, the absolute amount of import substitution in the food industry was larger than that in leather; assuming that the combined input intensity is similar for the food and leather

6. See *Israel's Industrial Future* (Jerusalem: Ministry of Commerce and Industry, 1961), pp. 208–09.

7. Algebraically, $(M_i)_{58} - (M_i/Z_i)_{51} (Z_i)_{58}$, where M_i is imports originating in branch i and Z_i is the total supply of branch i, or imports plus domestic production.

8. Implicitly, this assumes the same productivity per combined unit of total resources in all branches.

Table 4.2: Estimates of Absolute Import Substitution, 1950–58,
Labor Intensity and Cost of a Dollar Added

	Absolute import substitution (thousands of I£)	Total labor coefficient (man-days per I£ of output)	Direct labor coefficient (man-days per I£ of output)	Cost of a dollar added	Gross output 1958 (thousands of I£)
	(1)	(2)	(3)	(4)	(5)
Chemicals	69,630	.024	.013	9.94	141,222
Basic metals	} 36,752	.027	.019	} 2.00	} 182,080
Metal products		.041	.028		
Food processing	33,113	.038	.011	3.18	434,187
Leather and footwear	26,809	.037	.026	2.40	80,103
Machinery	17,302	.042	.031	2.46	55,334
Textiles	13,302	.038	.022	4.06	165,542
Stone and cement	13,859	.034	.021	3.21	106,403
Woodworking	7,658	.036	.026	2.50	139,492
Paper and printing	6,475	.042	.024	2.06	111,069
Electrical appliances	2,412	.040	.025	1.85	53,054
Clothing	1,718	.042	.023	4.56	205,473

Sources: Column 1: Calculated from import ratios in Table 4.1 and gross output data contained in Bruno, *Interdependence, Resource Use, and Structural Change*, p. 37.
Columns 2, 3: Ibid., pp. 137, 296, 297.
Column 4: Ibid., p. 111, except for leather, metals, and woodworking in which Ministry of Finance data on a number of firms in each branch were used.

branches, this implies a larger amount of total primary inputs allocated to food than to leather, although the latter experienced a much larger decrease in its import ratio.[9]

In nonconsumption branches substitution occurred in paper and printing, chemicals, metals, and machinery. These were branches in which import ratios were quite high in the early 1950s and thus offered significant substitution possibilities, though not necessarily efficient ones.

9. Although the import ratio is in current prices and the decline in the food import ratio is small (from 21 to 17 percent), other evidence also suggests a decline in the "real" import ratio. See Table 5.3.

We turn now to an evaluation of the import substitution process. The distribution of output or value added among the various branches at a particular point in time will not be analyzed explicitly. While this distribution may be of interest for purposes of historical comparisons, it is not fruitful to evaluate the social desirability of a particular constellation of output.[10] However, it is possible to evaluate changes in this structure attributable to import substitution, in terms of efficiency and, in an economy with a non-Keynesian unemployment problem, in terms of employment generation. To provide the reader with some perspective on the relative sizes of the various branches, gross output data for 1958 are presented in Table 4.2, along with data needed in analyzing the import substitution process.

To a considerable degree, import substitution was directed by the government, which used a variety of instruments (See Chapter 6) whose main impact was to channel investment to particular branches. Thus any evaluation of its success requires a specification of the objective function in terms of which it is to be evaluated; at a minimum, the variables to be included and, if possible, the relative trade-offs among the goals should be specified. As was shown in Chapter 1, the most important stated objectives (although not necessarily the revealed objectives) were the reduction of the current account deficit and the absorption of the immigrants into the labor force. Deferring an evaluation of these goals to Chapter 6, let us consider the success of the import substitution program in achieving them.

The total employment-generating effect of a unit of final output in manufacturing branch j is given by $E_j = \Sigma_i l_i r_{ij}$, where l_i is the direct labor input into branch i, and r_{ij} is an element in the inverse

10. Hollis B. Chenery, in "Patterns of Industrial Growth," *American Economic Review* 50 (Sept. 1960): 624–54, presented estimates for a number of branches of the relationship of a branch's share of total value added in manufacturing to per capita income. The equations were estimated for a large sample of countries. While Chenery himself did not use these equations as a guide to how a country's production structure *ought* to look, a number of authors since then have seemed to equate "normal" with "optimal." It is clear, of course, that such regressions cannot suggest anything about optimality, since the observed composition of production reflects the impact of government policy intervention, market imperfections, desire for prestige, etc. Moreover, endowment patterns and tastes for countries with the same per capita income are likely to be different.

matrix of the input-output table; E_j includes the employment generated in both nonmanufacturing and manufacturing branches. The value of E_j shown in Table 4.2 (column 2) may be compared with the two measures of import substitution shown in Tables 4.1 and 4.2. Food, machinery, and textiles, all of which have high employment-generating effects, did undergo substantial absolute import substitution,[11] as did metals and metal products. However, it is not possible to obtain a breakdown of the latter, so that it is not known whether the decrease occurred in metal products, which has a high coefficient, or in basic metals, which shows a low coefficient. In chemicals, the branch of greatest import substitution, the labor coefficient was small, and thus the intensive effort to stimulate the growth of this branch cannot be attributed to its employment effect.[12]

Thus there was no systematic relation between the extent of import substitution in manufacturing branches and the total labor coefficient, the rank correlation coefficient being negative, using either measure of import substitution.[13] The failure of employment considerations to be manifested in the import substitution process may have been caused by the weight given to other characteristics of the various branches such as their efficiency. To evaluate this latter aspect of the industrialization program, we use as the criterion of efficiency the *cost of a dollar added* (CDA) which shows the cost in domestic resources of saving a dollar of foreign exchange through import substitution.[14]

What would have constituted an optimal pattern of import substitution from the viewpoint of efficiency? As a first approximation one might desire the largest percentage decline in import coefficients to occur in those branches in which the CDA is lowest;

11. It should be noted that the high E_j value in food is attributable primarily to the agricultural employment generated, since direct labor requirements and those from the rest of manufacturing are fairly small. The same is true, though to a smaller degree, of textiles.

12. The government agencies responsible for investment allocations usually were furnished with estimates of the probable employment level which would be generated by a given investment proposal.

13. The rank correlation coefficient between the extent of import substitution and the percentage of workers with less than an eighth-grade education is also low, suggesting that absorption of unskilled workers was not an important subgoal.

14. See Appendix to this chapter.

however, in some branches with low CDA's, most of the possible efficient domestic production may already have been undertaken. Moreover, there are a number of problems relating to uncertainty, for example, changes in the world price, of either imported input or output that may alter the CDA. These variations are particularly important for projects in which both the value added per unit in foreign exchange and the CDA are low. To choose such a project, over one that has a higher CDA as well as a higher value added in dollars, may prove costly, since small price variations could completely eliminate the value added in the former, raising its CDA to infinity. Finally, the CDA may change over time, as the economy evolves and different factor scarcities constrain further development.

Despite these difficulties we shall evaluate the realized import substitution without considering uncertainty. A good or bad performance in terms of the CDA thus allows no definite inferences about the quality of planning, since the observed CDA's may not have been anticipated, for example, as a result of international price changes. Nevertheless, it enables us to evaluate the actual expost efficiency of the import substitution process. Moreover, since available data are limited to two-digit branches, some important differences at a more disaggregated level may be masked.[15] The inferences drawn from the aggregate data do correspond, however, to subjective impressions about particular industries, as well as to detailed data on the CDA (at the firm level) that the Ministry of Finance used in arriving at decisions on export subsidies.

As seen earlier, the chemical industry experienced the largest amount of absolute import substitution. However, its CDA (see Table 4.2) was the highest for any branch of manufacturing, and most firms within the sector exhibited very high CDA's. The decision to expand the industry apparently was based on its basic role in industrialization—its extensive forward linkages. Textiles and food processing were other branches in which considerable resources were devoted to import substitution. The latter branch was

15. In particular, a low CDA at the two-digit level may mask high CDA's in some subbranches. If substitution possibilities for the low cost subbranches are exhausted, further substitution would be undesirable.

expanded in an explicit attempt to become autarkic, partially for defense reasons, while the former was enlarged on the assumption that it would eventually become an efficient export branch. In both industries the overall CDA was high, as were most of the sub-branch figures. Indeed, the subbranch of textiles that was enlarged most, cotton spinning, was the least efficient within the industry.

Thus substantial import substitution occurred in three branches (chemicals, textiles, and food processing) which, at least in the short run, were inefficient by international standards. The high cost in the two latter branches was (and is) not necessarily due to any inherent comparative disadvantage that Israel suffers. Some of it may be attributable to the type of market structure that exists, particularly the duplication of small-scale facilities and an inability to capitalize on the possibilities of large-scale production in branches in which there are substantial economies of scale.[16] On the other hand, in chemicals the difficulty seems to have been the small size of the domestic market which, in many subbranches, made it impossible to support even one efficient firm.

However, there was also an increase in the relative importance of domestic production in leather, metals, and machinery, branches in which the overall CDA is lower than the average for all manu-facturing. Apparently, much of the recorded growth of output in machinery occurred in repairs and consumer appliances, and the branch did not begin to produce industrial machinery on a large scale until after 1958.[17] The machine industry's low CDA is a result of the fact that skilled labor, the most important input in the branch, is much cheaper in Israel than in the western countries in which machines are usually produced. Moreover, economies of scale are less important in this industry than in other branches, as most machines are produced to order, rather than on a large-scale, repetitive basis. The reasons for the efficiency of both metalwork-ing and leather products may be similar to those in machine pro-

16. The Bank of Israel, *Annual Report, 1962,* p. 244, and *Annual Report, 1963,* p. 239, suggest that part of the duplication may have reflected an attempt by the government to encourage entry in order to foster compet-itive behavior. On the size distribution of firms in the textile industry, see Ministry of Commerce and Industry, *Israel's Industrial Future,* pp. 152–58.

17. Ibid., pp. 242–45.

duction. Most of the increased output in the former occurred in metal products, a branch with a low capital-labor ratio and a high skill component.

The large absolute amount of import substitution in the chemical, food processing, and textile branches (I£116,000,000), compared to the more efficient branches, metals, machinery, and leather (I£80,000,000), and the greater capital intensity of the former, suggest that a disproportionate amount of capital resources were allocated to relatively inefficient branches. Had the resources going to these industries been reallocated to the lower cost branches, a greater reduction in total imports (or an increase in exports) would have been possible. When both employment and efficiency aspects are considered, the decision to increase the output of the textiles and food processing branches may be rationalized, although the same is not true of chemicals, which exhibited a low labor coefficient, as well as a high CDA.[18]

A major industrial branch that has not been considered is diamond polishing. Throughout the 1950–58 period, Israel's output of polished diamonds increased rapidly and, by 1958, was the major source of industrial export earnings.[19] The success of this branch was due to the presence of large numbers of emigrants from the Benelux countries who had had experience in diamond polishing and whose absolute wages were lower than those with similar skills in other countries. The exports in this branch were particularly profitable to the economy, the cost of a dollar added being the lowest of any industrial branch.

The growth of some relatively inefficient branches (in the sense that their domestic price exceeded their import price, c.i.f.) was made possible during the 1950–58 period by their isolation from international competition. The separation of private and social profitability was achieved mainly by quantitative import restrictions and substantial tariffs on those goods that were admitted. The only exception was investment goods; here tariffs were nil (until 1961), in order to keep the cost of investment low. This feature partially accounts for the relatively small amount of import sub-

18. The explanation of the underlying causes of the observed import substitution pattern is presented in Chap. 6.
19. Both in terms of gross earnings and value added in foreign exchange.

stitution in the capital goods industries despite their relatively high efficiency. Indeed, through most of the period, two-thirds of total machinery installed was imported.[20]

Although we have so far emphasized the impact of the import substitution program, it will be remembered from Chapter 3 that most of the *absolute* growth of manufacturing stemmed from rising domestic demand, especially consumption. The output of branches producing mainly consumption goods grew very rapidly between 1950 and 1958, and the importance of this growth for the manufacturing sector should be underscored. In order for new firms to enter the market and for old ones to expand, entrepreneurs must perceive either growing domestic or export markets. Since Israel has a small population, the only means by which the former can be achieved is through increasing per capita consumption.[21] Given the uncertainty of exporting, we find that the strategic role of domestic markets is apparent. The extent of the market is crucial because of the large minimum size required for efficient production in many branches. Even with the possibilities of substituting for existing imports, domestic demand may not be sufficient to warrant investment, unless it is expected to continue to grow. This by no means indicates that the policy which permitted rapidly increasing consumption (Chapter 7) was optimal; rather it suggests that, in a small economy, a growing domestic market may permit both increases in scale and learning-by-doing, which provide the basis for eventual exports.[22]

A final point on the growth of output during this period should be noted. Import substitution did not necessarily imply rapidly increasing domestic output. In those branches in which a substantial part of gross output ultimately was destined for construction (wood, stone, cement, and metal products), the domestic supply ratio increased without much additional capacity being built, because construction increased by only 4 percent in constant prices over the 1950–58 period. This is in contrast to the experience in other branches in which, as a result of rapidly increasing

20. Bank of Israel, *Annual Report, 1956.*
21. This, of course, implies increasing intermediate and investment good requirements.
22. Cf. Staffan B. Linder, *An Essay on Trade and Transformation* (New York: Wiley, 1961).

demands, a decrease in the import coefficient required a considerable augmentation of productive capacity.

1958–64

As was seen in Chapter 3, the manufacturing sector increased in
relative importance, vis-à-vis other sectors, between 1958 and
1964, mainly as the result of the high growth rate of exports. Table
4.3 shows the direct increases in final domestic demand, exports

Table 4.3: Increases in Industrial Domestic Final Demand,
Exports and Imports, 1958–64
(000's of I£, 1963 prices)

	Domestic final demand	Exports	Imports
Mining	1,868	41,905	284,774
Food processing	314,334	68,728	13,448
Textiles and apparel	164,474	171,855	44,903
Wood products	86,025	34,477	46,727
Paper, printing, and publishing	39,612	16,119	27,741
Leather	29,693	1,556	3,162
Rubber and plastics	9,177	24,324	7,247
Chemicals	80,296	58,790	77,686
Oil refining	15,425	28,891	1,162
Nonmetallic minerals	11,397	12,315	12,500
Diamonds	4,015	256,168	−931
Basic metals	6,139	9,452	110,950
Metal products	73,363	25,884	26,564
Machines and electrical appliances	629,587	22,431	410,503
Total	1,425,405	777,895	1,066,436

Source: Bank of Israel, unpublished data.

and imports; Table 4.4 shows the growth in gross output, the
changes in total output attributable to the direct and indirect effects
of changes in each final demand category and imports.[23]

In half of the two-digit branches the direct increase in export
demand exceeded that in domestic final demand; these were mining,
textiles and apparel, oil refining, rubber and plastics, diamonds,

23. For a discussion of the differences between the explained and the
observed output variation, see Chap. 3, p. 50.

Table 4.4: Changes in Total Output Requirements
Attributable to Changes in Final Demand, 1958–64
(000's of I£, 1963 prices)

	Gross output $X_{64} - X_{58}$	*Domestic demand* $P_{64} - P_{58}$	*Exports* $E_{64} - E_{58}$	*Imports* $M_{64} - M_{58}$	$(2) + (3) - (4)$
	(1)	*(2)*	*(3)*	*(4)*	*(5)*
Mining	107,749	151,698	281,439	346,381	77,766
Food processing	586,334	418,240	96,755	25,329	487,478
Textiles and apparel	735,048	346,895	331,740	103,665	570,326
Wood products	331,416	192,142	52,515	63,863	177,528
Paper, printing, and publishing	158,520	183,024	71,856	72,339	146,629
Leather	46,440	40,615	2,800	5,174	38,143
Rubber and plastics	133,488	46,156	35,454	19,967	59,546
Chemicals	233,754	257,458	124,944	154,685	221,001
Oil refining	114,815	117,173	72,857	44,201	135,219
Nonmetallic minerals	123,765	167,961	23,069	29,707	157,867
Diamonds	260,744	4,942	258,260	−434	263,608
Basic metals	129,653	280,932	58,035	276,082	55,326
Metal products	225,711	234,869	52,955	83,816	196,723
Machinery and electrical appliances	492,735	963,892	95,640	572,444	456,022
Total	3,680,172	3,405,997	1,558,319	1,797,219	3,043,182

Note: The Gross Output column shows the absolute change in this magnitude while the other columns show the total effect of direct and indirect requirements generated by the changed final demands of that column.

basic metals, and nonmetallic minerals. The importance of export growth in these branches is even clearer when the total impact (including indirect requirements of other branches' exports) is considered (Table 4.4).[24] In all but the last two branches, the total increased output requirements attributable to exports was at least 75 percent of that attributable to domestic demand. Despite the importance of exports in direct demand in basic metals and nonmetallic minerals, exports played a negligible role in their total expansion, since both are mainly used as intermediates in products absorbed in domestic markets. Of those branches in which the total increased demand stemming from exports was less important,

24. Table 4.4 is obtained by applying Equation 3.4 in the previous chapter to data for 1958–64.

wood, paper and printing and chemicals had more than 25 ptrcent of their increased output accounted for by export demand. Two others, food and leather, were clearly oriented toward the production of final goods for the domestic market, although in the former the increase in direct exports was substantial. In machinery the rapid increase in output was devoted to increased domestic demands, including some amount of import substitution.[25]

Although the main source of nonproportional growth after 1958 was attributable to exports (Chapter 3) in two branches, food processing and oil refining, import substitution was an important source of growth. The decreased reliance on imports in the former reflected the greater domestic availability of produce from the agricultural sector, particularly dairy products, wheat, and sugar beets; in the latter, refined oil products were produced from Iranian oil with new capacity that had been built in the late 1950s.

The export boom occurred in two phases. In the first, 1958 to 1961, the exports of almost every branch rose rapidly (Table 4.5) with total industrial exports, other than diamonds, expanding by an average annual rate of 31.5 percent. Since 1961 this rate of expansion has slowed considerably; the rates in each year from 1962 to 1965 being 13.3, 19.4, 13.5, and 11.6, respectively.

An explanation of the rapid growth in exports between 1958 and 1961 is necessarily multifaceted. One component is the increasing cartelization of the economy. Beginning in the mid-1950s a considerable amount of industrial capacity was installed. However, some excess capacity existed,[26] generated by the entry of new firms into industries that already possessed sufficient, and in some cases, excess capacity to satisfy existing demands.[27] These firms usually

25. The import ratio declined from .55 in 1958 to .48 in 1964. However, as the machinery branch includes repairs and electrical appliances, one cannot be sure about the extent of import substitution in machines per se without a further breakdown. The difference between the import ratio of .55 in machinery given here and that in Table 4.1, 57.8, reflects the inclusion here of appliances (in Table 4.1 appliances appear separately).

26. The Industry and Crafts Survey of 1960 provides detailed data on new firms and their relative importance in total employment for a two-digit industrial breakdown. In most industries firms begun after 1956 account for a substantial fraction (10 to 20 percent) of total employment. CBS, *Industry and Crafts Surveys, 1955–1960* (Jerusalem, 1964), Table 17. Such data, of course, do not prove that excess capacity was being generated by new firms. However, a number of sources suggest that this was an important phenomenon. See, for example, Bank of Israel, *Annual Report,*

Table 4.5
Industrial Exports 1958–65 (000's of U.S. dollars, current f.o.b. prices)

	1958	1961	1962	1963	1964	1965
Basic metals and pipes	495	1,732	2,815	3,494	3,470	6,059
Machinery and electrical equipment	339	1,313	2,003	1,975	1,531	2,250
Mining and quarrying	3,323	9,159	8,307	11,422	18,721	25,161
Glass, ceramics, cement, and their products	2,059	3,576	3,701	4,397	4,054	5,331
Chemicals	3,161	12,949	12,625	14,973	17,294	22,569
Metal products	823	9,764	12,107	18,718	10,557	12,996
Plywood	3,106	4,566	5,667	6,052	7,117	8,057
Clothing	3,268	8,891	9,602	8,450	9,396	10,213
Oil refining	–	2,003	3,731	7,854	9,566	10,188
Tires	5,687	8,382	9,874	8,788	8,428	8,816
Foodstuffs, except citrus	2,146	4,314	4,430	5,090	5,854	6,112
Citrus products	5,620	7,959	9,933	13,072	18,093	18,618
Leather and footwear	349	326	637	583	773	780
Textiles, except clothing	5,028	16,432	20,556	23,701	30,385	30,263
Paper, printing, and publishing	1,790	4,869	5,258	4,627	5,145	4,672
Rubber and plastics	459	1,338	974	1,975	1,843	1,504
Transport equipment[a]	2,237	1,719	2,755	2,835	4,284	3,466
Household equipment and appliances	2,893	5,787	4,711	4,772	6,366	4,717
Industrial exports, except diamonds	46,670	106,128	120,243	143,570	162,952	181,854
Polished diamonds	34,255	64,969	84,395	104,144	118,203	131,796
Total industrial exports	80,760	170,966	204,475	247,619	281,048	313,650

[a] Including production and repair; excluding the sale of ships and aircraft, which totaled $3.728 million in 1965.

Source: Bank of Israel, *Annual Report, 1965*, p. 277. Totals may not equal column sums because of rounding.

succeeded in obtaining a share of the market. They apparently operated at a fraction of their capacity, thus producing at high average costs. Despite this, they were able to achieve sufficient

---

1962, pp. 240–47. On the other hand, the Ministry of Commerce and Industry suggests that excess capacity was relatively small. See *Programme for Israel's Industrial Development, Second Outlook 1965–1970*, pp. 103–104.

27. Often there was government sponsorship of new firms, reflecting the assumption that the competition fostered would lead to efficient production methods.

profits to remain in the industry. Their success is best explained by the unwillingness of any of the established firms to cut prices for fear of evoking retaliation by firms with unused capacity.[28] Thus both old and new firms tended to operate with excess capacity.[29]

The obvious possibilities of the excess capacity for export promotion induced a shift in public industrial policy. The government, until the late 1950s, had encouraged the entry of new firms into industry, in the hope that competition would result in greater efficiency and lower prices. Realizing that the size of the domestic market precluded effective competition in most branches, the government reversed its policy and legalized the formation of cartels through legislation passed in 1959.[30] Although not stated explicitly, one of the premises implicit in the cartelization agreements was that an industry would be allowed to raise prices in the domestic market, provided that it agreed to engage in a strong export drive; even if export receipts covered only variable costs, the profit on total sales was guaranteed by high domestic prices. The prospective ability of a firm engaging in such a scheme was even incorporated in the evaluation of proposed industrial projects.[31] While excess capacity and the growth of cartels provides a plausible explanation of one aspect of export growth, it is important to note, in the face of difficulties in quantitatively establishing the existence of the former, that it is not a crucial component of the explanation; increased exports could have been produced with new capacity. What is vital in the explanation is the ability of the cartels to raise domestic prices in order to "finance" their exports; that is, domestic prices were set to cover fixed costs of all facilities whether used for domestic production or exports, while exports were sold at prices

28. For a theoretical analysis of a similar market structure and an analysis of the equilibrium of new firms, see Don Patinkin, "Multiple Plant Firms, Cartels, and Imperfect Competition," *Quarterly Journal of Economics* 61 (Feb. 1947): 173–205.

29. In the years after 1959, some excess capacity may have resulted partially from the optimizing strategy of those firms faced with the increasing difficulty of finding skilled labor, the high cost of unskilled labor, and the relatively cheap cost of machinery. In some industries it appears that this constellation of factors led to an adoption of capital intensive methods and that the minimum efficient size of many installations inevitably led to some initial excess capacity.

30. See Bank of Israel, *Annual Report, 1960*, pp. 166–68, for details.

31. Ministry of Commerce and Industry, *Israel's Industrial Future*, p. 161.

set to cover only variable costs. Thus, even in industries in which exports were produced with newly installed capacity, the profitable utilization of these facilities may have been dependent on cartel agreements.

Another aspect of the export surge between 1958 and 1961 might be found in the increasingly favorable exchange rate received by exporters. During the period from 1952 to 1962 Israel used a multiple exchange rate system.[32] From 1955 to 1962 the official exchange rate was I£1.8 per dollar. However, exporters received subsidies initially via an export retention system, which allowed the importation of scarce commodities with the value added portion of export receipts, and then through direct export premiums. Between 1955 and 1961 the effective exchange rate received by exporters on the value-added component of industrial exports, other than polished diamonds, increased from I£1.82 to I£2.77 per dollar, roughly 50 percent.[33] During this same period the consumption and investment implicit price deflators in the national accounts increased by about 35 percent. Thus, at least in the aggregate, it appears that changing relative prices between domestic and foreign sales may have accounted for some of the improved export performance. Detailed sectoral estimates currently being worked on by Michael Michaely may provide further clarification of this issue.

Another feature of the export expansion process deserves mention, namely, the provision, either by trade organizations or the government, of a host of important services such as establishing contacts with foreign purchasers, setting quality standards, improving packaging and designs, holding trade fairs, insuring against any unusual risks involved in exporting, low interest loans for working capital, and sharing of unusual transport costs. These seemed to have been of major importance in breaking down pro-

32. One part of this system, the export retention scheme, is discussed below. Halevi and Klinov-Malul, *Economic Development of Israel,* Chap. 10, provides a thorough description of foreign exchange policy.

33. Joseph Baruh, "Import Taxes and Export Subsidies in Israel, 1955–1961." These figures may overstate the actual increase, as the estimate for 1955 is a minimum one because of the difficulties involved in estimating the actual subsidy in the export retention scheme. By 1961 all subsidies were direct, and thus the estimates are a good indicator of the effective exchange rate. Ibid., p. 55.

ducers' reliance upon the domestic market, as a result of the high initial costs and greater risks of penetrating foreign markets.

One possible path in analyzing the factors underlying the observed export pattern has been neglected, namely, a detailed examination of the factor content (especially of high level skills) of exports.[34] This would allow us to ascertain whether the most rapidly growing exports exhibited high skill intensities, as might be expected in view of Israel's substantial pool of skilled personnel. This type of analysis is best fitted to a situation in which market prices play an important role in resource allocation. However, the extraordinary influence of the government in investment decisions (Chapter 6), including those leading to exports, suggests that such an approach would be of limited usefulness in Israel. While government attention to particular skill availabilities may have occurred, there is little evidence that during the period under consideration these were systematically considered. The results of a detailed study by Seev Hirsch at the level of individual firms lends support to this position, as he is unable to identify any statistical connection between good export performance and the skilled manpower employed by the firm.[35] However, in the post-1965 years there is evidence of the intention of the government to take advantage of the substantial technical community in the establishment of science-based industries, such as precision instruments, designed mainly for export.

The pattern of export growth is particularly interesting (Table 4.5). Although exports in most branches grew rapidly in the 1958–61 period, 75 percent of the total increment in industrial exports (other than diamonds) was concentrated in five branches: mining and quarrying, food processing, textiles and clothing, chemicals, and metal products. Over the next three years the concentration ratio increased; replacing metal products by oil processing in the previous group, five branches accounted for 83 percent of the increased exports. Thus, while cartelization and improved exchange rates may help to explain the growth in most export categories in 1958–61, the concentration of growth in a few industries, both

34. See, for example, Donald Keesing, "Labor Skills and Comparative Advantage," *American Economic Review* 56 (May 1966): 249–58.

35. Seev Hirsch, "Some Factors in Israel's International Competitiveness," in *Technology and Competition in International Trade* (New York: Columbia University Press, 1970).

before and after 1961, suggests the need for a more detailed explanation of the growth of capacity in particular branches. It will be shown in Chapter 6 that the branches of greatest export growth all received unusual government encouragement from 1955 onward, usually in the anticipation that exports would be realized. Thus capacity for the production of phosphates, the processing of citrus products, and the production of cotton textiles, three branches in which a large part of the export increment were concentrated, had been expanded considerably beyond the requirements for domestic usage.[36] However, chemical and petroleum product exports were often attributable to the excess capacity, resulting from the fact that the minimum scale plant often exceeded domestic requirements. As these topics are analyzed at length in Chapter 6 within a framework of overall government strategy, we omit further discussion at this point.

An evaluation of the impact of the growth of exports is difficult. Since they accounted for a large percentage of the growth in gross manufacturing output between 1958 and 1964, they contributed to the growth in employment. Nevertheless, an overriding goal remained the reduction of the trade deficit, and the question arises as to the efficiency of the allocation of domestic resources in attaining it. The question is as complex here as in the evaluation of import substitution. First, it is not necessarily correct to allocate resources to the branches in strict order of CDA because of the risks inherent in international price fluctuations.[37] Second, in some branches, for example, those utilizing agricultural products, the supply of intermediate inputs may be limited by land or water availability, so that the output of the processing branch is constrained. Third, as a result of economies of scale in marketing and servicing, it may be more rational to concentrate on potentially large export groups, even though some branches with small export potential have a lower CDA. While all of these qualifications apply essentially to long-run export planning, a further difficulty is presented by the fact that some exporting was undertaken to utilize unused

36. Ministry of Commerce and Industry, *Israel's Industrial Future,* pp. 73–96.
37. In a sense a similar risk is entailed on the import side if considerable substitution takes place in an industry whose current CDA is low but in which a decline in international price causes the CDA to rise eventually.

capacity in branches established to satisfy domestic requirements. In these branches the variable cost entailed in exporting was less than the average total cost relevant for long-run decisions.

Because of the multiple dimensions of the problem, it is better to examine briefly each of the major export categories separately, rather than attempt a summary measure.[38] The largest industrial export, polished diamonds, has the lowest cost of a dollar added of any industrial product, mainly as a result of the relatively low wages (compared to other countries) of the skilled workers in this branch. Moreover, there is little risk of price fluctuation in the branch, so that its export is clearly desirable.

After diamonds, the largest exporting branch is textiles, whose foreign sales expanded enormously over the period. There are two subbranches within the textile industry that have accounted for most of this growth, and their characteristics are quite different. Cotton yarns, which account for almost half of exports, is inefficient, with a CDA close to five, and its continued export growth has been made possible by substantial subsidies. Moreover, it is quite likely that the international price will decline, since many of the less developed countries are also attempting export programs in this branch. Paradoxically, the growth of cotton yarns reflects a planned increase in export capacity, rather than an unanticipated excess of supply over domestic demand, as was the case in some branches. The decision to build up this branch was based on the assumption that the success of Jewish-owned textile mills in Europe could be reproduced in Israel. Ironically, much of the new capacity was installed in development towns, which were settled mainly by immigrants from North Africa and the Middle East. The considerable factor allocations to this branch clearly represent one of the planning errors during the late 1950s.[39]

Synthetic yarns, which also had been set up primarily as an export branch, accounted for about one-third of textile exports. This is an efficient branch, neither being subsidized explicitly nor charging

38. The following discussion of the efficiency of detailed branches draws upon information in the chapters on industry in Bank of Israel, *Annual Reports; Programme for Israel's Industrial Development* (Jerusalem: Ministry of Commerce and Industry, n.d.).
39. See also Chap. 6.

prices that are higher in domestic than in foreign markets. Moreover, in the face of increasing world demand for these yarns, increased production involves relatively little risk.

Copper cement and potash, which make up most of the mineral exports, were both established as export branches. While potash is relatively efficient, having a low CDA, the CDA in copper cement is subject to frequent fluctuation because of variations in the richness of the ore currently mined. Moreover, copper has been subject to greater price fluctuations than potash. Therefore the desirability of having extensively supported copper exports is questionable.

The basic metals (including pipes) and metal products branches, which accounted for a large part of increased exports, were relatively efficient in terms of CDA as recorded in 1958. Pipe production benefited from the substantial domestic demand for irrigation in agriculture and became sufficiently efficient to become a competitive export branch. Many of the exports in metal products embodied highly skilled labor inputs that had been developed in the production of military hardware and irrigation equipment for domestic use.

Processed citrus products and chemicals are the two remaining major export branches. The former has a relatively low CDA, its exports being limited by the availability of fruits whose quality does not allow direct export. Their quantity is a function of the weather. Thus greater production of processed citrus could not have been undertaken, despite the favorable market generated by rising incomes in the principal purchasing countries.

Many of the chemical product exports are offshoots of planned import substitution, resulting from the technical need for building plants that had greater capacity than was required by domestic markets, although future growth will absorb any excess capacity. Regardless of whether the import substitution program was well-advised, as long as exports are currently covering variable costs (which they were), their export is warranted.

Thus export growth after 1958 seems to have proceeded along fairly efficient lines, with the exception (as in import substitution) of textiles and chemicals. As in the earlier analysis of import substitution, there was here no discernible systematic effort to expand

exports in branches having high direct (or total) labor input. However, by 1960, many types of labor had become scarce, and a labor
intensive policy would have been of little interest in any case.

Throughout the preceding discussion our evaluation of the efficiency aspects of the growth of manufacturing has relied heavily
upon the cost of a dollar saved estimates generated, with a few
exceptions, by the 1958 input-output study. While, for the purpose
of evaluating the earlier import substitution program, the CDA
was quite useful, at least as a static efficiency measure, there is a
possibility that over the next several years the changing structure
of the economy led to changes in the relative efficiency of the
various branches. Unfortunately, current estimates of the CDA
are not available. However, an indication of relative efficiency may
be gleaned from the levels of protection afforded to the various
branches of manufacturing. Such protection consists both of high
tariffs and administrative restrictions on the import of goods. Data
are available on both types of restrictions for 1965, the end point
of the period that we have just considered. Ideally, we would want
to use effective rates of protection, that is, those that show the net
protection received by a branch as a result of a tariff on its inputs
as well as its output. However, when quotas are extensively used,
effective rates lose much of their usefulness and direct price observations are needed.[40] In the absence of direct price observations we
are forced to use the available data for 1965. Table 4.6 shows the
average tariff rate for each branch, along with the percentage of
total output covered by quantitative restrictions.[41]

There is substantial correspondence between the figures in Table
4.6 and the CDA of 1958. For example, chemicals, clothing, and
textiles had the highest CDA's in 1958. In 1965, the latter two
had very high nominal rates of protection, and although chem-

40. For a discussion of effective rates of protection, see Bela Balassa,
"Tariff Protection in Industrial Countries: An Evaluation," *Journal of
Political Economy* 73 (Dec. 1965): 573–94. An example of the use of
direct price data will be found in Stephen R. Lewis, Jr., "Effects of Trade
Policy on Domestic Relative Prices: Pakistan 1951–64," *American Eco-
nomic Review* 58 (Mar. 1968): 60–78.

41. The data are from Flora Davidov, "The Liberalization of Imports,
February 1962 to May 1965," Bank of Israel, *Bulletin*, no. 26. The tariff
rates were arrived at by using domestic output as weights for subbranches,
a procedure that avoids the bias of giving undue weight to low tariff items
(the case if actual imports had been used as weights).

Table 4.6: Measures of Protection, 1965

	Average rate of nominal protection	*Percentage of output under administrative protection*
Food and tobacco	79	48
Textiles	231	6
Clothing	178	1
Wood and carpentry	60	–
Paper and paper products	50	60
Footwear and leather	130	–
Rubber and plastics	55	44
Chemicals	40	47
Oil refining	40	6
Nonmetallic minerals	35	13
Basic metals	37	1
Metal products	46	10
Machinery and electrical equipment	48	14
Household equipment and miscellaneous	69	6
Transport equipment	201	33

Source: Flora Davidov, "The Liberalization of Imports, February 1962 to May 1965," Bank of Israel, *Bulletin*, no. 26.

icals had a fairly low nominal protection rate, it was the third greatest beneficiary of administrative protection. Similarly, food processing exhibited a high CDA, and the rate of tariff protection and percentage of output protected by quotas were both high.[42] On the other hand, in 1958, the CDA of leather products, metals (mainly metal products), and machinery was found to be relatively low. Table 4.6 shows that all three groups received little administrative protection and, except for leather, had low nominal rates of protection. The high tariff rate in leather was attributable to the consumer good component, on which the tariff was used as a revenue-collecting device, leather imports of intermediate goods receiving only an average rate of protection.[43] Similarly, the high tariff in woodworking may be reconciled with the low CDA when the tariff is viewed as a convenient way to tax furniture and home purchases rather than as an attempt at protection. The data also

42. However, part of the high protection may reflect excise taxation on "luxury" goods, such as alcohol, tea, coffee, and tobacco.
43. Davidov, "Liberalization of Imports," p. 54.

suggest increasing competitiveness in nonmetallic minerals (stone and cement). The apparent decreased efficiency in paper and printing stems from the increasing weight of paper production, which is a high cost branch.[44]

In summary, then, our evaluation of the efficiency of the export drive in 1958–65, which used the CDA would have been similar if data on protection offered to domestic branches had been used. However, it should be emphasized that data on nominal rates of protection do not necessarily indicate the degree of protection offered by the tariff structure, as tariffs on inputs to a given branch must also be considered.[45] The calculation of effective tariffs in Israel is, as noted above, difficult, since the nominal rate of protection is of limited significance because of the extensive use of quantitative restrictions. Thus the correspondence between the CDA's of 1958 and the structure of nominal protection and quantitative restrictions in 1965, while suggesting roughly similar relative efficiency among industries, must still be regarded as a first approximation to a true ranking.

MANUFACTURING EMPLOYMENT

The traditional view of the development process assumes that a precondition for increased per capita income is increased productivity in the agricultural sector, which allows a movement of workers to the nonagricultural sectors and the production of wage goods for the workers who move. However, the absorption process envisioned is unlikely to proceed smoothly, unless the composition of demand in the nonagricultural sector and the technology adopted are sufficiently labor intensive to absorb the released workers. Thus, even when the productivity of agriculture grows enormously, as it has in Israel, a major obstacle to successful development remains the nonagricultural sector and its capacity for absorbing an influx of labor.[46] The recent history of Israel offers an important

44. *Programme for Israel's Industrial Development. Second Outlook, 1965–1970* (Jerusalm: Ministry of Commerce and Industry, n.d.), pp. 267–76.

45. See Balassa, "Tariff Protection in Industrial Countries."

46. Many of the crucial issues were first stated clearly by Richard Eckaus in "The Factor Proportions Problem in Underdeveloped Countries," *American Economic Review* 45 (Sept. 1955): 539–65. An explicit treatment of

exception to this general rule. Between 1950 and 1958 mining and manufacturing[47] accounted for roughly 24 percent of the total growth in employment, a percentage close to the share of industry in employment at the beginning of the period; over the next six years this percentage was 40.

By contrast, in many underdeveloped economies rapid rates of growth of real value added in manufacturing have been accompanied by only a slight growth in manufacturing jobs, employment growth rates equal to only 25 percent of output growth rates not being unusual.[48] In Israel in the two periods, 1952–58 and 1958–64, output growth rates of 9.5 percent and 14.2 percent were accompanied by growth rates of the labor force of 5 and 7 percent, respectively.[49] Although many reasons for the slow growth of employment may be suggested, for our purposes a critical difference between Israel and many other less developed countries is the absence of a dualistic industrial structure, that is, one exhibiting widely differing productivity among firms of different sizes within the same industry.

The employed labor force, L, within a branch can be represented by

$$L = \sum_i l_i Q_i \tag{4.1}$$

where l_i is the ratio of the labor force (measured in man-years) to value added (Q) in firms of size i. If we ignore for the moment changes in l_i, the rate of growth of the branch's labor force can be shown to equal [50]

---

the labor absorption problem in the industrial sector is provided in John Fei and Gustav Ranis, *The Development of the Labor Surplus Economy: Theory and Policy* (Homewood, Ill.: Richard D. Irwin, 1964), chaps. 3, 4.

47. Manufacturing includes a negligible number of workers in electricity generation.

48. For evidence on the poor employment performance, see Werner Baer and Michel Herve, "Employment and Industrialization in Developing Countries," *Quarterly Journal of Economics* 80 (Feb. 1966): 88–107.

49. It is worth noting that, during the 1960–64 period, employment growth may have been limited by the supply of workers.

50. Differentiating L with respect to Q_i, dividing by L and multiplying by Q_i/Q_i we obtain

$$\frac{dL}{L} = \sum_i \frac{l_i Q_i}{L} \frac{dQ_i}{Q_i} = \sum_i \frac{l_i}{\bar{l}} \frac{Q_i}{Q} \frac{dQ_i}{Q_i}$$

where $\bar{l}$ is the average labor coefficient.

$$\frac{dL}{L} = \sum_i \frac{l_i}{\bar{l}} \frac{Q_i}{Q} \frac{dQ_i}{Q_i} \tag{4.2}$$

where $\bar{l}$ equals the average labor coefficient for firms of all sizes within a branch, and Q is the total output of the branch. Equation 4.2 shows the rate of growth of employment within a branch to be dependent on three factors, namely, the rate of growth of output of firms of different size, their relative importance in total output, and the magnitude of their labor coefficient relative to the average. However, Equation 4.2 does not include the impact of changes in l_i. This is equal to

$$\frac{dL}{L} = \sum_i \frac{l_i}{\bar{l}} \frac{Q_i}{Q} \frac{dl_i}{l_i} \tag{4.3}$$

a weighted average of the change in labor coefficients. If we are given the rates of growth in each branch (4.2 plus 4.3), the rate of growth of employment may be obtained by aggregation:

$$\sum_j \frac{L_j}{L} \frac{dL_j}{L_j} \tag{4.4}$$

where the *j*s refer to branches.

It is convenient to analyze the employment performance of Israel's manufacturing sector, using the relevant concepts from Equations 4.2 and 4.3. First, it can be seen in Table 4.7 that the increase in value added per worker as the size of the firm increases was not very great in most branches in 1958. Typically, the value added per worker in large firms (300 or more employees) did not exceed that in firms with 25–49 workers by more than 50 percent, although of course there are exceptions. By contrast, Richard R. Nelson found in Colombia that large firms "tended to have a value added per worker three or more times greater than very small firms and roughly double that in middle size firms in the 20–49 employee range." [51] Thus, even if most of the growth in demand had been directed toward larger firms, the adverse effect on employment growth would have been limited; in terms of Equation 4.2, since there is relatively little dispersion in $l_i/\bar{l}$, differences in dQ_i/Q_i are

51. Richard R. Nelson, "A 'Diffusion' Model of International Productivity Differences in Manufacturing Industry," *American Economic Review* 58 (Dec. 1968): 1219–1248.

Table 4.7: Census Value Added per Worker by Size of Firm as a Percentage of Industry-wide Average

Number of employees

	1964						1958					
	1–9	10–24	25–49	50–99	100–299	300+	1–9	10–24	25–49	50–99	100–299	300+
Mining	.506	1.107		.646	.884	1.213	.451	1.027	.360	.748	1.253	
Food	.525	.726	.893	1.146	1.282	.994	.767	.879	1.064	1.034	1.125	1.255
Textiles	.864	.835	1.145	1.084	1.018	.997	.546	.835	.990	.868	1.068	1.437
Clothing	.742	.768	.882	1.285	1.562		.622	.940	1.386	.987	2.831	
Wood	.753	.927	1.033	1.228	1.309	1.321	.748	1.026	.972	1.350	1.234	1.556
Paper	.361	.462	.878	.891	1.400		.400	.493	.943	1.353		
Printing	.576	.740	1.100	1.095	1.389		.653	.952	1.039	1.110	1.230	
Leather	.836	.957	1.245	1.262		.000	.717	1.166	1.130	1.440		.000
Rubber	.471	.607	.928	1.072	1.147	1.346	.561	.622	.815	.932	1.404	
Chemicals	.816	.857	1.121	.851	1.055		.585	.760	.979	.898	.950	1.273
Nonmetallic minerals	.380	.462	.647	.714	1.405	1.484	.473	.694	.787	1.133	1.361	1.228
Diamonds	.618	.694	.939	1.379	1.371	.000	.852	.815	1.045	1.358	.652	.000
Basic metals	.409	.730	.650	.693	.792	1.349	.627	.605	.925	.828		1.181
Metal products	.697	.891	1.052	1.194	1.216		.648	.915	1.090	1.328	1.183	
Machinery	.393	.647	1.069	.741	1.014	2.271	.612	.925	.957	1.215	1.825	.000
Electrical machinery	.561	.840	1.092	.989	1.228	1.059	.667	.842	1.020	.899	1.236	.000
Transport equipment	.532	.775	.956	.917	1.096	1.292	.560	.845	.974	1.259		1.262
Miscellaneous	.773	1.224	.777	1.396		.000	.754	1.026	1.105	1.511		.000

Sources: CBS, Industry and Crafts Surveys (1955–1960), vol. 2, pp. 229–37; CBS, Industry and Crafts Survey (1964), pp. 44–45.

of less importance. By contrast, since in many less developed countries $l_i/\bar{l}$ is quite high for large firms, shifts of demand toward firms of a larger size have important retarding effects on the employment growth rates. The difference in this respect between these countries and Israel reflects the smaller gap in technology in the latter between small and large firms. In many less developed countries small firms often use an indigenous craft technology that is highly labor intensive, while large firms utilize modern, imported techniques with much lower labor output ratios. In this situation, even a rapid growth of industrial value added leads to a slow growth rate of employment, since much of the new demand is directed toward large firms.[52]

The second determinant of employment growth rates is the change in the labor coefficient within firms of a given size (Equation 4.3). The labor coefficient for a given firm-size group may decline as (neutral or labor augmenting) technological progress occurs or as the capital-labor ratio increases. Technical progress, when unassociated with new investment, may reflect better managerial coordination, learning-by-doing, and so forth, and may be expected to occur with some regularity. In economies exhibiting unemployment, however, the adoption of equipment that reduces the labor input requires a model to explain the behavior of input markets. Without developing such a model here, it is worth pointing out an often-noted characteristic of the industrial sector in the less developed countries, namely, that larger firms are the typical adopters of the more modern technology, so that their labor coefficient is not only low relative to the industry average but is also more likely to fall.

The preceding suggests that one aspect to consider in Israel's employment performance as compared to that in other less-developed countries is the ratio $l_i/\bar{l}$ in each size group of firms and the rate of change in the l_i's.

It seems to us that the similarity in labor coefficients is explained by the age structure of capital and the availability of foreign ex-

52. For an early statement of the technological dualism model, see Vera C. Lutz, "The Growth Process in a Dual Economic System," *Banca Nazionale del Lavoro, Quarterly Review*, no. 46 (Sept. 1958). Nelson, "A 'Diffusion' Model of International Productivite Differences" provides a rigorous statement of the model and links it with the international diffusion of technology.

change. Most Israeli industry is of recent origin (post-1950) and even relatively small firms (25–49 employees) were often aware of technological possibilities abroad and were able to import equipment of a modern type.[53] Thus a dualistic structure had little chance to evolve. Moreover, where it does exist, as in printing, its relative importance is usually fairly small, that is, Q_i/Q in Equation 4.3 is low.[54]

The rate of decline of l_i depends partly on the introduction of equipment from more developed western countries. The adverse employment effect of the adoption of advanced equipment is likely to be most pronounced in the first stages of industrialization, as firms switch from craft technologies to quite modern capital intensive ones.[55] However, once the latter have already been adopted, the possibility of further introduction of techniques using even lower labor coefficients is limited by the current flow of innovations in the equipment-producing countries. Because Israel is closer to best practice methods, we should expect other less developed countries to have a more rapid decline in their labor coefficients within firms of a given size.

This dualistic interpretation of the Israeli employment performance relative to that in other countries is, to be sure, only one part of a more complete explanation. Differences in factor market imperfections, including foreign exchange policy, labor force quality, product mix, among other characteristics of an economy, all require attention. The explanatory value of each of these aspects is still to be examined systematically in intensive cross-country studies.

FACTORS AFFECTING MANUFACTURING PRODUCTIVITY

In Chapter 2 we found that the residual in manufacturing accounted for less than 40 percent of the growth in total output, when observed factor shares were used as output elasticities, and

53. There was apparently less difficulty in obtaining foreign exchange for investment goods than for intermediate inputs.

54. In this sense a precise definition of *dualism* would have to consider not only the dispersion of $l_i/\bar{l}$, but a weighted dispersion, the weights being the percentage of output produced in firms of each size.

55. Of course, it is still necessary to explain why such techniques are adopted in the face of considerable urban unemployment.

even less, when elasticities from estimated production functions were used. If we use factor shares, the absolute residual rose from 3.9 in 1954–58 to 5.7 in 1959–64. While the use of residuals to evaluate differences in productivity growth among countries is certainly open to objections, the share of output growth explained by the residual [56] seems to be less than that observed in advanced countries, although considerably more than in other semi-industrialized economies, such as those of Latin America.[57] The residual calculation confirms a general impression of the difficulties faced by the manufacturing sector in achieving efficient growth.[58] Among the factors that may have led to a low relative (again the absolute was increasing) residual are the relative lack of experience of both employers and employees, the difficulties of the former being compounded by the inflationary process and the complexities of the foreign exchange system.

Between 1950 and 1963 the manufacturing labor force increased by over 6 percent per annum, whereas in most highly developed countries the rate is likely to be no more than 1.5 percent per annum. While the initial productivity of new workers in advanced countries may be lower than that of experienced ones, they have little impact on the average level of productivity because of their relatively small numbers. On the other hand, in Israel, new workers were a significant percentage of the labor force in many years; therefore the average experience of the entire labor force was relatively low. However, insofar as many of the skills required only a short time to learn on the job, the productivity depressing effect of the newness of the labor force stemmed not from purely technical learning problems but from difficulties in adjusting to the pacing required by factory work.[59] Relatively few of the manufacturing workers who had previously been employed abroad had manufac-

56. For a discussion of the relative merits of using this measure of the importance of the residual as opposed to the absolute level, see Chap. 2, p. 35.

57. For data on the United States and Canada, see Nathan H. Lithwick, George Post, and T. K. Rymes, "Postwar Production Relationships in Canada," in M. Brown, ed. *The Theory and Empirical Analysis of Production* (New York: National Bureau of Economic Research, 1967). For data on Latin American countries, see Henry Bruton, "Productivity Growth in Latin America." pp. 1099–1116.

58. See, for example, the chapter on "Industry" in various issues of Bank of Israel, *Annual Report*.

59. Cf. Eisenstadt, *Israeli Society,* pp. 128–38.

turing experience,[60] and many of the new entrants resented the routine of factory work; this manifested itself in high absenteeism, lateness, and sporadic slowdowns. Since workers' jobs were protected by the trade union and wages were determined on a national scale, which allowed relatively little incentive wage setting by individual employers, employee efficiency was relatively low.[61]

These productivity-depressing characteristics were transitory; the rate of growth of the manufacturing labor force has slowed. Most new employees have matured in an essentially modern economy that has inculcated, for better or worse, a modicum of discipline, and they have had at least a primary education, which probably enables them to learn a new job more quickly. Much of the early inefficiency of industrial management was also transitional. Many of the managers (who are frequently the owners) had little previous experience in manufacturing. In a normal economic setting with stable prices, a competitive domestic market, and relatively free entry of imports, inefficient producers would either learn and implement cost-cutting techniques or would be eliminated through the market process—in Israel, however, these conditions did not exist. Rather, profitability often depended on success in obtaining protection of output or foreign exchange to pay for imported inputs. In most firms, continued production required the availability of raw materials which, at least until the late 1950s, could be obtained only by receiving foreign exchange allotments from the government, an activity often requiring considerable time and ingenuity. The limited amount of organizational ability of the new managers was often devoted in disproportionate amounts to this activity.

The managers' problems were aggravated by the existence of the multiple exchange-rate system throughout the 1950s as a substitute for devaluation. Between 1953 and 1959 the multiple rates were implemented on the export side through a retention system, which enabled exporters to utilize their foreign receipts for either the purchase of imports used in their export production, or for finished goods or raw materials to be used in producing for the domestic market. These latter options constituted a bonus, since, as a result of quantitative import restrictions, domestic prices for

60. Population and Housing Census, 1961 (Israel), Publication no. 27, *Labour Force, Part 4,* Table 3.
61. While these problems differentiate Israel from more advanced countries, they are similar to those faced by other underdeveloped countries.

most goods were much higher than international prices. Exporters'
bonuses thus depended on the percentage of value added in foreign
exchange, that is, export receipts minus import costs, as well as
the price in the domestic market of the imported goods brought in
with the value added.

This system inexorably led to inefficient resource allocation. For
example, exporters were given an incentive to substitute relatively
high cost domestic inputs for lower cost foreign ones. The marginal
profit in domestic currency from exporting an additional unit of
output was

$$\pi = (P - M)(E + B) - C \qquad (4.5)$$

where π is the profit in I£, P and M are the f.o.b. price (assumed
constant) and the direct marginal import component of a unit of
exports, both measured in dollars, E is the official exchange rate,
B is the bonus received by selling an imported good in the domestic
market, and C the domestic marginal cost of producing a unit of
exports. Whereas in a situation without the retention scheme, imports would be substituted for domestic inputs when $ME < C$,
with the bonus arrangement such substitution will not occur until
$M(E + B) < C$. Thus producers were encouraged to use domestic inputs even when their costs were in excess of international
levels; moreover, domestic resources were allocated to firms not
on the basis of their ability to produce exports at competitive
prices, but according to the profitability in the domestic market of
the goods they were able to import with their value added in foreign
exchange.

For those firms that chose not to export, foreign exchange could
be obtained from the Treasury at one of several rates. The Treasury
selling rate depended upon the country of origin of the imports, the
type of good,[62] and whether they would be sold domestically according to the directives of the Ministry of Commerce and Industry.
Since decisions on the selling rate were usually made on an ad hoc
basis, and frequently changed, most companies devoted great effort
to obtaining favorable rates, usually through personal representatives at various ministries. In view of the large import component

62. Goods that constituted an important component of the consumer
price index received low rates. Alex Rubner, *The Economy of Israel*
(London: Frank Cass, 1960), p. 156.

in many branches, this may have been as effective a method for reducing (private) costs as more conventional cost-cutting procedures.

After 1959, the export retention system was abolished in favor of direct export subsidies based on value added, while import rates remained dependent upon the factors mentioned above. In the new situation there were still inducements to devote effort to cajoling higher subsidy rates; however, less attention seems to have been given to such activities than in the previous period, at least partially because the various government ministries had less discretionary power than previously.[63]

Thus, as in many other countries, the multiple exchange rate system led to some inefficiency in resource allocation. Although a quantitative evaluation of its impact upon productivity will not be attempted, studies of similar types of inefficiency in other countries suggest that their quantitative importance, measured in terms of alternative uses of resources, is likely to be limited.[64] The major impact of the multiple rate system in our view was the deflection of managerial attention from conventional concern with increasing internal efficiency through reorganization, the supervision of workers, and the introduction of more efficient techniques, that is, from the basic sources of potential productivity gains, or X efficiency in Leibenstein's terms. For example, Rubner points out that, as effective exchange rates on both imports and exports were those concluded by private negotiation between importers (or exporters) and the officials of the Ministry of Finance and/or Industry and Commerce:

> Large manufacturing concerns were forced to maintain full time representatives in Jerusalem and Tel Aviv to arrange for the granting of import licenses. Criteria governing the accept-

63. The delimitation of discretion was attributable to the increasing number of trained economists who worked for both the Ministries of Finance and Commerce and Industry. Within the government they fought vigorously for standardization of subsidies, based mainly on the cost of a dollar added rather than value added. Although political intervention certainly occurred, the possibilities of adverse publicity if subsidies were given to branches with a high CDA became a constraint on the arbitrariness of subsidy rates.

64. See, e.g., Arnold Harberger, "Using the Resource at Hand More Effectively," *American Economic Review* 49 (May 1959): 134–46.

ance or rejection of applications were usually not formalized
in written instructions, and oral instructions were subject to
considerable flexibility of interpretation.[65]

One might argue that, given the small level of exports, these ma-
nipulations would have affected relatively few firms. However,
almost all firms required imports in their production process and
inevitably became entwined in the system. As rates were changed
frequently and often arbitrarily, even firms producing only for the
domestic market inevitably devoted considerable effort to importing raw materials at low prices, rather than producing at low costs.

Thus the effects of the multiple exchange rate system, the general
lack of experience, and occasional, rapid inflation with its adverse
effect on cost consciousness help to explain some of the relatively
slow growth of productivity in manufacturing. Another characteristic of the economy, which undoubtedly depressed productivity
levels, was the small size of firms. As we have noted several times
in this study, the limited size of the domestic market should have
exerted an important influence on policy decisions. In particular,
in those branches of manufacturing in which the minimum efficient
plant size permitted no more than a few efficient firms, the
optimality criterion (in the sense of maximum output per unit of
combined input) would have suggested that entry should have been
limited by the government, and the industry regulated, either
directly as a utility, or indirectly, through the use of tariffs or the
establishment of a government-owned firm that could inhibit
oligopolistic practices on the part of the other firms.[66] However, in
most branches a structure evolved in which a few firms (three to
ten) were responsible for a majority of sales, while a large number
of other firms held a small share of the market. The oligopolistic
structure of manufacturing may be seen quite clearly in a study by
Meir Merhav. Examining 450 subbranches of manufacturing, he
found that "62.7 percent of total industrial output is accounted for
by the three biggest enterprises making each item, 75.8 percent by

65. Rubner, *Economy of Israel,* p. 142.
66. For a theoretical analysis of the possible functioning of a government
owned firm operating along with privately owned firms, see William C.
Merrill and Norman Schneider, "Government Firms in Oligopoly Industries:
A Short Run Analysis," *Quarterly Journal of Economics* 80 (Aug. 1966):
400–412.

the top six and 84.2 percent by the top ten."[67] Price leadership and other manifestations of oligopolistic markets resulted, and most firms produced quantities smaller than those at which minimum cost occurred for their existing plant. Moreover, because of the excessive number of firms, the plant that was being operated at too low a level was in most cases not the optimal size plant, that is, firms were producing along a short-run average cost curve which was above the lowest such curve attainable.

Another adverse effect of the oligopolistic structure has been the tendency of firms to begin production in new lines in order to escape the price uniformity imposed by the cartels in their branch.[68] This has led to a considerable amount of small-order production designed to satisfy local demands. Such production has proved attractive, since it provides an opportunity to utilize unused capacity. Inevitably, such production occurs at a high cost because of its small scale, but still it has been profitable because of the high tariff protection afforded most local production. As a result of this trend the manufacturing sector produces a much larger range of products than could possibly be produced efficiently on a small scale.

While the oligopolistic structure did result in some large firms, even these were small by international standards.[69] Thus, in 1958, only 163 plants had more than 100 employees and only 40 plants employed more than 300 workers. Moreover, only 25 percent of manufacturing value added was produced by those with more than 300 employees; thus those firms that might have been reaping the benefits of scale economies accounted for only a small part of total

67. Bank of Israel, *Annual Report, 1962*, p. 242.
68. Ibid., pp. 240–47.
69. Economies of scale are usually considered to result from changing the size of the physical plant and adjusting other factors simultaneously. In the absence of data on plant size we assume that the number of employees is correlated with capital capacity, and that the possibilities of increasing labor specialization and the introduction of more efficient equipment are indicated by the number of workers.
Economies of scale are extremely difficult to estimate empirically without engineering data by firm, which is unavailable in Israel. However, a recent survey of such data for advanced countries indicates that substantial scale economies do exist through most ranges of production. See John Haldi and David Whitcomb, "Economies of Scale in Industrial Plants," *Journal of Political Economy* 75 (Aug. 1967): 373–85.

output.[70] However by 1965 the number of plants with more than 300 employees had almost doubled; if this trend continues it may have an important impact on the structure of future growth.[71]

While the combined effect of the inability to capitalize on economies of scale, the oligopolistic structure of production, and the tendency toward producing a large spectrum of products cannot be quantified, it may be assumed that they lowered the level of productivity. The dramatic change in the number of large-scale firms between 1958 and 1965 bodes well for the future. It may be assumed that this change in structure was at least partly responsible for the increase in both the absolute residual and its share in output growth between 1961 and 1965. Despite the increase in large-scale activity in these years, small-scale production was still of considerable importance at all times, and it may well be true that part of the good employment performance was attributable to this phenomenon. Had scale economies been more fully exploited, the average labor coefficient might well have been reduced even more and the difference in labor productivity between large and small firms increased; given the increased concentration of demand in large-scale firms, this would have reduced the rate of growth of employment. Moreover, the full realization of cost savings from large-scale production might have accelerated the shift of output toward large firms. The extent of the trade-off between employment and productivity cannot be measured, although in some branches it was undoubtedly quite large.[72] These remarks should not be interpreted as suggesting that a conscious choice between employment and output was made by the government. Instead, to the extent that the government influenced market structure, the multiplication of firms was attributable to the desire to foster competition among firms, rather than to solve employment problems.[73]

70. CBS, *Industry and Crafts Surveys* (*1955–1960*), p. 272. The measure is of census value added, which differs from the national income measure in that it includes advertising and insurance payments.

71. *Statistical Abstract of Israel, 1966*, p. 422.

72. For a clear example in textiles, see *Israel's Industrial Future, Outlook, 1960–1965* (Jerusalem: Ministry of Commerce and Industry, 1960), pp. 152–53.

73. See Chap. 6 for a detailed discussion of the trade-off between employment and other policy objectives.

APPENDIX

Since its first efforts to industrialize, the government of Israel has been concerned with the balance of payments implication of every investment over which it had significant influence. This concern led to two distinct methods of evaluating the contribution of a proposed project to the eventual independence of the economy. The first, which was used until 1955, calculated the value added in foreign exchange of the product(s) of a new plant, whether for importation or export. Value added is defined as the selling price (in dollars) minus the import component (in dollars) of the product, $P - M$, and the percentage of value added is $(P - M)/P$. However, this method was subjected to criticism, as it considered only the foreign exchange value of a project and ignored the cost to the economy of earning this exchange. For example, two plants producing two different products may both have the identical percentage of value added in foreign exchange; yet one may require twice as many domestic resources in order to produce a net dollar of foreign exchange. Thus the government adopted the criterion of "cost of a dollar saved" for import-substituting projects and "cost of a dollar added" for export-oriented projects. To implement this concept, a very elaborate method for project evaluation was developed, which may be summarized briefly here. The basic rationale of the evaluation is to calculate the real gains to the economy from the building of a new project. Here the word *real* may be taken as synonomous with the value of the project if all costs are evaluated at their shadow price to the economy.

For each project all costs are broken down into foreign exchange and local currency components.[74] Costs are defined to include both variable costs and the amortization of initial fixed investment, as well as of start-up expenses and interest charges for working capital. Then, to take the calculation for import substitutes as an example, the dollar and I£ costs of the replaced import are calculated. The saving in dollars (the c.i.f. price of a unit of the replaced import minus the dollar value of the import component) is divided

74. For a detailed explanation, see *Memorandum on Economic Evaluation of Industrial Projects* (Jerusalem: Ministry of Commerce and Industry, 1960).

into the I£ cost of production to obtain the cost of a dollar saved.

Algebraically, the cost of a dollar added (CDA) for a given project is equal to:

$$\text{CDA}_j = \frac{W + iK}{P_\$ - M_\$} \tag{4.6}$$

where W represents the labor cost of a unit of the product, whether used directly in production of j or embodied in inputs from other sectors; iK is the return on locally produced total capital used in the project; $P_\$$ is the f.o.b. dollar price at which a unit of output will sell, if an export, and the c.i.f. dollar price, if an import substitute; and $M_\$$ represents the total import component, including current inputs as well as the imputed rate of return on total imported capital. In input-output notation

$$W = \sum_i w_i r_{ij},$$

$$iK = i \sum_i k_i r_{ij},$$

$$M_\$ = E(\sum_i m_i r_{ij} + i \sum_i \bar{k}_i r_{ij}),$$

where w_i is the direct wage input into each branch; k_i and $\bar{k}$ are the amounts of domestically produced and imported capital, respectively; m_i is the current import coefficient in branch i; E is the pound price of a dollar; and i is a shadow rate of interest.[75] A "shadow" rate of interest, rather than observed returns to capital that may include elements of rent, is used in order to arrive at the real cost of the capital input. The interest rate used in most calculations is 8 percent, assumed to be the marginal cost of foreign borrowing; however, calculations using alternate interest rates are also analyzed to ascertain the sensitivity of the project to the assumed interest rate.

In practice it is not possible to use total input coefficients, since detailed input-output data are not available. The CDA is then arrived at by estimating the domestic and foreign cost components of purchased commodity inputs, such as raw materials, packaging materials, and so forth. The following data used in an analysis of

75. For simplicity we omit total depreciation in both numerator and denominator, e.g., the former should include depreciation on domestically produced capital goods.

the profitability of citric acid production may serve as an example.[76] (See Table 4.8.)

Table 4.8: Calculation of Cost of a Dollar Added in Citric Acid Production

	Foreign exchange component in dollars	*Local currency component*
1. Variable costs		
Chemical inputs	277,100	179,700
Fuel	46,000	26,500
Electricity	35,600	28,500
Labor		158,000
Other	31,200	46,300
2. Fixed costs		
Overhead, depreciation, and interest on fixed assets	170,400	379,200
Amortization and interest on running-in costs	54,800	34,100
3. Freight charges and commissions	16,700	13,700
4. Total cost of sales	631,800	866,000
5. Proceeds from exports and replacement value of imports	818,500	
6. Foreign exchange gained (5 − 4)	186,700	
7. Net expenditure in local currency		866,000
8. Cost per dollar gained (7/6)		4.56

While this procedure assumes that market labor cost is roughly equal to its shadow price, adjustments are made for both fuel and electricity, in which it is known that, as a result of government subsidies, market price understates real costs.

The CDA criterion thus formulated does not explicitly consider risk in terms of the changing prices of imports or exports. These variations are particularly important to consider for projects in which both the value added per unit in foreign exchange and the CDA are low. To choose such a project over one in which both characteristics are less favorable may prove costly, since small price variations could completely eliminate the value added in the former, raising its CDA to infinity. As a result, when profitability calculations were made, both the percentage of value added and the CDA were considered.

76. *Economic Appraisal of a Project for a Citric Acid Plant in Israel* (Jerusalem: Industrial Advisory Group, 1959).

The CDA calculation has been part of the evaluation process since 1955, although calculations less elaborate than the one presented above have been used. However, as will be suggested in Chapter 6, it was rarely this feature alone that determined a project's acceptance or rejection.

The CDA criterion was developed in the early 1950s by the Economic Advisory Staff of the Prime Minister's office. In a series of papers Michael Bruno has given it rigorous content, by deriving its validity as an investment criterion from an explicit linear programming formulation of the choice of import and export activities,[77] and has shown the sensitivity of the CDA to differing factor constraints within a development programming framework.[78]

As indicated in the text, the CDA's used in evaluating the efficiency of the various manufacturing sectors were taken, for most branches, from the 1958 input-output table. This does not fully correspond to the theoretically correct criterion, as the observed input-output coefficients may reflect inefficiencies. For example, the coefficient representing the delivery of basic metals to metal products may be higher than the usual such coefficient in other countries[79] as a result of either high cost production in the basic metals sector or inefficient use in the metal products branch.[80] Similarly, the calculation made by Bruno uses the actual wage rates, rather than a shadow price. Thus the CDA's actually used represent a first approximation to the desired measure.

77. Michael Bruno, "The Optimal Selection of Export Promoting and Import Substituting Projects," in *Planning the External Sector: Techniques, Problems and Policies* (New York: United Nations, 1967).

78. Michael Bruno, "A Programming Model for Israel," in Irma Adelman and Eric Thorbecke, eds., *The Theory and Design of Economic Development* (Baltimore: Johns Hopkins Press, 1966); Michael Bruno, "Optimal Patterns of Trade and Development," *Review of Economics and Statistics* 49 (Nov. 1967): 545–54.

79. Assuming the same product mix.

80. Bruno is aware of this difficulty. See Bruno, *Interdependence, Resource Use and Structural Change,* pp. 112–13.

5

The Agricultural Sector

The agricultural sector in Israel is relatively small, accounting for less than 10 percent of value added in 1965 and about 13 percent of total employment. Yet, of all the sectors of the economy, this is the one that has drawn the widest attention internationally. Indeed, to some it has become a model of agricultural performance. Although the increase in agricultural production has resulted in an almost self-sufficient food supply—an achievement that fulfills both ideological and security goals—and has also been a source of foreign exchange saving, through both import substitution and increased exports, these goals have been achieved at the cost of substantial factor commitments, which domestic critics feel might have been better utilized in other sectors. Moreover, government policy in the sector has become the focus of much criticism because of its extensive interference with the market mechanism, which, it is alleged, has resulted in substantial resource misallocation within agriculture.

Before beginning an analysis of the sector, it is important to note that, of all branches in the economy, agriculture was the legatee of more ideological and social pressures than any other. Nonoptimizing behavior on the part of a large percentage of farms, attributable to the pursuit of the goal of individual self-sufficiency, reinforced by the desire of the government to utilize the sector as an instrument of immigrant absorption, limited the extent to which the sector could be molded into an efficient economic engine for improving the economic position of the entire country.

Farming is carried out on three types of farms: collectives (kibbutzim), cooperatives (moshavim), and privately owned farms.[1] The first two are part of the Histadrut sector. In kibbutzim

1. From an enormous literature existing on the cooperative and collective sectors, see Eliyahu Kanovsky, *The Economy of the Israeli Kibbutz* (Cam-

all factors of production are owned jointly,[2] with labor services being provided by members of the community; the allocation of factors is decided by an elected governing body in each settlement. Each kibbutz is run as a single, competitive firm; given the prices of inputs and outputs that it faces, the kibbutz acts as a profit-maximizing unit, with the important exception that it will not hire workers. Thus labor inputs are limited to those that can be provided by the members of each kibbutz. Consumption is provided on an egalitarian basis to members of the community out of the net earnings from the farm's activities.[3]

A moshav is a settlement consisting of farms operated by individual families, each family performing all of the requisite work on its farm and making all of its production decisions. They differ from private family farms insofar as in each moshav, the individual units purchase inputs and sell output on a joint basis.[4]

In 1967 the kibbutzim and moshavim provided somewhat less than half of the agricultural labor force,[5] and cultivated about 67 percent of the land of the agricultural sector.[6] Private farms account for the remainder and are mainly devoted to citriculture in the Jewish sector and to field crops and fruit plantations in the non-Jewish sector. In 1959, the last year for which data on income originating by form of ownership are available, the kibbutzim and moshavim accounted for about 28 percent of net product originating in agriculture, and their share of both land and labor was similar to that in 1967.[7]

---

bridge, Mass.: Harvard University Press, 1966); Haim Darin-Drabkin, *Patterns of Cooperative Agriculture in Israel* (Tel-Aviv: Israel Institute for Books, 1962); and R. Garfunkel, ed., *The Role of Cooperation in Rural Development, papers presented to the International Symposium* (Tel-Aviv: Gvil Press, 1966).

2. Land is rented by each kibbutz from a quasi-government agency on a ninety-nine year basis.

3. Manufacturing activities performed on the kibbutz have become an increasingly important source of income. However, we shall consider only the role of the Kibbutz in agriculture.

4. Further taxonomies of moshavim are possible but they are not relevant for our purposes.

5. *Statistical Abstract of Israel, 1968*, p. 266.

6. Ibid., pp. 315–20.

7. The data on product originating are given in Barkai, *The Public, Histadrut and Private Sectors in the Israeli Economy*, Table 7. He also provides an analysis of the possible reasons for the low share of the Histadrut farms relative to their share of labor and land, ibid. pp. 39–40.

The size distribution of the land available to kibbutzim is shown in Table 5.1. A dunam is roughly one quarter of an acre, so that

Table 5.1: Size Distribution of Cultivated Area in Kibbutzim, 1959

Number of cultivated dunams	Number of kibbutzim
Less than 2,000	7
2,001–3,000	31
3,001–4,000	36
4,001–5,000	21
5,001–6,000	23
6,001–8,000	50
8,001–10,000	24
10,001–15,000	24
15,001–20,000	7
Total	223

Source: H. Darin-Drabkin, *Patterns of Cooperative Agriculture in Israel* (Tel-Aviv: Israel Institute for Books, 1962).

almost all have at least 500 acres and many considerably more. On the other hand, most of the moshav farms have thirty to forty dunams.

While many kibbutzim would be large enough to produce one or two industrial crops efficiently, the dominant ideology that sanctioned the development of mixed farms has often prevented the realization of potential productivity.[8] A similar state of product diversification exists in the moshavim, even though farm size is quite small. The commitment to mixed farming set limits to productivity in such industrial crops as wheat, cotton, sugarbeet, and peanuts, which are best cultivated in large quantities, and which were producible at lower prices (relative to international levels) than many of the products of the typical mixed farm. A system of government price supports, tariffs, and subsidies was used to make this system profitable and delayed a switch in production to products in which the country enjoyed a comparative advantage.

In addition, as indicated earlier, the rural sector was viewed as an excellent setting in which to integrate the immigrants from both Europe and the Islamic countries of the Middle East and North Africa. While it was hoped that these settlers would eventually

8. On the mixed farm ideology, see Rubner, *Economy of Israel*, **pp.** 107–09.

become productive in farming, other objectives, such as the learning of Hebrew, adjustment to a relatively modern society and the establishment of settlements in militarily important areas, were viewed as being at least equally important through the mid-1950s. These noneconomic aspects of the agricultural development process, as well as those mentioned previously, constitute a backdrop to the discussion that follows and must be considered in any evaluation of the sector's performance and of government policy toward it.

Thus we may summarize the goals of agricultural policy. The first and overriding aim was the achievement of self-sufficiency in food production. This was partially the result of military considerations because of the possibility that the country might be isolated from outside supplies during a war. It was also a fulfillment of the Zionist goal to "return to the soil."

A second objective was the reduction of foreign exchange expenditure, primarily through import substitution. This is broader than the first goal, insofar as an attempt is made to produce domestically not only food, but all agricultural goods. Still a third goal was the absorption of immigrants and the regulation of their entrance into urban areas. Moreover, important subgoals such as the fostering of mixed farming and the promotion of the Kibbutz sector for ideological reasons also played an important role in determining government policy.

We turn first to an examination of the extent to which each of the major goals was met and then to an evaluation of the effects of government policies.

THE GROWTH OF OUTPUT

Table 5.2 shows the growth of gross agricultural output in current and constant prices between 1950 and 1965. The greatest increase occurred in meat production and "other fruit," representing on the demand side high income elasticity of demand,[9] and on the supply side a rapid augmentation of capacity in response to high profitability. Output growth in other branches was much slower than in

9. See Yair Mundlak, *Long-Term Projections of Supply and Demand for Agricultural Products in Israel* (Jerusalem: Falk Project 1964). Mundlak's estimates show income elasticities of 1.3 for beef and .8 for fresh fruit.

Table 5.2: Agricultural Output, 1950–65
(millions of I£)

	Current prices				1949 Prices				Implicit price deflator (1949 = 100)				Price of food relative to other components of consumer price index	
	1950	1955	1960	1965	1950	1955	1960	1965	1950	1955	1960	1965		
Field crops	11.2	79.1	124.5	252.9	10.4	21.7	33.4	50.9	108	365	373	497	1952	96.3
Vegetables and potatoes	7.0	45.1	60.6	121.6	8.0	14.8	19.5	23.1	87	306	311	526		
Citrus fruit	7.5	62.6	110.7	240.3	7.5	11.5	17.5	21.9	100	547	634	1097	1955	100.0
Other fruit	3.1	29.3	78.7	154.3	2.8	5.7	14.4	29.5	110	518	546	523		
Milk	8.2	46.5	84.5	131.6	8.8	16.2	26.0	32.9	94	286	325	400	1960	94.1
Eggs	7.8	36.3	93.7	130.6	9.0	14.2	31.5	37.8	87	256	298	346		
Meat	4.7	48.6	146.4	252.9	5.2	12.8	37.4	58.7	92	379	392	431	1965	89.5
Fish	2.3	11.6	18.7	33.8	2.7	4.9	6.3	9.5	84	234	295	356		
Other	4.4	18.3	31.8	37.0	3.7	4.8	9.0	8.7	118	378	354	425		
Total	56.3	377.4	749.8	1354.8	56.3	106.5	194.9	273.0	97	354	385	496		

Note: Output includes intermediate produce. (Items may not add to totals because of rounding.)

Sources: Columns 1–12: Statistical Abstract, 1968, pp. 322–23.
Column 13: Mundlak, Long-Term Projections for Agricultural Products, p. 76; Statistical Abstract of Israel, 1964, p. 234; 1968 p. 234.

fruit and meat, mainly reflecting relatively low income elasticities.[10] The growth in these branches would have been even slower had the consumer price of these products not fallen relative to nonfood prices (Table 5.2), particularly during the 1950s. The importance of the decline in food price may be judged by Mundlak's estimate of the price elasticity of food to be −.625 for the 1952–61 period.[11] The failure of food prices to fall even more than they did was a result of output restriction in response to falling prices; such restrictions were sometimes suggested by the government.[12]

In a number of branches a significant portion of increased output was attributable to import substitution. Thus, between the years 1951–53 and 1961–63, the ratio of imports to total supply declined from 1.00 to .17 in cotton, .38 to .04 in butter, .85 to .39 in beef;[13] whereas powdered milk was an important source of milk consumption in the earlier period, its use had decreased considerably by the latter set of years.

AGRICULTURE AND THE BALANCE OF PAYMENTS

Despite the rapid rise in the population and general living standards, imports of food and other agricultural products increased by only 15 percent between 1952 and 1959. (See Table 5.3). However, since 1960, imports of both processed and nonprocessed foods have risen significantly, primarily meat, edible oil seeds, and sugar. Increased sugar imports between 1960 and 1964 were transitory, primarily attributable to the building up of stocks in an attempt to smooth the effects of price fluctuations;[14] in 1965 they declined significantly.

The possibilities for further improvement in the import side of the current account are limited. Many of the components of

---

10. This refers to food products, not to such products as cotton.
11. Mundlak, *Long-Term Projections for Agricultural Products*, p. 78.
12. A detailed description and analysis of the development of the various agricultural branches for the period until 1961 is provided by Mundlak, *Long-Term Projections for Agricultural Products*, Chap. 2. A lengthy study of the mechanics and the impact of agricultural planning is provided in Raanan Weitz and Avshalom Rokach, *Agricultural Development: Planning and Implementation* (New York: Prager, 1968).
13. CBS, *Israel's Foreign Trade*, various issues and food balance sheets and production data in issues of the *Statistical Abstract of Israel*.
14. See Bank of Israel, *Annual Report, 1965*, p. 43.

Table 5.3: Imports of Food and Other Agricultural Products, 1952–65
(millions of U.S. dollars)

	1952[a]	1956[a]	1959[a]	1963[a]	1965[a]
Grain and flour	31.8	38.6	43.5	50.4	43.7
Feeding stuffs for animals[b]	3.1	5.1	6.1	2.4	1.9
Meat and meat products[c]	3.7	9.6	2.0	7.0	19.7
Eggs and dairy produce	5.2	5.4	2.4	2.0	5.7
Fresh fruits, nuts, vegetables	1.3	0.2	.1	.4	4.7
Other foodstuffs	26.5	18.6	19.6	25.5	17.3
Subtotal	71.6	77.5	73.7	87.7	93.0
Tobacco and beverages	1.1	0.9	1.5	3.1	5.5
Seeds for edible oil and extraction	6.7	8.8	15.5	22.6	29.7
Raw cotton	3.6	3.8	4.2	4.8	8.4
Total food and other agricultural products	82.8	90.9	94.9	118.2	136.6

[a] Calendar years.

[b] Other than whole grains included in "grain and flour."

[c] Including animals, live, for food.

Sources: 1952, 1956, 1959: Mundlak, *Long-Term Projections for Agricultural Products*, p. 100.
1963, 1965: *Statistical Abstract of Israel, 1966*, pp. 236–38.

"other foodstuffs" are goods that Israel cannot produce, especially coffee, tea, and cocoa. However, further import substitution may occur in cotton, sugar, and wheat, although land and water limitations will presumably limit the quantities produced, unless there are further cutbacks in fodder production, which has a similar input structure. This would require larger feedgrain imports but would lead to a decline in the cost of total imports, as these are less expensive in the international market.

Exports of processed and unprocessed products expanded rapidly during the period 1952–65, with the principal export being citrus fruit (Table 5.4). The export of poultry products, particularly eggs, has also increased but may be expected to decline, since they were attributable to large surpluses and are uneconomical exports, given their high cost of a dollar added. Since 1960 the export of processed fruits and vegetables has become important. Continued export gains here will require a conscious export effort, not ad hoc reliance on surpluses. Until the early 1960s exporting was viewed

Table 5.4: Exports of Edible Agricultural Products, 1952–65
(millions of U.S. dollars)

	1952[a]	1956[a]	1960[a]	1960[b]	1965[b]
Citrus fruit	16.7	40.3	46.7	46.6	74.5
Fresh fruit and vegetables	0.0	0.2	1.1	2.4[c]	4.4[c]
Livestock and poultry products	–	0.8	11.7	11.8	6.7
Peanuts	–	1.4	2.1	2.0	1.4
Hard wheat and feeding stuffs	–	0.3	0.8	1.0	0.9
Processed fruit and vegetables	3.3	4.1	7.4	7.9	19.0
Miscellaneous	0.6	1.7	7.4	3.4	12.3
Total	20.6	48.9	77.1	75.1	119.2

[a] Pre-1958 customs classification.
[b] SITC classification.
[c] Including dried fruits and vegetables.

Sources: 1952, 1956, 1960[a]: Mundlak, *Long-Term Projections for Agricultural Products*, p. 101.
1960[b]: *Statistical Abstract of Israel, 1963*, p. 442; *1964*, pp. 201, 203, 205; *1967*, p. 221.
1965: CBS, *Israel's Foreign Trade, Part 1 (1965)*, pp. 40, 41, 46; *Statistical Abstract of Israel, 1967*, pp. 213, 215, 221.

as a residual activity; given the higher (and more certain) profits in the domestic market, output was planned with the domestic market in mind and no relatively certain continuing flow of produce to the processing industries for export was available. The growth of marketing boards with their emphasis on serving export markets and their pooling of receipts from domestic and foreign sales has undoubtedly been an important factor in the rapid expansion in processed food exports.

As a summary measure of the impact of agriculture on the balance of payments, the trade deficit for processed and unprocessed food as well as cotton has been calculated. This deficit was $62.3 million in 1952 and declined to $49.4 million in 1964, while constant price GNP more than doubled during the period. This calculation must be taken only as a rough approximation of the total balance of payments effect, since it omits industrial imports used in agricultural production, as well as domestic agricultural output embodied in nonfood exports (particularly clothing and textiles).[15]

15. In addition, processed food contains some elements of industrial value added.

Nevertheless, these magnitudes are suggestive of the success of the government in utilizing agriculture to reduce the trade deficit. However, given resource and climatic limitations, there is little hope that the deficit can be reduced much below these levels. Indeed, as will be discussed below, there are many who doubt whether, on purely economic grounds, agricultural expansion should have proceeded as far as it did.[16]

GROWTH IN INPUTS

The factor growth implicit in the above production gains are substantial, even though actual factor requirements were reduced as a result of productivity growth. As we saw in Chapter 2, of the 12.6 percent annual rate of growth of net output, over the 1950–64 period, only 6.6 percent was attributable to capital and labor growth, where the observed factor shares are used to indicate output elasticities. Even if the share of capital used to measure the elasticity of output with respect to capital were arbitrarily raised, for example, to 25 percent above its recorded share, the residual would still be large.

Before examining possible sources of the residual, let us consider in some detail the growth of the primary factors. Between 1950 and 1965 the agricultural labor force increased from 72.9 thousand to 117.6 thousand. A labor force peak of 121.6 thousand was reached in 1961, and it has since declined steadily. Simultaneously, the agricultural capital stock increased rapidly, from I£559.2 in 1950 to I£2,299.3 million in 1965 (in 1955 prices). Table 5.5 shows investment in agriculture as a percentage of total fixed investment and of fixed investment exclusive of dwellings. Until 1960, investment in agriculture accounted for more than one-quarter of nonhousing investment in all years and often for more than one-third.[17] The distribution of this investment among types of assets is unusual; almost one-third of gross investment went toward increasing irrigation facilities. The stock of irrigation capital increased to six times its initial level during the 1950–65 period,

16. Chapter 6 considers agriculture within a broader framework of comparative advantage.
17. During this period agriculture accounted for only 12 percent of national income at factor cost, excluding the imputation for housing.

Table 5.5: Agricultural Investment, 1950–65

	Investment in agriculture as percentage of total fixed investment		Investment in agriculture as percentage of total fixed investment exclusive of dwellings	
	In current prices	In 1955 prices	In current prices	In 1955 prices
1950	17.6	16.9	32.1	28.9
1951	16.5	16.3	30.9	27.6
1952	17.9	18.2	29.2	28.8
1953	23.4	24.5	36.4	37.3
1954	22.8	22.3	36.4	36.9
1955	20.2	20.2	32.5	32.5
1956	19.6	19.3	29.6	28.9
1957	17.7	17.5	26.9	26.5
1958	19.5	19.2	28.6	28.3
1959	17.4	17.3	25.8	25.6
1960	16.2	16.1	23.4	23.1
1961	13.6	13.7	19.9	19.8
1962	13.2	13.7	19.8	20.9
1963	11.9	21.2	17.2	17.8
1964	8.8	9.1	12.4	13.1
1965	8.2	8.2	11.8	11.3

Source: Unpublished data of A. L. Gaathon.

whereas the stock of all other agricultural capital went up less than fourfold.

There have been cycles in the composition of investment by asset type, reflecting primarily changes in the private profitability of the various branches. In most years, investment in fruit plantations (both citrus and deciduous) has been important. More than half of this has been allocated to citrus groves, the planting of which has proved to be extremely profitable, both privately, and from the viewpoint of the national economy. In the late 1950s there was considerable investment in livestock, mainly as a result of the increasing private profitability of this branch, which was due to both high demand and substantial government subsidies and protection. This type of investment fell off with the rapid growth of output and the resultant downward pressure on prices. Recently, machinery purchases, which include tractors, have become the single largest element of agricultural investment. Much of this represents the replacement of caterpillar-type vehicles with wheeled vehicles, which are more suitable for use on irrigated land. Investment in irrigation fell off sharply with the completion of the national water carrier in 1963; it is likely to continue to fall. Other farm investment has been declining continuously since 1958 in both current and real terms, although even during the 1958–64 period, nonirrigation capital stock grew at an annual compound rate of 7.5 percent.

After several years of rapid growth the labor force has remained almost constant since 1958, increasing by only 2,500 workers. Since 1961, in fact, its absolute size has decreased. The agricultural labor force had been recruited mainly from among new immigrants, often as a step in the integration process, as well as to augment productive capacity. The failure of the labor force to grow after 1958 reflected the improved demand for labor in the nonagricultural sector and the adequate potential output of agriculture without additional productive factors. As a result the government decided not to place new immigrants in farm settlements, relying rather on industries in Development Towns for the provision of employment.

An important determinant of the growth of agricultural output in Israel has been the increasing availability of water. We have noted the sixfold growth in irrigation capital over the period. However, in evaluating the effects of capital formation on the growth of production, the relevant variable is capital services. For irrigation facilities there is an unambiguous measure of services, namely, cubic meters of water pumped through the system each year (see Table 5.6).[18] Water use rose much more slowly than the corresponding capital stock, increasing slightly more than threefold between 1950 and 1963, when water usage reached a peak from which it has since declined. The expanded use of water was extremely important in the agricultural growth process because irrigated land had substantially higher yields than unirrigated land. It is difficult, however, to estimate the quantitative significance of water, using either production function estimates or residual-type calculations; the former because the multicollinearity of the variables precluded the estimation of reliable output elasticities, the

18. It will be remembered that, in the productivity calculations in Chap. 2, agricultural capital exclusive of irrigation was used.

Table 5.6: Land Use and Water Supply[a], 1949–65

Year	Total agricultural land	Irrigated	Distribution of Irrigated Land					Unirrigated	Water used in irrigation
			Field crops	Vegetables, potatoes, peanuts	Fruit plantations	Fish ponds	Miscellaneous[b]		
1949	1,650	300	65	54	150	15	16	1,350	257
1950	2,480	375	79[c]	90	158	22	26	2,105	332
1951	3,350	470	118	120	166	27	39	2,880	413
1952	3,475	540	127	–[d]	–	–	–	2,935	468
1953	3,550	650	165	208	193	35	49	2,900	563
1954	3,560	760	191	241	236	35	57	2,800	660
1955	3,590	890	265	237	285	37	66	2,700	760
1956	3,685	965	305	235	311	40	74	2,720	830
1957	3,820	1,100	368	250	365	41	76	2,720	830
1958	3,940	1,185	414	240	410	43	78	2,755	1,000
1959	4,105	1,240	431	242	448	46	83	2,865	990
1960	4,075	1,305	434	248	493	49	81	2,770	1,060
1961	4,150	1,360	467	235	522	53	83	2,790	1,025
1962	4,030	1,445	486	241	577	56	85	2,585	1,125
1963	3,970	1,505	492	249	615	58	91	2,465	1,140
1964	4,110	1,500	468	230	651	59	92	2,610	1,025
1965	4,190	1,550	477	253	666	61	93	2,640	1,100

[a] Area data is measured in 1,000 dunams; the water supply in millions of cubic meters.
[b] Auxiliary farms, nurseries, flowers, etc.
[c] Fodder and other crops.
[d] Dash indicates data not available.

Sources: 1949, 1951, 1953, 1956, 1959, 1962–65, Statistical Abstract of Israel, 1966, p. 358.
  1950: Statistical Abstract of Israel, 1954/1955, p. 72.
  1952: Statistical Abstract of Israel, 1956/1957, p. 65.
  1954: Statistical Abstract of Israel, 1959, p. 141.
  1955, 1957, 1960: Statistical Abstract of Israel, 1964, p. 316.
  1958: Statistical Abstract of Israel, 1962, p. 186.
  1961: Statistical Abstract of Israel, 1965, p. 366.

latter because the price of water was subsidized and, therefore, the observed expenditure shares are not indicative of output elasticities. Moreover, in many instances water was allocated on the basis of fixed amounts to each farm unit, so that marginal productivity cannot have been equated to price in any case. Although the effect of water on overall output growth cannot be isolated, Table 5.7

Table 5.7: Output of Selected Agricultural Crops
on Irrigated and Nonirrigated Land
(kilograms per dunam)

Crop	Irrigated	Nonirrigated
Sorghum	525	215
Green fodder	7,300	1,500
Cotton lint	125	50
Cottonseed	195	90

Source: Statistical Abstract of Israel, 1965, p. 373.

shows measures of the difference in yields in kilograms per dunam on irrigated and nonirrigated land for some major field crops in 1964. Although, in the absence of information on the use of other factors, these output differences cannot be assumed to be attributable solely to the use of water, they are probably indicative of the importance of water to the sector.

Like other inputs the amount of cultivated land increased significantly until the late 1950s, and has remained almost constant since then. The total cultivated area grew from 2,480 thousand dunams in 1950 to 4,190 thousand dunams in 1965 (Table 5.6). However, by 1959 cultivated area had already reached 4,105 thousand dunams; the succeeding years have seen little growth. Two-thirds of the increase in cultivated land during the 1950–65 period has been in irrigated land, which expanded from 375 thousand dunams in 1950 to 1,550 thousand dunams in 1965. Further, the amount of irrigated land has continued to rise since 1959, despite the constant total under cultivation. This points to an interesting feature of recent agricultural development, namely, that the amount of water being utilized has remained almost constant since 1960, despite the continuous increase in irrigated area. The main expansion in irrigated area has gone to fruit plantations, which have relatively high water usage (see Table 5.8). However, the number

Table 5.8: Water Consumption in Various Irrigation Uses, 1951–65
(millions of cubic meters per 1,000 dunams)

	1951	1955	1959	1961	1963	1965
Field crops	.69	.69	.68	.65	.71	.67
Vegetables, potatoes,						
peanuts	.66	.65	.62	.57	.56	.47
Fruit plantations	.72	.76	.73	.70	.72	.67
Fish ponds	4.19	4.41	3.91	3.17	2.93	2.62
Miscellaneous	.51	.67	.60	.63	.66	.59
Total	.88	.85	.80	.75	.78	.71

Sources: 1951, 1959, 1961, 1963: *Statistical Abstract of Israel, 1965*, pp. 366, 399.
   1955: *Statistical Abstract of Israel, 1963*, pp. 218, 258.
   1965: *Statistical Abstract of Israel, 1966*, pp. 358, 392.

of cubic meters of water used per 1,000 dunams in this branch decreased from .73 to .67 million, or by 8 percent, between 1959 and 1965. Similarly, the water inputs in all other categories fell. Thus, despite the fact that irrigated area was increased by 25 percent, water use increased by only 10 percent between 1959 and 1965. From the available data it is impossible to ascertain whether the reduction in water use was attributable to within-branch crop changes or to reduced needs per crop, or both. Part of the explanation is undoubtedly improved rainfall, but this factor appears to be insufficient to account for the observed decrease in water use. There is some evidence that increased training in efficient utilization has resulted in significant saving.[19]

From this survey of the growth of inputs, one aspect stands out. The period of the most rapid rate of growth of output, 1949–58, was associated with extremely rapid increases in inputs. However, since 1958 a slower, although still substantial, rate of growth of output has occurred, but there has been virtually no increase in any input with the exception of capital; water, total land and labor all remained fairly constant, although the amount of irrigated land did increase by approximately 34 percent.[20] It is evident that much of the recent rapid growth in output can be attributed to causes

19. Bank of Israel, *Annual Report, 1959*, p. 131.
20. The residual using labor and capital as inputs for the 1958–64 period is 7.3 percent per annum and accounts for about two-thirds of the growth in gross output. This may be compared with the residual for 1954–58 of 5.0 percent, which accounted for 40 percent of gross output growth.

other than the material inputs considered thus far, although it is possible that changes in their quality, along with the maturation of earlier investments, have contributed to this growth.

The measured increase in productivity of primary inputs undoubtedly includes the effects of the accumulation of experience (especially in the new settlements and among the new workers), the impact of extension programs, the education of agricultural workers, and the considerable efforts devoted to agricultural research.

Table 5.9 shows the changes in the number of agricultural settle-

Table 5.9: Changes in the Number of Agricultural Settlements, 1948–65

	Moshavim[a]	*Kibbutzim*	*Other*
1948–50	141	37	50
1951–53	79	13	52
1954–56	34	1	10
1957–65	10	2	−59

[a] Including collective Moshavim.

Sources: 1948–49 to 1959–60: Mundlak, *Long-Term Projections for Agricultural Products*, p. 23.
   1960–61: *Statistical Abstract of Israel, 1961*, p. 11; *1962*, p. 39.
   1961–62: *Statistical Abstract of Israel, 1962*, p. 39; *1963*, p. 25.
   1962–63: *Statistical Abstract of Israel, 1964*, p. 21.
   1963–64: *Statistical Abstract of Israel, 1965*, p. 29.
   1964–65: *Statistical Abstract of Israel, 1966*, p. 29.

ments, by type, from 1948 to 1965. The largest increase in the number of settlements occurred among moshavim (from 104 in 1948 to 358 in 1956), with most of the expansion occurring in the early 1950s as part of the immigrant absorption program. The number reached a peak in 1957 and has since remained near this level. Although thirty-seven Kibbutzim were established in 1948–50, over the next decade only fourteen new ones were begun. The number of other settlements, mainly private farms, also increased substantially. The population in these rural settlements more than tripled between 1948 and 1957.[21] At the time of the 1961 census

21. There is some ambiguity in numbers, as definitions were changed in 1957, so that numbers before and after cannot easily be compared. However, the main difference is in "other types," and the orders of magnitude are still large.

the total population in moshavim was 121,770 persons, of whom 57,160 had arrived after 1948. In the kibbutzim the situation was reversed: of the 82,125 members, only 15,580 had arrived after the founding of the state.[22]

There is evidence that few of these new workers had previous agricultural experience. The 1961 Census showed that only 7.9 percent of male immigrants engaged in agriculture in that year had been employed in farming abroad. Among females this percentage was 2.7.[23] The workers included were only those less than sixty years old, who had been between twenty-four and fifty-four years of age at the time of their immigration. They constituted about one-fourth of the agricultural labor force. It may be assumed, however, that the percentages would not be much different among other new, immigrant farmers, who together made up almost two-thirds of the Jewish agricultural labor force and more than half of the total agricultural labor force in 1961.[24]

The effect of the lack of experience manifested itself mainly in the sphere of farm management.

> Although most new settlers had had no previous experience in farming, the acquisition of manual and mechanical skills did not present any particular difficulties. However, great variations in adaptation were noticeable in the theoretical and decision making spheres and in the mastering of organizational problems, such as management, marketing, etc.[25]

Not only was the lack of experience an obstacle to high productivity on new farms, but serious sociological problems also had to be overcome. Initially, an attempt was made to mix immigrants from diverse areas of origin and social background. Often these settlements were unsuccessful, exhibiting much lower productivity than similarly endowed, but cohesive villages. Gradually, a new basis

22. Population and Housing Census, 1961. It is not possible to identify the private farm population. However, the data available on these villages suggest that, if anything, they would raise the percentage of new immigrants in agriculture.

23. Population and Housing Census, 1961 (Israel), Publication no. 27, *Labour Force*, part 4, table 3.

24. *Labour Force Surveys (1955–1961)*, p. 64.

25. Weitz and Rokach, *Agricultural Development*, summarizing a study of productivity in moshavim.

for deciding on the composition of villages was established, emphasizing extended family groups as the core of the community.[26]

One would expect new settlers to rapidly improve the productivity of their own labor input as they gained experience and to close the gap between themselves and the veteran settlers. Moreover, one would also expect other primary factors to be used with increasing efficiency. The rate of technical change would be higher for the new settlements than for the old, although the absolute level of the productivity index would be higher for the latter.[27] Thus the rising share of output of new settlements before 1958 or 1959 probably led to a lower average level of productivity than would have existed had all output been undertaken by established farms; this probably reduced the size of the residual. However, after 1958, with few new settlements and with production being shared in proportion to previous output, part of the increased residual during the post-1958 years reflects the effect of experience. Increased experience, however, is only one element of unexplained productivity growth.

It is also possible that part of the residual stems from omitted or incorrectly measured factor inputs and that correct estimates would eliminate any unexplained growth in output.[28] In a series of studies by Griliches, the most important factor corrections were found to be research expenditures and the educational level of the agricultural labor force.[29] While our subjective impression is that "learning by doing" [30] has been the most important source of productivity growth, the increasing number of students who have attended four-year agricultural schools, the increasing availability of extension

26. Ibid., pp. 141–44. These and other not strictly economic problems were often handled with considerable ingenuity. Weitz and Rokach provide numerous examples of important innovations in regional agricultural planning.

27. If the production function for each sector is written as: $Q_t = A(t) \, f[K(t), L(t)]$, then $A^V(t) > A^N(t)$, where V denotes veteran and N, new. But $\dot{A}^N/A^N(t) > \dot{A}^V/A^V(t)$, when $\dot{A}$ is the time derivative of $A(t)$.

28. For an analysis of this type performed for the United States, see Zvi Griliches, "The Sources of Measured Productivity Growth: U.S. Agriculture 1940–1960," *Journal of Political Economy* 71 (Aug. 1963): 331–46.

29. Zvi Griliches, "Research Expenditures, Education, and the Aggregate Agricultural Production Function," *American Economic Review* 54 (Dec. 1964): 961–74.

30. "Learning by doing" is here meant to indicate the movement of newer farmers toward the efficiency levels of the established farms.

services and the rapid growth of agricultural research, have undoubtedly contributed to growing productivity.[31]

AGRICULTURAL POLICY

Agricultural policy was directed toward the attainment of several
proximate goals whose ends were to improve the trade balance on
agricultural account and to encourage people to stay in the agricultural sector. To achieve the latter, substantial efforts were made
to reduce the farm/nonfarm income differentials, as well as to
guarantee attractive incomes to new settlements. As for the former,
relatively little attention was given specifically to encouraging the
growth of economically profitable import substitutes or export
goods during the 1950s, although general agricultural development
was encouraged in many ways. However, since about 1960 there
has been a significant move toward encouraging those branches
whose output would be most beneficial to the national economy.
One additional objective of policy has been the stabilization of
food prices to consumers, since the tying of wages to the price
index (see Chapter 7) means that increases in food prices tend to
generate further inflationary pressure.

To achieve these goals the following instruments have been used
at one time or another; quantitative restrictions on output; subsidies; tariff and quantitative import restrictions on agricultural
commodities; low cost, long-term financing, and preferential loans
for working capital. Regardless of the immediate objective of a
given instrument, it is likely to influence several other variables
that may be important; thus subsidies intended to maintain farm
income will change the relative profitability of different branches,
as well as the pattern of inputs.

Before turning to a discussion of specific policies, let us consider
the general situation of Israeli agriculture and the policies that
most analysts of the sector have counseled.[32] Since the problem of

31. Some data suggestive of the importance of these facts are: the number of research workers at agricultural research stations increased from 85
in 1954 to 1,300 in 1964 (*Israel Government Yearbook 1954,* p. 48, *1964,* p.
58); the enrollment in four-year agricultural schools increased from 1,900
in 1953 to 7,000 in 1965 (*Statistical Abstract of Israel,* various issues.)

32. See, for example, the chapters on agriculture in the annual issues of
the Bank of Israel, *Annual Report*; Mundlak, *Long-Term Projections for
Agricultural Products*: Rubner, *Economy of Israel,* chaps. 13, 14.

closing the foreign exchange gap appeared to be the critical one during the entire period, purely economic criteria suggested that production be governed by the cost of a dollar saved or added (CDA).[33] By 1954 or 1955 it had become apparent that the CDA of citrus fruit and a number of industrial crops was significantly lower than that for animal products.[34] Nevertheless, in conformity with the mixed farming ideal mentioned earlier, and possibly because of a desire for self-sufficiency regardless of the economic costs, the production of meat, dairy and egg products was encouraged. However, even after the decision was made to engage in livestock production, there still remained the choice of producing or importing animal feeds. A decision to produce fodder was made, although its CDA was above that for alternative industrial crops and cereals which could be grown with similar resource combinations. While the decision to produce livestock products was mistaken on purely economic grounds,[35] the growth of animal feed production compounded the error and precluded an increase in the output of other socially profitable field crops.

A similar problem arose in the choice of production between vegetables and a number of industrial crops. Throughout the period small subsidies were given for cotton and peanuts (the one on cotton rising rapidly in the 1960s),[36] two industrial crops, which in terms of their CDA's were more profitable than most agricultural output to the national economy. Moreover, sugar beet production, which promised to be more profitable than vegetables, was subsidized via payments to processors, who were enabled to purchase the product at prices higher than they would otherwise have paid.[37] However, despite subsidies to these branches, the continued high subsidization of vegetables (intended as an income supplement) maintained the latter's higher private return and slowed the move-

33. See Chap. 4, Appendix.
34. See, for example, Bank of Israel, *Annual Report, 1956*, p. 142.
35. For some settlements livestock production may have been the best product choice, given the possibilities of substituting capital and labor for land and water in this activity. For the kibbutzim, which refused to hire labor and were running into a labor shortage, another attractive feature was the possibility of increasing mechanization.
36. The increase in cotton subsidies reflected a change in emphasis from agricultural self-sufficiency to the improvement of the balance of payments.
37. See Mundlak, *Long-Term Projections for Agricultural Products*, p. 13.

ment of resources to these alternative uses, despite the saturation of the domestic market for vegetables.

It had become clear by the late 1950s that, as the result of the rapid growth of agricultural inputs and productivity, the agricultural problem in Israel was going to be a unique one for a relatively underdeveloped economy, namely, the limitation of the growth of certain branches, while maintaining farm incomes by encouraging the increased growth of output profitable to the national economy. Product subsidies constituted the main instrument for inducing changes in the composition of output and for maintaining income. Table 5.10 shows that subsidies increased very rapidly after 1955 and that much of the increase was concentrated in milk and egg output,[38] two of the most important income sources for mixed farms.

Other measures have also been extensively used to increase the viability of the agricultural sector. Land is allocated on an acres-per-family basis, and a low uniform rate is charged for land of all qualities and in all locations. Water is subsidized insofar as the water company's prices did not cover costs and their resultant deficits were covered by general government revenue. In 1962 subsidies were also used to alleviate the effects of the currency devaluation on the agricultural sector. Payments were made to importers to prevent the price of imported fertilizer from increasing; the effective exchange rate on fodder did not increase until nine months after the devaluation, which meant price increases on the accumulated stock of imported inputs were therefore delayed.[39] Tariffs have been used extensively to protect most branches, in particular meat and dairy products. In addition, when prices have fallen for particular commodities, quantitative import restrictions have been utilized for short periods of time.

A number of favorable financial arrangements have also been offered to the sector. A considerable part of the fixed and working

38. There were relatively small subsidies in these branches until 1958, designed to elicit greater output. These may not have been necessary, since livestock farming, which uses relatively little land and water, became increasingly attractive to many farms as water and land became scarcer. Furthermore, after 1963, concentrated feeds were imported and fodder production was significantly reduced, so that cattle raising did not require any significant input of land.

39. Bank of Israel, *Annual Report, 1962,* pp. 197–200.

Table 5.10: Agricultural Subsidies and Value of Output, 1955, 1960, and 1965
(millions of current 1£)

	1955		1960		1965	
Output	*Subsidy*	*Value of output*	*Subsidy*	*Value of output*	*Subsidy*	*Value of output*
Milk	4.3	44.5	12.5	81.4	33.1	128.6
Poultry	0		} 3.3	125.6	5.5	135.9
Beef	0				1.2	87.0
Eggs	.1	32.6	19.4	80.9	25.0	107.1
Vegetables	5.5	47.0	5.1	60.8	11.6	117.8
Cotton	.3	4.8	6.8	25.7	10.3	56.0
Peanuts	1.4	8.9	0		1.2	11.0
Fruit	1.7	30.4	0		2.3	160.0
Fish	.1	11.8	0		2.3	5.4
Tobacco	0		1.1	2.8	.3	
Wheat	0		0		3.6	33.2
Miscellaneous	1.1		2.9		1.4	
Total	14.5	312.1[a]	51.1	649.5[a]	97.8	1294.8[a]
Input						
Fodder	0		0		15.1	
Fertilizer	7.3		3.4		2.9	
Water	0		0		13.2	
Frost and drought compensation	0		23.2		.2	
Total	7.3		26.6		31.4	
Total output and input	21.8		77.7		129.2	

[a] Including the value of products not subsidized.
Sources: 1955: Bank of Israel, *Annual Report, 1956*, pp. 153–57.
1960: Bank of Israel, *Annual Report, 1962*, p. 204.
1965: Bank of Israel, *Annual Report, 1965*, p. 250.
CBS, *National Income Originating in Israel's Agriculture* (Jerusalem, 1964), Table 8.

capital needs has been provided by the public sector through the government Development Budget and the Jewish Agency Settlement Department. Thus, in addition to public development projects, such as irrigation and afforestation, the government has financed a large percentage of ordinary farm investment. For example, in 1962, 85 percent of total agricultural investment (including public projects) and 78 percent of private farm investment were financed by public funds. Loans were made to farms at low interest rates, frequently so low that the real rate of interest (after adjusting for inflation) was negative. The Jewish Agency, for example, made loans to kibbutzim at an interest rate of 3.5 percent for thirty years, while the price level during the years immediately preceding these loans had been increasing by about 10 percent per year. After the 1962 devaluation the government did not insist on linkage provisions, even for those farm loans on which they had previously been required, and this induced further borrowing by the sector.[40] Moreover, subsequent linking provisions were very liberal. Funds for working capital were also made available at low rates, and the uses to which they were put were determined by the government. In addition, industrial firms processing agricultural products received credits that were passed on to farms in the form of advances for raw materials and supply credits.[41] Finally, the Bank of Israel exempted private banks from liquidity requirements on loans to certain agricultural branches, varying the extent of exemptions in accord with suggestions from the Ministry of Agriculture.

Some insight into the government's intentions in agriculture can be gleaned from movements in such "directed" credit. The distribution of such credit by branch is shown in Table 5.11. In the years 1959–61, cotton, which, as we have noted above, was a profitable crop for the economy, received about 18 percent of all directed credit. Citrus fruit and peanuts, two other profitable crops, received about 27 and 5 percent, respectively. Thus, about one-half of the total directed credit was being allocated to the most profitable activities, mainly in the older settlements. However, the credits to new settlements undoubtedly encouraged livestock and vegetable production despite their lack of social profitability. The decline in the amount going to citrus fruit probably reflects the increased ability of producers to finance themselves commercially.

EVALUATION OF GOVERNMENT POLICIES

The above set of policy measures may be thought of as an attempt to improve the agricultural balance of trade whenever this was consistent with raising agricultural incomes. Where the aims conflicted,

40. Bank of Israel, *Annual Report, 1962,* p. 211.
41. Bank of Israel, *Annual Report, 1965,* p. 163.

Table 5.11: Average Annual Balance of Directed Credit
by Destination, 1959–65
(percentage)

	1959	1960	1961	1962	1963	1964	1965
Cotton fibers	16.6	18.3	20.2 ⎫				
Field crops	9.8	8.4	7.1 ⎬ 39.9	42.2	35.8	40.0
Peanuts	6.1	6.2	3.4 ⎭				
Citrus fruit	26.3	26.8	27.0	17.5	9.6	10.6	12.0
Livestock	a	a	a	12.0	11.8	11.4	9.1
Buyers' organizations	9.3	9.5	10.1 ⎫				
New settlements	6.9	5.9	5.6 ⎬ 30.6	36.4	42.2	38.9
Miscellaneous	25.0	24.9	26.6 ⎭				

a Included in miscellaneous.

Sources: 1959, 1960: Bank of Israel, *Annual Report, 1960,* p. 140.
  1961: Bank of Israel, *Annual Report, 1961,* p. 189.
  1962, 1963: Bank of Israel, *Annual Report, 1963,* p. 225.
  1964, 1965: Bank of Israel, *Annual Report, 1965,* p. 261.

it appears that the latter was accorded priority. The maintenance or improvement of agricultural incomes was a reflection of the continued importance of Zionist egalitarian philosophy in economic decisions in the post statehood period. The implementation of this policy was made considerably easier by the initial agricultural background in Palestine of most of the nation's leaders as well as the disproportionate influence (in comparison to actual voters) of farmers in the councils of the political parties.[42]

Our previous discussion has indicated some of the distortions introduced by government policies. It is interesting to attempt a qualitative estimate of their impact on agricultural incomes. The measures taken by the government can usually be reduced to a change in prices which farmers receive (where price is defined to include product subsidies) or a change in the prices which they pay for intermediate inputs, as well as for land and water.

The distortion of product and factor prices results in a rearrangement of production, so that neither the combination of outputs produced nor the factor combinations used to produce them are

42. The importance of high agricultural incomes in preventing the flow of population from rural to heavily populated urban areas is duscussed below.

the same as in the case of nonintervention. Let us consider first the impact on the factor side of allocating land and water by fiat. Instead of the sector's producing at a point on the potential production transformation curve TT (in Figure 5.1), it will produce

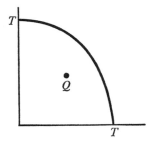

Figure 5.1. Effect of input distortions.

somewhere within the curve, for example, at Q.[43] The loss in value added could be measured by weighting the increased output that could result solely from resource reallocation by some set of output prices.[44] Against this loss there are no inevitable offsetting benefits. It would be necessary to determine whether the decreased input costs resulting from (the implicit) subsidies were as great as the output foregone.

While the net effect of input subsidies is thus not unambiguously income-augmenting, product subsidies almost certainly involve a net gain in farm income. The subsidization of one sector within agriculture, say the dairy and poultry branches, increases the price cum subsidy received by the producer and lowers the price to the purchaser. As a result, resources are shifted to such production, the quantity sold rises and total receipts (including subsidies) increase (as they must if any resource shift is to occur); inputs are withdrawn from the nonsubsidized sector, so that output decreases; and the price received by farmers increases, the change in receipts

43. This would correspond to being off the contract curve in an Edgeworth Bowley box. This distortion does not occur because factor prices faced by two activities differ, but as the result of fixed allocations to each farm regardless of the marginal productivity of the farm in using the land or water.

44. The relative output prices after the reallocation would almost certainly be different than the initial set of prices at Q, unless the output of each good were expanded proportionally and the community indifference map were homothetic.

depending upon the elasticity of demand for the nonsubsidized product. For the large nonlivestock branch this elasticity is unlikely to be greater than unity, so that (at the worst) the total receipts from unsubsidized products remain the same.[45] Thus income for the entire agricultural sector will increase.

Product subsidies have accounted for as much as 28 percent of income originating in recent years, and it seems likely that these more than offset any negative effect on income to which the distortions on the input side led. In addition to product subsidies, value added in agriculture has been raised by the use of tariffs for protection of domestic production and by quantitative restrictions. Nominal and effective tariff rates are shown in Table 5.12.[46]

Table 5.12: Nominal Tariff Rates and Protection of Value Added
in Agriculture, 1958

	Tariff rates	
	Nominal	*Effective*
Cereals and fodder	.21	.23
Industrial crops	.23	.22
Other livestock	.37	.07
Poultry and eggs	.56	−.19
Citrus	.00	−.04
Vegetables and fruit	.91	.18

Sources: Joseph Baruh, "Import Taxes and Export Subsidies in Israel, 1955–1961," Bank of Israel, *Bulletin* no. 18; Michael Bruno, *Interdependence, Resource Use and Structural Change in Israel.*

All branches except citrus and poultry had a higher value added as a result of the tariff structure. However, in poultry, quantitative restrictions were important, and it would not be correct to infer

45. It is assumed that subsidies are paid for out of general tax revenue, most of which is obtained from nonagricultural sources.

46. The implicit tariff is calculated according to the formula used by Ronald Soligo and Joseph Stern, in "Tariff Protection, Import Substitution and Investment Efficiency," *The Pakistan Development Review* 5, no. 2 (1965): 249–70. It represents the percentage increase in the value added in a branch resulting from the protection afforded its output and the additional cost of its inputs resulting from tariffs. If Z_i is value added in a branch when domestic prices are used and W_i, the value added at world prices, the implicit rate is $(Z_i - W_i)/Z_i$. The 1958 input-output table was used, along with tariff data for 1958 contained in Bank of Israel, *Bulletin*, no. 18. The data in Table 5.12 refer to 1958.

that the tariff structure reduced its value added; more generally, these figures are only partial—they do not reflect the impact of quantitative restrictions in a number of branches.[47]

Although we have shown that agricultural policy increased aggregate agricultural income, how successful was it in achieving parity between farm income and incomes in alternative employment? As a first approximation to these relative changes, agricultural income per nonhired farm worker (other salaries, interest, and rents having been deducted) was compared to per person wages in other sectors.[48] We are assuming here that, in general, farm owners would have become employees, rather than employers, had they moved to nonagricultural employment. Between 1955 and 1960 the ratio of income per farm owner to wages per employee in the nonagricultural sector increased from 67 to 80 percent,[49] and between 1960 and 1965 from 80 to 87 percent.[50] Thus there was a significant gain during the 1955–65 period, attributable in large part to government product subsidies and tariffs. A comparison of relative incomes must be made in terms of relative purchasing power. A study of kibbutzim in 1957 indicated that, when adjustments were made to allow for imputations and discounts resulting from cooperative purchases, the consumption expenditures per kibbutz member were the approximate money equivalent of those of the skilled urban worker.[51] To what extent similar adjustments would affect other types of farms is not clear.

47. Insofar as quantitative restrictions were applied to the inputs of the agricultural sector, they resulted in prices of inputs higher than those suggested by the nominal tariffs, so that the net impact of quantitative restrictions is not known. However, subsidies on purchases of major inputs such as fertilizers suggest that the cost-raising impact of quotas probably was less than the price-increasing effect of quotas on farm output.

48. In 1963, 32 percent of the agricultural labor force consisted of employees; by 1965 this percentage had risen to 39.8.

49. The 1955 and 1960 figures are calculated from *Labour Force Surveys* (*1955–1961*), pp. 42, 74; CBS, *Israel's National Income and Expenditure* (*1950–1962*), p. 105.

50. A qualification is necessary here to avoid too literal an interpretation of these changes. Within the agricultural sector, there are considerable variations in income; old, established Jewish farms have much higher incomes than new Jewish settlements or Arab farms that are less capital intensive. Thus net average earnings in 1959 were I£2,830 for all farms and I£5,300 for the older established ones alone. (Bank of Israel, *Annual Report, 1959*, p. 108.)

51. S. Rosen, "The Kibbutz Movement," *Hedim* (July 1958), cited in Kanovsky, *Economy of the Israeli Kibbutz*, p. 69.

We have yet to examine the incomes of agricultural employees; these have consistently been among the lowest for any sector. In 1955 their annual income was only 60 percent of that of workers in other branches; this declined to 58 percent in 1961 and 53 percent in 1965.[52] While the government undertook a set of measures designed to raise agricultural incomes, employees (who constituted between 30 and 40 percent of the agricultural labor force) benefited little. During much of the period, there was considerable unemployment in the rural areas, and in development towns where many of the new immigrants were settled;[53] thus market forces kept wages relatively low, the only nominal increases being those ordered by the national government in response to changes in the cost of living. The failure of the government to improve these low incomes, despite a general concern for agriculture, apparently reflects a dominant concern with farm owners, rather than employees.

As urban unemployment virtually disappeared between 1960 and 1965, the number of owners in the branch decreased by 5.5 percent, while the number of employees remained constant. Had the government not, in fact, subsidized owners' incomes, many more would undoubtedly have left in response to increasing opportunities in the cities. While direct income payments, rather than the extensive product subsidy scheme, would have been a more desirable method for maintaining farm owners' incomes, in view of the need to instill and maintain self-respect, particularly among new immigrants, subsidies on output rather than transfers for restricting output may have been the only alternative.

Nevertheless, even if subsidies were to be used, one mistake was made that cannot easily be rationalized, namely, the offering of capital to the agricultural sector at rates much below the real cost to the economy, thus encouraging the substitution of capital for labor in agriculture, while at the same time trying to combat unemployment in other sectors. There is substantial empirical evidence that considerable variation in capital intensity was possible.[54]

---

52. For the calculation of the 1955 percentage, Bank of Israel, *Annual Report, 1959*; for those in 1961 and 1965, Bank of Israel, *Annual Report, 1965*.

53. Such unemployment persisted even in the 1960s when there was virtually no unemployment in urban areas.

54. Kanovsky, *Economy of the Israeli Kibbutz,* p. 55.

Although it is true that capital intensive techniques are more productive, the added productivity was not necessary, since by the mid-1950s the rapidly growing supply began to exceed the growth of demand in some branches. The impact of this capital intensive policy and the distributional objectives which it may have served are considered in the next chapter.

6

The Role of Government

The Israeli government has been a major participant in economic activities: financing the private sector, providing tariff protection, and offering preferential tax treatment to a large number of businesses. These instruments have been applied by policy makers in the belief that they would increase the possibility of fulfilling the overriding goals of the economy, namely, the elimination of the balance of payments deficit, the productive absorption of immigrants into the labor force, and the dispersal of the population from the coastal plain to other areas of the country. Although it appears that the entire set of instruments usually did move the economy in the desired directions, individual instruments were occasionally used in a manner that had perverse effects. The purpose of the following analysis is to indicate the extent of governmental influence and to evaluate the consistency, in terms of its stated goals, of the entire constellation of policies. The increasing number of empirical studies of government influence on development suggest that similar problems arising from public sector intervention occur in many other less developed countries. While few economists would advocate the pursuance of laissez-faire policies in these countries, it is to be hoped that, if existing levels of governmental control are continued, they will be implemented in a more consistent manner.

The instruments discussed in this chapter are microeconomic in the sense that they were designed to achieve the economy's aims via the sectoral allocation of resources, rather than through the control of aggregate demand. The following chapter considers the impact of macroeconomic policies on the same goals.

POLICY INSTRUMENTS

Although a number of government agencies, for example, the Ministry of Commerce and Industry and the Ministry of Finance, jointly administered each of the instruments, it is convenient to analyze policy by discussing the instruments themselves.[1] These were the Development Budget, the granting of tax and other benefits to approved businesses, the use of tariffs and quotas, and finally, direct employment by the government.

The development budget

The Development Budget is a special budget that supplements the ordinary one, its main functions being to channel funds to the private sector and to finance social overhead facilities.[2] Outlays from the Budget include both loans and direct investment in privately owned corporations, as well as the financing of research expenditures. In the early 1950s a large percentage was devoted to residential construction, but this type of expenditure has diminished in relative importance due to the slowing of immigration.

While it does not include all forms of governmental aid, the Development Budget may be viewed as a document that reflected broad trends in the relative importance which the government attached to given activities or sectors. In most years the largest individual expenditures were for housing construction and debt redemption, both of which may be considered nondiscretionary outlays. The former reflect the intention of the government to provide all members of the population with a relatively high minimum housing standard. Although the magnitude of the expenditure may not have been warranted on purely economic grounds, internal social and political pressures left the government with little choice concerning the size of the outlays. However, a high housing standard may well have served to increase output in other sectors by improving the health of new immigrants, and perhaps by inducing an increase in either the quality or quantity of work effort.[3]

1. The actual use of any instrument was the result of compromises among various ministries and cannot be interpreted as implementing a unified development plan.
2. The Development Budget is not a capital budget, as many of the expenditures financed by it are on current account, for example, agricultural research. However, under a broadly interpreted definition of capital formation, most of the expeditures could be interpreted as such.
3. There is no rental housing in Israel. Flats built by the government must be purchased from it, and the mortgage payments for many groups constitute a substantial percentage of income. Given the demonstration

Table 6.1: Sectoral Distribution of Development Budget Expenditures, 1952–63[a]
(percentage)

	Agriculture and national water project	Mines and quarries	Electricity	Industry and crafts	Communication and transport
1952–53	56	10	4	11	19
1953–54	58	6	13	12	11
1954–55	51	9	12	12	16
1955–56	47	8	20	12	13
1956–57	47	9	9	20	15
1957–58	48	12	9	19	12
1958–59	48	6	12	24	10
1959–60	52	7	5	24	12
1960–61	51	2	8	26	13
1961–62	49	2	2	26	21
1962–63	39	6	4	22	29

[a] After subtraction of outlays on housing and debt redemption.

Source: Central Bureau of Statistics, unpublished data.

Table 6.1 shows the percentage distribution of the Development Budget after housing expenditures and bond redemption allocations are subtracted. During the years through 1962, agriculture (defined to include the national irrigation project) received 45 percent or more of total outlays. Manufacturing, on the other hand, received 12 percent or less of total budget allocations until 1957, the rapidly rising percentage thereafter presumably reflecting an increasing awareness by the government of the reliance it would have to place upon manufacturing if the import surplus were to be reduced. Outlays on electricity and transportation were concomitants of the general growth process, since the growth of output in agriculture and industry necessitated both the increasing availability of electricity (particularly in irrigation) and improved internal transport facilities. In addition, both a commercial airline system and an extensive merchant marine were developed.

The Development Budget had several effects. First, it was an important determinant of the relative availability of funds to the various sectors. For all sectors except industry, the primary

---

effect of foreign consumption patterns and the spending constraint imposed by mortgage payments, it is conceivable that either more hours were worked where possible or that the labor force participation rate was increased.

source of financing in most years was the public sector, of which the Development Budget was the major component. Table 6.2

Table 6.2: Percentage of Sectoral Fixed Investment
Financed by the Public Sector, 1958–59

	1958	*1959*
Agriculture (including irrigation)	74	72
Manufacturing and construction	42	32
Mining and quarrying	75	71
Electric power	69	54
Transport and communication	59	68
Services	48	56
Housing	44	44
All sectors	54	52

Source: Bank of Israel, *Annual Report, 1965,* p. 102.

shows the share of government financing of the major sectors for 1958 and 1959, these figures being typical of those for much of the period since 1956.[4] Although these percentages are quite high, even they underestimate the importance of public sector financing influence, since they do not include the ability to determine the policies of commercial banks and other financial intermediaries which provided additional sources of funds.

The distribution of capital to the major sectors was not determined on a competitive basis in which the interest rate is set by the supply and demand for capital and only those projects whose internal rate of return was greater than the equilibrium rate receive funds. Rather, the government set sectoral priorities and then allocated a fixed amount of resources accordingly; the interest rate thus played no role in intersectoral resource allocation. Interest rates were set at arbitrarily low levels, with funds being allocated to specific enterprises by the Ministry of Finance and the Ministry of Agriculture. As a result, excess demand existed at the given interest rate, and the marginal productivity of investment in each sector was determined by the size of its allocation, rather than by the competitive mechanism. In fact nominal interest rates were set at such low levels that the real rate (after allowing for price in-

4. Since the early 1960s explicit public financing of manufacturing has been declining and has been replaced by the Industrial Development Bank, a quasi government agency.

creases) was often negative. The nominal interest rate on all loans from the Development Budget ranged between 5.0 and 5.7 percent between 1950 and 1962.[5] However, since the implicit price deflator of GNP increased in all years through 1957 by more than 9 percent per annum, borrowers using a naïve model of extrapolating recent increases in the price index would have anticipated a very low or negative real rate of interest. Even after 1957 when the rate of inflation slowed, the real rate on most loans was quite low, since the nominal rate remained between 5 and 6 percent.

The practice of tying both the principal and the interest on loans to either the consumer price index or the dollar probably had little impact on the ex ante cost as viewed by borrowers. First, only part of each loan was linked: 50 percent of two- to five-year loans and 70 percent of loans for eight years or more. Thus, even when price increases were anticipated, only a fraction of the existing liability was affected. Moreover, a choice of the form of tying was granted until 1961 and the dollar was most often selected, since loans obtained and repaid before devaluation occurred were never affected by increased liability. Devaluation was, in most years correctly assumed to be unlikely, despite the existence of considerable domestic inflation.[6]

The Development Budget thus had two major effects on the economy. First, it influenced the relative sectoral growth rates; in particular neglecting manufacturing while encouraging the expansion of agriculture. Secondly, the low interest rates charged on such loans, combined with the arbitrarily high price of labor[7] and a low price for imported machinery,[8] encouraged excessive capital intensity (from the social viewpoint) in all sectors.

5. Haim Ben Shahar, *Interest Rates and the Cost of Capital in Israel, 1950–1962* (Basel: Kyklos Verlag, 1962), p. 39.

6. Ben Shahar has calculated the ex post real rate of interest, which includes the effect of the actual increases in liability due to the tying agreements. This rate (for all sectors) increased from −6.7 on loans granted in 1950–53, to 4.2 on loans granted in 1960–61. Even this latter figure was clearly below the marginal cost of funds to the economy, as measured by the cost of borrowing abroad. See Ben Shahar, *Interest Rates and Cost of Capital*, pp. 82–84.

7. See Chapter 7.

8. See the discussion below.

Approved investment status

While the Development Budget was used to channel funds to all sectors and was the main instrument available to the government for affecting the sectoral composition of investment, a second important instrument, used primarily to influence industrial investment, was the Law for the Encouragement of Investment.

This law was initially designed to stimulate direct foreign investment, although domestic investors could also benefit from its provisions. The first law, passed in 1950, and continued with modification until the present, contained the following benefits for approved investments:[9]

1. Annual repatriation by foreign investors of up to 10 percent of their initial investment in the same currency that they brought in.

2. The exclusion of imported capital goods and raw materials from custom's duty.

3. An exemption from property tax for five years with a possible extension.

4. Accelerated depreciation, which made it possible to write off the initial cost of a machine in four and a half years.

5. A maximum tax of 25 percent on business income.

6. The refunding of Israeli tax liabilities to foreign owned companies if the same income were being taxed in the company's home country and the Israel tax liability were not deductible.

Although the law was designed primarily to encourage investment in manufacturing, its provisions also benefited investors in service branches, particularly in tourism. The structure of the law has become familiar in the less developed countries, differing only in detail, for example, providing complete income tax exemption for five years, rather than a maximum tax of 25 percent. It is impossible to estimate the additional investment induced by such a law, since observed data on the number of new firms or the amount of investment benefiting from its provisions cannot indicate how much of this investment would have occurred in any case; such a

9. *Israel Economic Bulletin* 2, no. 14.

distinction would require knowledge of the ex ante investment plans of firms and the effect of the law on these plans. However, there is little doubt that the government was able to induce some investment that otherwise would not have occurred. It did not simply choose among a given set of projects suggested by the private sector; rather it was often responsible for conceiving industrial needs (usually designed to fill lacunae in the existing production structure), finding entrepreneurs and inducing them to undertake the project, by the offer of approved status and substantial financing from the Development Budget. An examination of actual approvals can thus provide a measure of government preferences, as well as a partial explanation of the evolution of the branch structure of the industrial sector.

Tariffs and quotas

In the two previous chapters we have indicated the important impact of both tariffs and quotas on the development of agriculture and industry. Until at least 1958 quantitative restrictions were placed upon almost all imports that were competitive with domestically produced goods, both agricultural and manufactured, these being imposed regardless of the domestic cost of production. Since 1959 there has been increasing liberalization, particularly on industrial products. Nevertheless, tariffs have remained high.[10] The only major branch of industry that received neither tariff nor quota benefits was machinery. The primary impact of this practice was the reduction of the domestic price of imported machinery to levels considerably below their scarcity value, given the overvaluation of the exchange rate; this, combined with low interest rates increased the likelihood that excessively capital intensive modes of production would be adopted. The other effect of the extensive protection and quotas was to allow the growth of some branches that did not possess a comparative advantage. However, as seen in the two previous chapters, given the multiple dimensions of a desirable import substitution and export promotion policy, there were relatively few egregious violations of the broad dictates of efficiency. This, of course, does not imply that the process would not have been more efficient had liberalization been greater.

10. See Chap. 4, Table 4.6.

Direct employment

Government civilian employment has accounted for a high percentage of total civilian employment. In 1961, a year of full employment, about 25 percent of the total civilian labor force was employed by the government, while in most countries the comparable figure is at most 15 percent. Labor absorption by the government was a significant contributor to the economy's move toward full employment. While public employment was 18.2 percent of total civilian employment in 1951, by 1964 it had increased to 23.3 percent. This implies that the government employed over one-quarter of all additional labor force members during this period. Such an unusual distribution of the incremental labor force may be attributable either to the government's acting as an employer of last resort or to an atypical set of demands for public services. If the former explanation is correct, then government employment was in fact a conscious instrument of policy, designed primarily to meet the employment goal, whereas, if the latter is true, direct employment should not be considered an instrument at all.

SECTORAL IMPACT OF GOVERNMENT POLICY

Agriculture

As we saw in the previous chapter, the policy toward agriculture, which included investment financing, subsidies on both inputs and outputs, and protective tariffs, had a pervasive effect. The autarkic policy followed by the government was more often limited by climatic conditions and resource scarcities than by economic desiderata. As a result of the enormous resource inputs into the agricultural development program, other sectors were deprived of funds and sectoral investment bore little relation to the output configuration dictated by the country's resources, demand patterns, and trading opportunities. Thus, between 1952 and 1955, agriculture and irrigation accounted for 21.1 percent of total fixed investment (in constant prices), the same percentage that went into industry (manufacturing, construction, mining, quarrying, and electricity). Indeed, through 1958 the cumulative investment in the agricultural sector was 94 percent of that in industrial activities.

To some extent the demand for funds, particularly on the part of existing farms, was induced by the possibility of borrowing at negligible real rates of interest and the absence of any import taxation on agricultural machinery. Even if one agreed with the sectoral priorities of the government, the wisdom of following a capital intensive mode of production in agriculture was open to question, given the extensive general unemployment in the economy through 1959 and the lack of skills of most of those unemployed. How much additional employment would have been possible depends upon the (partial) elasticity of factor substitution in the agricultural sector between the types of investment that could have been cut back, primarily machinery and structures, and labor. We do not have production functions detailed enough to allow an estimate. However, comparisons between techniques on kibbutzim and moshavim suggest that considerable possibilities did in fact exist, particularly in the dairy and poultry branches, which were the most capital intensive subsectors.[11] Thus the same agricultural output (and improvement in the balance of payments) could have been produced with a greater absorption of labor and a smaller use of capital, freeing more funds for other sectors.[12]

Two questions are suggested by the analysis of the previous paragraph. The first concerns the feasibility of the process envisioned; specifically, could more workers have been induced to work in agriculture and would they have been hired? Second, what would have been the income distribution implications of labor-capital substitution?

With regard to the willingness to work, it is necessary to remember that most of the new immigrants were located in areas designated by government agencies and had little choice in the matter. Moreover, many immigrants undoubtedly anticipated a change in occupation upon arrival in Israel; while many were far from anxious to adopt an agricultural mode of life, for a number of years the only real choice for many was employment in farming or un-

11. See Chap. 5, n. 54.
12. It has also been suggested that the irrigation system was another area in which considerable funds could have been saved by adopting alternate techniques. See Albert G. Black, "Reflections upon Israel's Recent Agricultural Development and Its Relationship to General Development," *Symposium on the Challenge of Development,* Hebrew University, 1957 (Jerusalem, 1958), pp. 199–212.

employment, and it is likely that most would have selected the former. Indeed, given the relatively large-scale job switching that did, in fact, occur, there is little reason to believe that it could not have been greater.[13] However, two constraints operated on the government's ability to implement such a policy: (1) the unwillingness of kibbutzim to employ hired labor, a factor that limited the absorptive role to be played by the collective sector; and (2) the effect on farm family incomes if capital intensity were reduced in the non-Kibbutz sector. Only the second need be considered, as the first constraint represented an institutional feature that had wide support.

Since the moshav-type organization with individual units owned by families was the most prevalent, greater labor absorption would have implied a decrease in the average land holdings;[14] thus substitution of labor for capital would have led to a decline in both the land/labor and capital/labor ratios for individual farms and to lower family incomes across the entire sector,[15] thus increasing the inequality of income between agriculture and other sectors. This outcome would have been quite distasteful to many people, including those outside of agriculture.

Traditional analysis would suggest that the substitution of previously unemployed labor for capital in agriculture, and the productive use of the latter in other sectors, would have increased national income and that a tax on the incremental income could have been used to achieve desired distribution goals. While the intellectual appeal of such a mechanism is great, the actual potential of the tax system for implementing it is debatable. In view of this, and taking explicit cognizance of distribution goals, the capital intensive mode adopted in agriculture may be said to have resulted in some output loss, compensated for by a step in the desired direction in income distribution for those actually employed. The continued unemployment of labor that might have been absorbed poses further, well-known problems in evaluating

13. See Chap. 1.
14. This assumes that increased labor absorption would have occurred in the form of additional individual farms within the moshav framework, rather than from an increase in hired labor. Within the Israeli institutional framework this would appear to be the most plausible assumption.
15. We are assuming factor substitution which maintains the output of the entire sector.

the overall welfare implications of the capital intensive policy, which it would be fruitless to pursue. All we can do is to note that, once the evaluation procedure extends beyond the pure allocation question and other goals are considered, one's misgivings about the policies followed becomes much more open to question.

Until now we have taken the size (in terms of value added) of the agricultural sector as a datum. However, many observers have questioned whether the sector was expanded beyond a desirable level. If the only variable in the social welfare function had been the reduction of the balance of payments deficit (or the maximization of real national income), then the criterion for deciding the optimal size of each sector would have been its productive efficiency in relation to world competition. We have seen that this concept could be approximated by the cost of a dollar added for each branch. Despite the casual impression of inefficiency in agriculture,[16] the major subdivisions all had CDA's lower than many of those in industry, which indicates that, at least until 1958, there had been no excessive overall expansion in agriculture. Moreover, although CDA's are not available for the post 1958 period, the residual for agriculture has been both absolutely higher and greater as a share of total product growth than that in manufacturing,[17] suggesting that, at least in the aggregate, the farming sector has more than maintained its relative efficiency.

Thus, if any major error was made in agricultural planning, it would be that of excessive capital intensity; here the benefits in terms of income distribution suggest that a more broadly defined welfare function might not lead to this being evaluated as a serious mistake.[18]

It is worth noting that had less capital been allocated to agriculture as a result of a decision to expand the sector somewhat less and/or to proceed with the expansion along less capital intensive lines, it is not obvious that the freed capital would have been allo-

16. Black, *Reflections upon Israel's Recent Agricultural Development.*
17. The residual calculation excluded land and water inputs, but as seen in Chap. 5 these rose very slowly after 1958.
18. The tariff and subsidy policies that encouraged a shift toward capital intensive branches, particularly dairy farming and chicken raising, partly reflected income distribution considerations, as small farms could, with sufficient capital, enter into the production of milk and eggs. However, protection of these branches undoubtedly was also beneficial to large, well-established farms.

cated to those manufacturing branches that exhibited the lowest CDA's. As a result of tariff-subsidy distortions, a low CDA in manufacturing did not necessarily indicate high private profitability, which would have allowed efficient firms to attract nongovernment finance. Moreover, the government itself often ignored the CDA in allocating investment funds. Thus it cannot be assumed that the efficient branches of manufacturing would have benefited from a release of resources from the agricultural sector.

Manufacturing

In Chapters 3 and 4 it was seen that the development of the manufacturing branch went through two distinct phases, one of significant import substitution through 1958 and the other a major expansion of exports thereafter. However, the sector did not always develop along lines dictated by comparative advantage, nor does it appear that the program was intentionally directed toward labor absorption. The opportunity for expansion, which often did not coincide with comparative advantage, is attributable in large measure to substantial government intervention in the private sector—in particular to its tariff sheltering, as well as its sectoral loan and investment approval policy.

Throughout the post-1950 period protective tariff policies, along with quantitative restrictions, have been major ingredients in the Israeli policy mix. Although quantitative restrictions have been gradually decreased in number, they are still important in many branches.[19] Quotas on imports were imposed whenever a good could be manufactured domestically, with almost no regard for its cost of production. There is some evidence that as early as 1953 any product that could be produced domestically at a cost of I£2.5 or less per dollar of imports would be protected by quantitative restrictions.[20] Thus any imported product whose c.i.f. price was $100 would no longer be imported if the domestic cost of production were I£250 or less, although the official exchange rate was I£1.8 per dollar. Moreover, this calculation understates the degree of protection, since it ignores the import component. Thus, if the import component were $50, the domestic resources required

19. See, e.g., Table 4.6.
20. Rubner, *Economy of Israel,* p. 171.

to save \$50 of foreign exchange would be I£160.[21] Despite the liberality of this criterion, even when costs of production were higher than I£2.5 per dollar, pressure groups often succeeded in obtaining quotas. Apparently the only products on which quantitative restrictions were not put into effect were those that were important in determining the level of the consumer price index.

Since they were essentially nondiscriminating, in effect completely protecting any branch in which output was physically feasible, the use of quantitative restrictions and tariffs cannot explain the differential degree of import substitution among branches. Rather, sectoral growth patterns were decisively influenced by the offer of funds and approved status for new investments. The quantitative importance of government policy in the development of the manufacturing sector may be seen in the following data. The total amount of investment in industry during 1950–58 in current prices was I£956 million. Although a complete breakdown between manufacturing, on the one hand, and construction, mines and quarries and electricity, on the other, does not exist, available data suggest that about 40 percent of this investment was not in manufacturing.[22] Thus about I£574 million was invested in manufacturing. In the same period loans from the Development Budget to manufacturing totaled about I£140 million.[23] However, since private participation in projects was usually at least 100 percent of the government's contribution, the total amount of investment coming under the direct influence of the government was of the order of I£280 million or roughly 40 percent of the total investment. In the period since 1958, public sector financing has been about 40 percent of total manufacturing investment;[24] matching private participation probably brings the percentage subject to immediate government influence to perhaps 60 to 75 percent.[25]

21. I£250–I£1.8 (50).
22. *Statistical Abstract of Israel, 1964,* pp. 146–47.
23. These were concentrated in the 1955–58 period.
24. See Table 6.2.
25. In the period since 1958 private participation relative to that of government apparently declined somewhat, primarily as a result of the government's willingness to finance almost all the capital needed by firms in some development areas. For similar conclusions on the importance of government financing, see Halevi and Klinov-Malul, *Economic Development of Israel,* pp. 204–208; Patinkin, *Israel Economy: The First Decade,* pp. 88–91.

An analysis of detailed data on the branch allocation of loans from the Development Budget and the branch pattern of investment approvals provides a guide to understanding the observed evolution of the industrial structure, as well as a rough indicator of the relative importance the government assigned to each of its policy objectives. Had the government allocated funds from the Development Budget in a manner consistent with its goals, one would expect that the sectoral allocation of funds would depend on three characteristics, namely, the sector's efficiency as measured by its CDA, its anticipated capital-labor ratio, and the possibility offered for population dispersal, since some branches can locate away from the central areas more easily than others. As the economy evolved, the response to changing values of the goals, for example, the unemployment rate or the balance of payments on current account, should have led to alterations in the relative importance of the various objectives in determining each period's policy actions. Thus, between 1955 and 1963, for example, we should expect the employment-generating characteristics of investments to explain less and less of the investment allocation, while the explanatory power of the CDA and dispersal opportunities should have become more important. These expectations are also in conformity with official statements of industrial policy.[26]

To evaluate the validity of this hypothesis, we have analyzed detailed data on the branch distribution of Development Budget loans to manufacturing.[27] Regression equations were estimated, in which the dependent variable in each year was the percentage of total loans going to each branch (I_i/I) and the independent variables were for each branch the labor-capital ratio (l), the CDA, and a measure of the dispersal effect, the percentage of loans going to development areas, (D). If the authorities followed their stated goals, presumably the proportion of total loans made available to a sector (I_i/I) would exhibit a positive correlation with D and l and a negative one with the CDA. As the empirical equivalent of each of these measures we have used the labor-capital ratio

26. See, for example, *Programme for Israel's Industrial Development, 1965–70* (Jerusalem: Ministry of Commerce and Industry, 1962).
27. Data on loans were obtained from the *Report on the Industrialization of the Development Areas* (Jerusalem: Ministry of Commerce and Industry), various issues.

estimates from the 1958 input-output study, the CDA estimates shown in Chapter 4, and the percentage of loans in each branch actually lent to firms in development areas.

The use of the 1958 labor-capital ratios is imposed by the lack of any alternate ones with the same breadth of coverage.[28] The ratios are the average for 1958, whereas for investment allocation decisions the marginal is the relevant magnitude. It is thus implicitly assumed that the marginal can be approximated by the average and that the relative labor-capital ratios remained constant between 1955 and 1964.

The cost of a dollar added is available for only a limited number of branches. In these there was no significant correlation (linear or rank) between a branch's share in investment funds in any year and its CDA. The lack of importance of this variable does not, of course, mean that balance of payment considerations were ignored; rather it indicates that the process of import substitution and export promotion did not necessarily follow an efficient pattern.[29] There is also no systematic relation between the absolute size of imports in 1955 in the various branches and their share of loans, although in individual sectors such as chemicals the existence of large imports clearly motivated attempts at domestic production.

Table 6.3 shows the results of the regression of I_i/I on D_i nad l_i using a 23-branch disaggregation. The data for contiguous fiscal years were pooled to eliminate random, year to year variations. Until the 1958–60 period the two variables explain little of the variation in I_i/I. However, after 1959 the coefficient of determination becomes considerably higher and the coefficient of each variable becomes significant, at least at the .05 level. The coefficient of l_i is initially not significantly different from zero and after 1959 becomes significantly negative. This pattern might be inter-

28. The Ministry of Commerce and Industry used these figures in their 1960–65 plan. It is quite possible, of course, that actual project labor-capital ratios diverge from those for the sector. We are assuming that the within sector labor-capital ratio variance is less than that among sectors.

29. The lack of significant relation between the CDA and a sector's share of investment funds does not preclude the possibility that the former would be a significant variable in a multiple regression. It has not been included because of the absence of CDA's for a number of branches for which the other variables were available. However, a multiple regression for those branches for which the CDA was available yielded an insignificant coefficient.

Table 6.3: Regression of Sectoral Share of Investment Funds
(on D_i and l_i)

	D_i	l_i	R^2
1955–56/1956–57	.0302	−5.97[a]	.1223
	(.0370)	(4.07)	
1956–57/1957–58	.0478	−7.19	.1248
	(.0496)	(6.22)	
1957–58/1958–59	.0582	−11.64[a]	.1573
	(.0472)	(7.13)	
1958–59/1959–60	.1272[c]	−16.09[c]	.4121
	(.0385)	(6.03)	
1959–60/1960–61	.1315[c]	−16.09[b]	.3527
	(.0437)	(6.90)	
1960–61/1961–62	.1534[b]	−17.56[b]	.2464
	(.0662)	(9.44)	
1961–62/1962–63	.0865[b]	−14.05[b]	.2724
	(.0412)	(7.01)	
1962–63/1963–64	.0858[c]	−16.05[c]	.4384
	(.0312)	(4.94)	
1963–64/1964–65	.0850[b]	−14.69[b]	.2860
	(.0424)	(6.13)	

[a] Significant at the .10 level.
[b] Significant at the .05 level.
[c] Significant at the .01 level.

preted as indicating no specific government interest in employment generation, even during the period of high unemployment.[30] However, the increasing negative sign after 1959 might imply that, although the government may always have believed that the capital intensive branches were the ones to be expanded, until 1959 employment considerations had led to a favoring of industries offering substantial employment possibilities. An examination of project evaluations and publications of the Ministry of Commerce and Industry reveal that some attention was given to the employment potential of a given project but that other characteristics were more heavily weighed. The changing coefficient of l_i is, moreover, readily interpretable in terms of the development of the industrial sector. Before 1958 or 1959 there were sufficient unmet needs in the

30. The interpretation of policy based on the regressions discussed in this and the following paragraph must be considered tentative, as covariance tests of the differences in the coefficients between groups of years do not show statistically significant changes.

economy (in a physical sense), so that investment was needed in most industries, including ones that primarily produce consumer's goods, which were relatively labor intensive, such as parts of the food processing branch, clothing, and leather. However, by 1959 industrial policy became oriented toward production for export and filling the interstices of the existing production structure. In particular, textiles, chemicals and mining were encouraged, all of which had higher than average capital-labor ratios. Thus it was not as a result of an explicit response to the improving employment picture that a switch towards capital intensive branches occurred, but rather as the outcome of the evolution of the industrial structure away from consumer goods toward intermediates. The negative sign of l_i therefore occurs because l_i serves roughly as a proxy variable for important sectors in which either further import substitution or export possibilities were present.

The interpretation of the dispersal coefficient is also not straightforward. It is readily admitted by government officials that, until 1959 or 1960, little effort was devoted to insuring the location of new firms in development areas. Since 1960, once a desirable industrial project has been agreed upon, an attempt has been made to induce location in the development areas, using both tax incentives and a very high ratio of loans to equity capital as lures.[31] This implies that the truly independent variable is the branch allocation of investment and the dependent one the percentage of loans going to development areas, while the form of our regression suggests the opposite, that the government faced a set of investment proposals and systematically favored those which, regardless of branch, proposed location in development towns. Whichever way one interprets the causality, it is clear that the government evinced more concern with dispersal after 1959, a finding that corroborates the statements of officials.

31. Much of the recent literature on capital budgeting suggests that a high leverage ratio may be undesirable because the impact of fluctuations in earnings upon earnings per share of common stock will be amplified as a result of fixed interest charges. However, the high loan-equity ratio was attractive to firms for two reasons. First, interest payments did not begin immediately after the business was begun but were delayed for a considerable time. Secondly, it was usually anticipated that, even when such payments became due, if earnings were still low (or fluctuating), they would be further deferred.

We began this section by attempting to explain the branch allocation of resources in the industrial sector, given the fact that the
price mechanism which would normally have been the basis for
efficient allocation was prevented from working by trade restrictions. While government concern with both employment and dispersal exerted some influence on the allocation of Development
Budget loans, these factors do not provide an adequate explanation, given the relatively low coefficient of determination. It appears that the main determinant of the allocation process was the
possibility of import substitution or increased exports in a few
branches. In the pre-1960 period the branches that received large
loans were food processing, basic metals, and textiles; the first two
produced goods that were still being imported in large quantities,
while textiles were generally assumed to be an important future
source of export earnings. After 1960 textiles received even larger
loans; rubber, nonmetallic minerals, and chemicals also became
major recipients, the first two because of the expected export potential and the latter because of a desire to deepen the import
substitution process that had occurred earlier. This suggests that
balance of payments considerations were of considerable importance in explaining the branch distribution of investment funds.
This does not contradict the previous finding that the CDA was not
closely related to investment allocation, only that the import
substitution-export expansion program did not closely follow the
"efficiency" path suggested by a CDA ranking.[32]

We still have to consider the role of approved investment status
on the sectoral pattern of growth. The Law for the Encouragement
of Investment was quite important, especially in the years before
1956, since Development Budget loans to the manufacturing sector
did not assume major importance until that year. In 1953, Levi
Eshkol, then Minister of Finance, suggested the principles that
guided the investment approval process:

> In industry we want to direct investments to basic industry.
> Our industry has developed mainly in tertiary branches, those
> which provide for current consumption . . . whenever we
> increase our consumption we have to import more raw ma-

---

32. However, see Chap. 4, pp. 79–80, for a discussion of the difficulties
encountered in using a strict CDA ranking of performance.

terials. [Our next] campaign is to deepen the structure of industry. As long as the primary stages of production will lag the final stages, we shall be dependent on the import of raw materials. The government will help to the best of its ability to establish basic industries.[33]

In effect, this was a policy of expanding branches that have extensive forward linkages and it was followed to a considerable extent. The cumulative investment approvals as of December 1957, which may be seen in Table 6.4, reflect these guidelines.[34] Again,

Table 6.4: Loans to Approved Enterprises Reaching Production
by 31 December 1957

	Capitalization in millions	
Branch	I£	Dollars
Food production	9,194	5,399
Food storage facilities	4,607	2,950
Spinning, weaving, knitting	12,612	8,811
Wearing apparel	138	1,246
Wood and wood products	1,188	2,036
Paper and printing	4,628	4,686
Metals and metalworking	12,437	8,730
Machinery and cars	1,879	2,999
Electrical appliances and precision equipment	3,518	5,304
Quarries	95	957
Building materials (including cement)	5,565	8,867
Glass	1,115	1,464
Chemicals	11,735	6,932
Rubber and plastic	3,157	6,865
Miscellaneous	5,344	4,511

Source: Israel Economic Bulletin 3, no. 3.

the same pattern is present that was observed in the Development Budget process; the branches in which the largest approvals occurred were textiles, nonmetallic minerals, metalworking, food processing, and chemicals. This pattern corresponds closely to the

33. *Minutes of the Knesset, 1953,* p. 913 (in Hebrew), quoted in an unpublished manuscript by Moshe Mandelbaum and Haim Roet.
34. As a result of the lack of similar data for the period since 1957, we cannot examine the role of the Investment Center. However, it appears to have been closely coordinated with the Development Budget allocations.

structural changes through 1958 discussed in Chapter 4, particularly the substantial import substitution in the latter three branches and the buildup of capacity that laid the basis for the expansion in textile and cement exports.[35] The importance of food processing is again partially a reflection of the concern with building up an autarkic food sector; however, there was some expectation of the future export of processed fruits, which was in fact realized after 1958.

In noting the important role of the government in the differential expansion of the branches, it must be emphasized that the Investment Center was not a passive agent in the approval process. Rather, it was often the prime instigator in the entrepreneurial process, perceiving areas of needed investment, seeking private entrepreneurs, and often using loans in addition to tax benefits to encourage the undertaking of the proposed enterprise.[36]

In summary, the combined effect of all government policies directed toward industry was to encourage the growth of those branches that could improve the balance of payments (though not necessarily in an efficient manner). Little systematic attention to the problem of labor absorption is evident. Indeed, the combined effects of excessively low real interest rates, low tariffs on imported machinery, and accelerated depreciation allowances on new investment[37] probably intensified the process of capitalization and reduced employment opportunities. From 1960 onward increasing importance was given to the dispersal effort, although this was achieved within the framework dictated by balance of payments considerations.

Services

In 1961, 41 percent of the total labor force was employed in agriculture, manufacturing, and mining; and another 11 percent in construction and public utilities. The remaining 48 percent was engaged in what are considered the service branches, an unusually high ratio when compared to other countries. In Chapter 3 it was seen that a country with a large import surplus would be likely to exhibit a relatively large service sector: service intensive domes-

---

35. See Tables 4.1 and 4.2.
36. See, for example, *Israel Economic Bulletin* (Dec. 1953), p. 30.
37. This, in effect, results in an interest-free loan.

tic production supplements a goods intensive import surplus to yield a balanced final bill of goods. It is nevertheless possible that part of the disproportionately large service sector may reflect disguised unemployment resulting from inadequate absorption of labor in agriculture and industry.[38]

In other countries disguised unemployment in the service sector has taken several forms: large numbers of workers in petty retailing and personal services, each providing services during a full day that could be performed in a fraction of the time; featherbedding in some activities owned by the government, particularly transportation; finally, in some countries in which there exists a considerable divergence between the stock of workers possessing particular skills (typically resulting from extensive but unusable education) and the demand for such skills, government employment of an unproductive sort is provided, primarily designed to prevent the political disaffection of those who would otherwise be unemployed. All three types of disguised unemployment exhibit a common factor: the worker is not an employee of a firm subject to market pressures that require that the employee's marginal value product equal his wage. Thus in retailing and personal services the typical structure is one of self-employment, the income earned providing a low subsistence standard of living. In transport and government there is again no market pressure; unneeded employees' salaries are covered by general tax revenue.[39]

Let us look more closely at the structure of the aforementioned sectors in Israel. The bus and taxi subbranch of transport is owned cooperatively, and entrance requires very large initial investment outlays. Moreover, very few employees are hired, since almost all of the labor force consists of member-owners. Railroads, on the other hand, are publicly owned. However, their absolute employment is miniscule, accounting for less than 5 percent of total employment in transport, and thus could not be an important source of disguised unemployment.

In trade activities, there may have been some disguised unem-

38. In this section industry refers to construction and utilities, as well as manufacturing.

39. Of course, there may be some resistance to the increased taxes necessary to finance these workers, but since revenues are rarely earmarked it is unlikely that opposition to featherbedding will crystallize.

ployment. In 1956,[40] 10.1 percent of the labor force was employed as "traders, agents, and salesmen," but by 1963 this figure had fallen to 8.1 percent,[41] although the absolute number had risen considerably. Had disguised unemployment in trade been substantial in 1956, a year of high aggregate unemployment, one would have expected a decline or at least a plateau in trade and sales employment as the unemployment rate declined. However, the continuing growth in absolute numbers in this occupation in the face of a tightening labor market from 1960 onward suggests that underemployment, if present, was limited.

We are thus left with the government as a possible sector of disguised unemployment. The government, committed to full employment, could have absorbed workers, regardless of their skills and of the real requirements of the public sector. Had this occurred, it would have corresponded to a situation of disguised unemployment. An alternative explanation is that the provision of necessary services may have required the employment of new workers whose skills coincided with those of the workers not currently being absorbed by the other sectors of the economy. A detailed study by Ofer suggests that the actual situation was close to the latter, although admittedly there are difficult problems of identification.[42] To support this view, let us consider employment in the public sector. Since 1951 the overall weight of this sector in civilian employment increased substantially, from 18.2 percent of total employment in 1951 to 23.3 in 1964 (Table 6.5). Within

Table 6.5: Public Employment as a Percentage of Total Employment

	1948	1951	1954	1959	1961	1964
Public sector	18.9	18.2	21.8	24.0	24.2	23.3
General government	7.7	10.3	8.6	9.5	8.6	8.0
Other public services (including education, health)	11.2	7.9	13.2	14.5	15.6	15.3

Sources: 1948, 1951, 1954, 1959: Gur Ofer, *The Service Industries in a Developing Economy: Israel as a Case Study* (New York: Praeger, 1967), p. 88.
1961, 1964: *Statistical Abstract of Israel, 1965*, p. 309.

40. This is the first year for which detailed occupation data are available.
41. *Labour Force Surveys (1955–1961)*, p. 95; *1963*, p. 42.
42. The following analysis is based on Ofer, *Service Industries in a Developing Economy*.

the public sector the percentage of employment in general government actually declined between 1951 and 1964, while that of public services rose.

Comparisons with other countries suggest that much of the unusually high percentage of services in Israel is concentrated within the public services subbranch of the government sector, particularly in health and educational services. This finding is explicable mainly in terms of demand factors. First, although the demographic structure of Israel is similar to that of an underdeveloped country, exhibiting a high percentage of school-age children, its educational standard is that of an advanced country. This combination requires an unusually large educational labor force, stemming solely from the demand side. One fact casts some doubt on the likelihood that the concentration in education stems solely from the demand side—the student-teacher ratio, in primary schools, 24, is among the lowest to be found in any country in the world.[43] This could have been the result of a governmental decision to create additional teaching openings to absorb the large stock of educated people who could not find employment in the rest of the economy. However, it is difficult to find evidence that such a policy was pursued. In any case it is the demographic and educational standard that accounts for most of the difference between the percentage of workers employed in education in Israel and the United States, and not the student-teacher ratio.[44]

Health services employment may similarly be explained in terms of the health standards desired. In particular, new immigrants exhibited relatively poor health; bringing them up to the status of the rest of the population required considerable manpower. In this area the supply of available medical personnel undoubtedly aided the goal, but it does not appear that their availability induced the desire to provide higher standards than would have been set without them.

The continued growth of employment in the health-education subsector despite the continued fall in unemployment and the appearance in the early 1960s of labor shortages at all skill levels

43. *Ibid.,* p. 63, and Appendix C.
44. The percentage of the civilian labor force employed in education in Israel is 7.2, while in the United States it is 3.5. About two-thirds of this gap is explicable in terms of differences in the demographic structure, and one-third by the differential student-teacher ratio. Ibid., p. 64.

in nongovernment sectors provide further support for the hypothesis that the high level of public services has a demand sanction and is not the result of the government's need to act as employer of last resort.

Employment in general government also accounts for a higher percentage of the labor force than that observed in other countries. Several factors may account for this. First, the government has been extensively involved in regulating the economy and has assumed an enormous administrative burden resulting from immigration, and the ensuing need to obtain and administer the large inflows of foreign aid. Secondly, in view of its large range of activities, some inefficiency undoubtedly resulted from the lack of specialization and the inability to capitalize on scale economies.

In summary, the impact of government employment complemented the growth in employment opportunities in other sectors, absorbing many educated labor force members who probably would not have found jobs in those sectors. While it is possible that the composition of governmental demand which generated the employment of a highly educated stratum of the labor force may have been induced by the availability of these workers, other objective considerations, such as the health, educational, and administrative requirements of the immigrants, appear to be the dominant causes of the high government employment. On the other hand, if there are economics of scale in general government, future employment patterns may require increased absorption in the private sector of many employees with advanced education.

Neither the absence of a direct employment policy nor the encouragement of capital intensive techniques in agriculture and manufacturing is sufficient evidence for the conclusion that the government gave little systematic attention to employment objectives, for it is possible that the government may have induced the expansion of employment in the nongovernment home goods sector (construction, utilities, transport, services), while using the traded goods sector for its balance of payments contribution. The high share of construction employment in most years (over 9 percent) was attributable to continued immigration, requiring new housing and the upgrading of existing housing standards. While the latter undoubtedly seemed to increase employment, upgrading (in terms of rooms per person) was initiated not by the government, but in the private sector, often by recipients of personal restitution payments from West Germany. Similarly, we have shown above that in trade, finance, and personal services, which constitute the nongovernment service sector, it is difficult to identify the mechanism by which the government could have induced either greater hiring or larger demand.

Thus there is little evidence of conscious government stimulation of employment in construction or private services. Nevertheless, this does not preclude the possibility that the government correctly (implicitly) forecast the continued growth of private demand in these sectors and decided that no special incentives were necessary. One cannot preclude the possibility that the implicit strategy of using the labor intensive home goods sectors for reducing unemployment was a correlate of the relatively capital intensive policy in the traded goods sectors. To the extent that this was true, some of the criticism of this policy loses its force, although the continuation of high unemployment until 1960 suggests that a more labor intensive expansion of the traded goods sector would nevertheless have been appropriate.

The foregoing analysis suggests that the government paid little attention to accelerating the absorption of labor in agriculture and industry during the 1950s, a period of high though declining unemployment. Neither the choice of branches to which funds were made available nor the factor price ratios, resulting from the set of government policies, provided an inducement to labor absorption. Thus, in the face of a rising wage-capital cost ratio, full employment[45] was only achieved after six years of sustained growth, during which real GNP almost doubled.[46] The government's direct employment policy did little to alleviate the general unemployment situation. Although it employed many whose particular skills made employment in the private sector unlikely even had the private sector chosen more labor intensive techniques, this was a result of social goals, rather than "government employment as a last resort."

45. *Full employment* is defined as unemployment of less than 5 percent. At this aggregate unemployment level, many regions exhibited a labor shortage, unemployment being concentrated in development towns.

46. We are here assuming that 1960 was the year in which full employment was achieved. As seen in Chap. 2, growth was quite irregular until 1953, after which it occurred in a steady manner.

Moreover, the rapid augmentation of the capital structure in the agricultural sector prevented other sectors, particularly manufacturing, from expanding as rapidly as might have been desirable. Against this it is necessary to balance distributional gains that may have accrued to those employed in agriculture.

One aspect of factor allocation policies is of particular interest. Assume that labor-capital substitution was feasible and that full employment had been achieved with lower levels of aggregate investment. What could have been done with the released investment funds, in particular their foreign exchange component, other than simply augmenting the reserves of the latter. The most obvious answer is to have invested in socially profitable export activities. However, another possibility would have been the use of the freed foreign exchange to cover the costs of an import liberalization program. Whether this could, in fact, have been implemented is debatable as significant internal pressures existed for the continuation of both quotas and excessively high tariffs. However, the availability of more free foreign exchange, especially in the 1950s, would have at least allowed the possibility of liberalization to be more strongly considered, and as should be clear from our earlier discussion of resource allocation, this policy could have provided substantial benefits to the economy.

Although there were flaws in factor allocation policies, it is easy to overstate one's criticism of the government's policies. Full employment was achieved by 1960, only eight years after the termination of mass immigration, and in the face of continued rapid growth of the labor force. During much of the 1952–60 period, the short fall from full employment (taken to be 5 percent unemployment) was, at most, 5 percent of the labor force, including part-time workers seeking more hours of employment. If the government had an implicit time horizon in mind for achieving full employment, say ten years, there were indications year by year (indeed, often quarter by quarter) that it was being approached. Although policies that did not make a maximum contribution to the reduction of interim unemployment may be faulted (unless a trade-off between employment and output or output growth is posited), this is probably an overly strict standard. Viewed in a comparative, cross-country context, Israel's employment performance was quite remarkable.

The success of the dispersal program is demonstrated by the rapid increase in the population in areas other than the coastal plains; thus in the southern part of the country the share of population rose from about 1 percent in 1948 to about 11 percent in 1965, and in the northern district from 7.6 to 10.4 percent over the same period. Moreover, unemployment rates were only slightly higher than in the coastal plain. Much of this is attributable to employment opportunities in agriculture, as most of the expansion in agriculture occurred in these regions; in both districts the share of agriculture in total employment was twice the national average. Thus the substantial buildup of the agricultural sector served to aid the dispersal process, as well as to achieve a step toward autarky. Indeed, the proportion of the labor force engaged in agriculture in both major development areas understates its importance, since much of the employment in other branches was a response to the direct needs of the agricultural settlements. There is still, of course, uncertainty about whether the dispersal already achieved can be maintained, particularly as the growth in demand for agricultural products is slowing. This is one of the reasons for the government's emphasis on the industrial development of these areas. It is hoped that, as agricultural productivity gains encourage an exodus from the farm, the availability of other jobs in the area of the current residence will prevent a move to the major cities.

The major policy goal throughout the period considered was an improvement in the import-export gap. While, in agriculture, it may have shared in primacy with the distributional objectives, in manufacturing there can be little doubt that the potential for saving foreign exchange was the dominant criterion motivating most government policies. Although an efficient path for achieving this aim may not have been followed, the differential growth rates among branches of manufacturing seem to be explained best by the government's perception of their relative potential for achieving foreign exchange savings. As we saw in Chapter 3, import substitution and export promotion explain most of the increasing importance of the manufacturing sector in the economy, and these patterns may be attributed largely to government policies. However, despite these efforts, the import surplus was reduced only gradually. The following chapter will show that this was a result of the failure of the government to restrict domestic demand adequately; the microeconomic measures adopted, while successful, were inherently too small in magnitude.

This chapter has emphasized the static allocation effects of government policy, while neglecting important questions of its contribution in a broader framework. Specifically, because of the shortage of skilled entrepreneurs and business managers, it is unlikely that many of the (socially) profitable investments undertaken by the private sector at the instigation of the government would have been perceived as desirable ventures by these decision makers. In this sense the government may be thought of as having engaged in a type of indicative planning, foreseeing future requirements and encouraging investment in these projects. While the actual implementation of this plan and the incentives offered may occasionally have led to inefficiencies of one type or another, in the absence of government prodding the private sector might well have foregone many of these projects. The growth thus generated would have to be weighed against the costs of the inefficiencies with which part of this chapter has been concerned. We have emphasized resource allocation aspects, as they are more readily identified, simpler to quantify, and more amenable to straightforward policy recommendations. The dynamic questions are much more intractable, yet a total evaluation of government's role must consider them; we shall pursue some of the questions of the broader role of government in the final chapter.

7

Macroeconomic Policy

The macroeconomic background against which the microeconomic developments took place is integral to a complete understanding of the development of the economy. Many of the policies leading to distortion on the micro level such as import controls and multiple exchange rates represented an attempt to use a series of ad hoc micro measures to ameliorate problems that were essentially macroeconomic in nature. While trade restrictions might increase the domestic price of imported goods and encourage import substituting activities, these measures could perforce have limited impact upon the current account deficit, unless the rate of growth of domestic absorption were slowed. When this slowdown occurred in 1966–67, it was a result of a serious recession, rather than the product of a policy that altered the relative importance of exports and domestic uses within a full employment context.

As discussed in Chapter 2, the periods before and after 1954 were essentially different. Between 1950 and 1953 there were substantial year-to-year fluctuations in GNP as a result of the dislocations caused by mass immigration, and GNP per capita did not grow. Since 1953 the processing and absorption of the much smaller number of immigrants has been routinized and has freed both human and material resources. Between 1954 and 1965 real GNP rose by a (compound) rate of 10 percent per annum; it is in this period that the fundamental macroeconomic issues that the country continues to face crystallized, namely, the reduction of the import surplus and the achievement and maintenance of full employment.

The achievement of the latter objective necessitated a rapid rate of growth of investment, as the wage rigidity imposed by the Histadrut and the low cost of using equipment, resulting from a combination of overvaluation of the exchange rate, a failure to impose tariffs on machinery imports, and low interest rates, precluded a labor intensive technology. However, a rising level of investment could not automatically lead to an improvement in the trade deficit, unless policies were pursued to insure that an increasing share of the additional output would be devoted to import substitution or export. In the last chapter it was seen that Development Budget allocation, investment incentives, and trade restriction were apparently designed with these objectives in mind. By 1958 the opportunities for further efficient import substitution had been exhausted, with a few exceptions, and the main direction in which a solution to the balance of payments problem could proceed was improved export performance. This could be achieved only by restraining domestic demand and, if necessary, changing the structure of relative prices to make the utilization for export of the released resources a profitable activity.

The direction of developments in the post-1958 period conformed to this outline, exports rising more rapidly than all components of domestic demand. However, by 1965 the absolute size of the current account deficit had risen to $521 million from $334 million in 1958; despite the much more rapid growth rate of exports than of imports, the large initial discrepancy between the two led to an increase in the absolute size of the deficit. The growth of the deficit partly reflects the failure of the government sufficiently to restrict domestic demand; underlying this are a number of social and political difficulties that must be explicitly considered.

We shall now consider some relevant aspects of demand in detail and then discuss the use of the various macroeconomic instruments.

THE BEHAVIOR OF THE MAJOR AGGREGATES

Table 7.1(A) shows the distribution of total resources (GNP plus imports) among the major demand components, along with the share of GNP in total resources, and Table 7.1(B) the distribution of GNP itself. The unusual nature of 1950 can be seen in the enormous investment undertaken, much of it in housing for immigrants, and in the great importance of the import surplus relative to later years. By 1954, with mass immigration no longer important, the

Table 7.1: Resources and Uses of Resources, 1950–67

A (*percentage of total resources: 1955 prices*)

	1950	1954	1958	1962	1965	1967
Private consumption	49.5	54.9	53.5	50.9	51.0	51.5
Public consumption	14.6	14.2	14.2	13.5	12.9	17.7
Investment	32.1	21.5	22.1	21.4	20.6	12.2
Exports	3.8	9.4	10.3	15.1	15.5	18.6
Total uses	100.0	100.0	100.0	100.0	100.0	100.0
Gross national product	60.8	69.6	70.7	68.1	68.9	68.9
Imports	39.2	30.4	29.3	31.9	31.1	31.1
Import surplus/Total use of resources	35.4	21.0	19.0	16.9	15.6	12.5

B (*percentage of GNP*)

	1950	1954	1958	1962	1965	1967
Private consumption	81.4	78.9	75.7	74.7	74.0	74.7
Public consumption	24.0	20.4	20.1	19.5	18.7	25.7
Investment	52.8	30.9	31.3	30.5	29.9	17.7
Exports	6.3	13.5	14.5	22.6	22.5	27.0
Imports	64.5	43.7	40.8	49.7	45.1	45.1

C (*percentage of total resources: current prices*)

	1950	1954	1958	1962	1965	1967
Private consumption	57.9	55.4	53.6	47.6	49.3	49.9
Public consumption	15.5	13.4	14.7	15.0	15.3	20.9
Investment	24.1	21.4	21.8	22.3	20.8	11.4
Exports	2.5	9.8	9.9	15.1	14.6	17.8
Total uses	100.0	100.0	100.0	100.0	100.0	100.0
Gross national product	77.9	74.3	74.3	67.3	71.7	73.0
Imports	22.1	25.7	25.7	32.7	28.3	27.0
Import surplus/Total use of resources	19.6	15.9	15.8	17.6	13.7	9.2

D (*percentage of GNP*)

	1950	1954	1958	1962	1965	1967
Private consumption	74.7	76.0	72.1	70.7	68.7	68.4
Public consumption	20.0	18.4	19.8	22.3	21.3	28.6
Investment	31.1	29.4	29.4	33.2	29.0	15.7
Exports	3.3	13.3	13.3	22.4	20.4	24.3
Imports	29.1	37.1	34.6	48.6	39.4	37.0

Sources: 1950–62: CBS, *Israel's National Income and Expenditure*, (*1950–1962*). 1965–67: *Statistical Abstract of Israel, 1968*.

distribution of the components of GNP had assumed more normal values, which changed slowly over the next decade. Between 1954 and 1965 both private and public consumption, as well as investment, decreased relative to total resources, while exports rose from 9.4 to 15.5 percent. Gross investment was maintained at about 30 percent of GNP during this period, an unusually high share. However, when investment is compared with total resources, the ratio is roughly .20, a figure similar to the ratio in a number of other countries. Although in 1954 the import surplus provided almost all of the saving for financing gross investment, its importance declined steadily over the next decade.[1] Unlike the absolute values of the other major components of GNP, which exhibited fairly smooth upward trends over time, both imports and exports moved with considerable irregularity and, consequently, so did the import surplus. It may well have been this characteristic, particularly the unpredictability of imports, that led, in 1965, to the decision to deflate the economy following a rapid rise in the import surplus.[2]

We turn now to a detailed examination of the behavior of the various components of domestic absorption.

Consumption and saving

As we are primarily interested in aggregate consumption rather than its composition, it is convenient to analyze private saving rather than consumption per se. Total private saving is available only as a residual after subtracting the import surplus, the government surplus, and errors and omissions from gross investment. The result of this process is a savings estimate that contains the compounded errors of other estimates. Moreover, private saving defined in this manner combines both business and household saving (as well as that of private, nonprofit institutions), precluding estimates of the relation between household saving and disposable income. However, budget surveys of saving have been carried out for four years, and provide some of this information.

The saving rates for *all* families obtained in these surveys were:[3]

1. The measured decline may not, however, be an accurate assessment, as difficult problems arise in measuring saving in a system with extensive trade distortions and multiple exchange rates. These problems will be discussed later in this chapter.
2. See below, pp. 215–17.
3. Source: 1954, 1957–58, 1958–59: Bank of Israel, *Bulletin,* no. 21, p. 53. 1963/1964: Bank of Israel *Annual Report, 1965,* chap. 19.

$$1954 = 4.0$$
$$1957-58 = 5.1$$
$$1958-59 = 4.2$$
$$1963-64 = 4.3$$

A personal savings rate of from 4 to 5 percent, if it were to hold for the national accounts, would place Israel in a relatively low position in international comparisons of savings; most countries with as low a rate as Israel's exhibit considerably lower per capita income.[4]

There are two sets of factors which, when taken account of, suggest that the normal savings rate would be similar to that found in other countries as measured by national accounts data. First, the survey and national accounts definitions are not consistent, and it is the latter from which savings rates of other countries are derived. Second, a substantial percentage of the population received one-time windfall income, which raised their consumption levels above what might be considered permanent levels.

To allow for the first factor, Ablin has attempted to build up the personal savings ratio in the national accounts, using survey results as a basis.[5] The saving-income ratio was adjusted for items that are treated differently in the national accounts and in surveys: saving through the provident funds, severance pay, imputed income on own housing, and depreciation of unincorporated businesses and housing. These adjustments indicate a personal saving ratio on national accounts definition of 6.1, as compared to 5.1 recorded in the 1957–58 survey.

However, even this adjusted measure underestimates the normal savings rate, as it does not allow for the impact of German restitution payments, which constituted windfall income. Although many families received these one-time payments during the survey period and they led to higher consumption levels than would have occurred without such receipts, they are not recorded as current disposable income. Thus the recorded savings ratio for the entire

4. See Hendrik Houthakker, "On Some Determinants of Saving in Developed and Underdeveloped Countries," in E. A. G. Robinson, ed., *Problems in Economic Development* (London: Macmillan, 1965).

5. Richard Ablin, "Household Saving in Israel," *Bulletin of the Oxford University Institute of Economics and Statistics* 28 (May 1966): 131–43. These points were first made by Patinkin, *Israel Economy: The First Decade,* p. 100.

survey population is considerably less than that for the non-recipient population, and the observed saving rate may be viewed as being transitionally lower than may be expected over the longer run, when such payments are no longer received. The reduction in saving attributable to windfalls is perhaps one half of recorded saving.[6] With an adjusted saving rate of 6.1, this implies a long run personal saving rate of 8 to 9 percent, still less than many Western European countries but similar to that of Canada, Sweden, and the United States.

While these adjustments attempt to put survey and national accounts data on a comparable base, another method for evaluating the deviation from normal is to compare the available budget data with those from other countries.[7] The recorded saving ratios in Israel are above the 2.5 percent recorded in a British survey in 1953–54, but below the 8.6 percent recorded for the United States in 1950. However, if the U.S. data are adjusted according to the British age and occupation distribution, the saving rate is reduced to 4.2. Thus "the savings behavior of Israel families would appear to differ only slightly from that of the U.S. with British weights." [8] Although this does not consider the impact of reweighting the Israeli data by these weights, one may assume that, given the demographic structure, which contains an unusually high percentage of young people, such a reweighting would make the Israeli saving rate even higher.

In summary, then, the saving pattern of the household sector does not appear to be much different from that found in developed countries. If allowance is made for the importance of transfers,

6. For example, in the 1958–59 survey, 4 percent of families received restitution payments, the average additional expenditure of these families (compared to those of similar income), including lagged effects, was I£1,589 per family; thus the average increase for *all* families in the survey attributable to the payment was I£63.6 (.04 × I£1,589), which was approximately half of the recorded per family saving. See Bank of Israel, *Annual Report,* 1959, p. 326.

7. This paragraph is based upon a Bank of Israel study by Edmond Lisle, "Household Savings in Israel, 1954 to 1957/58," Bank of Israel, *Bulletin,* no. 21.

8. Ibid., p. 49. The comparison was made by John B. Lansing and Harold Lydall in "An Anglo-American Comparison of Personal Saving," *Bulletin of the Oxford University Institute of Economics and Statistics* 22 (Aug. 1960): 225–58.

realized private saving is perhaps two-thirds of its long-run value.[9] It is also noteworthy that the saving ratio declined between 1957 and 1964, and this decline offset part of the increased level of direct taxation;[10] if this was a response to increased taxes, it suggests that the government would have had some difficulty in restricting consumption, as shifts in the propensity to consume might have offset part of any tax increase.

Investment

A high percentage compared to other countries, approximately one-third (in most years) of the investment/GNP ratio of 30 percent was accounted for by dwellings. Housing construction was dependent upon population growth, particularly immigration, until perhaps 1954. The doubling of the population between 1948 and 1952 led to a considerable backlog of demand, despite the large construction program undertaken during these years.[11] However, by 1954 the temporary quarters in which many immigrants had been housed were no longer in use, and from this date onward new construction reflected an effort to increase the quality of existing housing, which was quite overcrowded, as well as to provide living quarters for new immigrants. Other factors that also had some impact on private housing expenditures were the availability of funds, especially restitution payments, and the possibility that the purchase of housing was perceived as a hedge against inflation.

Attempts to estimate an equation to explain housing investment for 1955–65 suggest that the main determinants of expenditures were immigration and the change in the median number of persons per room, the latter representing the impact of the upgrading of existing housing standards. Both restitution payments and first and second differences in the consumer price index have little explanatory power, although they may have been important in particular

9. For further results on testing the permanent income hypothesis, see Bank of Israel, *Annual Report, 1959,* chap. 18; Mordecai Kreinin, "Windfall Income and Consumption—Additional Evidence," *American Economic Review* 51 (June 1961); Michael Landsberger, "Windfall Income and Consumption—Reply," *American Economic Review* 56 (June 1966): 534–39.

10. See below, pp. 186–87.

11. Although some housing was available on abandoned Arab property, this was limited, relative to the influx. However, these dwellings were important in the early years of heavy immigration in reducing crowding.

years. The best variable to represent the effect of immigration was found to be a four-year unweighted moving average (including the current year). This is fairly reasonable, as new immigrants were often housed in temporary quarters if existing facilities were over-crowded, and adjustments to overcrowding took place only after the passing of some time. The best equation was found to be

$$I_{Ht} = 1909.8 + \underset{(.0004)}{.0008} \sum_{r=0}^{3} P_{t-r} - \underset{(93.0)}{727.7R_t} \qquad R^2 = .92$$

where I_{Ht} = millions of I£ invested in housing in year t,

P_t = immigration in year t

R_t = median persons per room

The number of persons per room is the more important variable in the equation.[12] Although the Durbin-Watson statistic shows no significant pattern in the residuals, it is worthwhile noting that, for the 1962–64 period, the residuals are negative; it is in this period that considerable amounts of housing purchases, as inflation hedges, are believed to have occurred.

The housing equation may appear unusual insofar as it contains no variables reflecting the availability or cost of financing. This reflects the fact that a large part of the demand for housing was not subject to market determination, as almost half of the total investment was undertaken by the government. The funding for these projects came from the Development Budget and hence was not dependent on the state of local money markets. The other half was carried out by the private sector, but much of it, being financed by German restitutions and personal (family) loans, was not subject to the usual market pressures. To the extent that rapid upgrading was undesirable because such investment did not con-tribute to the reduction of the trade deficit, it is possible that it could have been slowed had the government provided alternative investment opportunities. Even with the inflation and the presence of restitution payments, high yield securities might have provided an attractive alternative use for funds and slowed the process of upgrading.[13] Nevertheless, it would be erroneous to assume that all of the upgrading was wasteful, for purchasers of these larger dwell-

12. The beta coefficient for R_t is .84 as compared with .22 for the immigration variable.
13. See below.

ings vacated smaller existing ones, thus reducing the net required amount of new publicly financed housing.

Not only was a large percentage of dwelling investment carried out independently of market pressure, but so was most of the fixed capital formation in sectors other than manufacturing. Thus three-quarters of total construction in trade and services[14] occurred in medical institutions, universities, government and municipal services, and other public buildings. (See Table 7.2.) While such government investments are partially a response to the need of the private business sector, for example, more highly trained graduates and a healthier labor force, and thus have an indirect market sanction, most of such expenditures are undoubtedly a reflection of social welfare concerns independent of the immediate demands of the private sector and thus of profitability considerations. Similarly, agricultural investment, as we have seen in earlier chapters, was often influenced by noneconomic factors. Finally, capital formation in transport,[15] communication, and utilities was almost completely undertaken by the government and was primarily a function of anticipated physical needs with little reference to a rate of return calculation.

Of total investment, only about 20 percent, that in manufacturing, private transport companies, and private services, was dependent upon a profitability calculus. The major component, manufacturing investment, fluctuated about a trendless line between 1950 and 1957, and began to grow steadily only after that (Table 7.3). Over the entire 1950–57 period, investment in manufacturing (in 1955 prices) constituted only 16 percent of total investment in the economy.

A detailed econometric examination of the determinants of investment in manufacturing would be of limited usefulness here;[16]

14. In most years construction accounted for over 80 percent of total investment in trade and services. CBS, *Israel's National Income and Expenditure (1950–1962)*, pp. 98–99. Such construction excludes that in public corporations (included in mining and manufacturing), and in roads and ports (included in transportation). Total investment in trade and services constituted 15 percent of total investment in all sectors.

15. Including railways, posts, roads, ships, aircraft, vehicles, ports, airports, and pipelines.

16. Although, in developed economies, investment functions based on neoclassical or accelerator theories of investment demand have been useful, the basic theoretical constructs underlying them are not valid in countries

Table 7.2: Sectoral Distribution of Investment, 1952–67
(percentage)

At current prices

	1952	1953	1954	1955	1956	1957	1958	1959	1960	1961	1962	1963	1964	1965	1966	1967
Agriculture, forestry and water projects	.178	.234	.227	.202	.197	.177	.195	.174	.162	.134	.127	.116	.084	.074	.090	.116
Manufacturing and construction, mining and quarrying	.206	.205	.215	.118	.152	.118	.167	.197	.166	.171	.174	.189	.170	.155	.129	.122
Electricity				.076	.080	.056	.054	.036	.037	.028	.039	.029	.022	.038	.038	.041
Transport and communication, trade and services	.225	.205	.182	.224	.231	.300	.261	.264	.322	.338	.304	.331	.408	.399	.415	.445
Dwellings	.389	.355	.374	.378	.337	.345	.320	.326	.314	.327	.353	.332	.313	.332	.326	.273

At 1955 prices (1952–1958) / **At 1964 prices** (1959–1967)

	1952	1953	1954	1955	1956	1957	1958	1959	1960	1961	1962	1963	1964	1965	1966	1967
Agriculture, forestry and water projects	.181	.244	.222	.202	.194	.175	.193	.164	.155	.129	.128	.116	.084	.074	.086	.109
Manufacturing and construction, mining and quarrying and electricity	.227	.209	.202	.194	.239	.179	.224	.243	.211	.208	.211	.214	.192	.194	.168	.164
Transport and communication, trade and services	.223	.202	.178	.224	.232	.301	.260	.261	.321	.346	.298	.329	.408	.401	.416	.448
Dwellings	.367	.342	.395	.378	.333	.343	.321	.329	.311	.317	.362	.340	.313	.331	.327	.276

Source: *Statistical Abstract of Israel, 1968*, pp. 150, 151.

Table 7.3: Gross Investment in Manufacturing and Mining, 1950–65
(1955 prices—I£ million)

1950	97.0	1958	135.0
1951	135.8	1959	173.0
1952	110.0	1960	169.3
1953	85.1	1961	202.7
1954	83.0	1962	224.6
1955	75.3	1963	254.2
1956	102.6	1964	273.5
1957	93.8	1965	251.4

Source: Unpublished data, A. L. Gaathon.

available aggregate evidence suggests that, since 1954 or 1955, investment in the sector was probably limited by the availability of financing rather than perceived profit opportunities, although in some branches, and for certain periods, low profitability may have been a cause. For example, in 1955, one of the first normal years after the cessation of mass immigration, the ratio of the nonwage share of value added to the stock of fixed capital (in 1955 prices) was 23.6 percent. However, the nonwage share includes both interest and rent. Assuming that 10 percent of all interest recorded in the national accounts and 5 percent of rent is chargeable to manufacturing,[17] and that one-third of the remainder represents wages of the self-employed, the average rate of return on total fixed assets is about 15 percent.[18] However, even this relatively high figure understates the return on equity capital, as the latter is

---

in which government influence, in the form of loans, protection via tariffs and quotas, etc., are major determinants of new investment. Insofar as import substitution and export growth are an important objective of government investment policies, accelerator models are inappropriate, as are neoclassical models in the face of disequilibrium capital markets.

17. Although there are global items for rent and interest, they are not distributed by sector. Our assumed percentages are in line with other information on borrowing and rent.

18. Calculations were made from data in CBS, *Israel's National Income and Expenditure (1950–1962)*, Tables 57 and 63, and unpublished data of A. L. Gaathon on the capital stock. In an unpublished study, Ephraim Kleiman has performed similar calculations, although without these adjustments. He reaches similar conclusions on the profitability of manufacturing. His estimates are presented in "The Structure of Israel Manufacturing Industries," mimeographed (Falk Project, 1964).

smaller than fixed assets.[19] Moreover, fixed assets are calculated at 1955 prices, while most were acquired earlier at much lower prices, so that the profit on historical cost would be even greater. Thus the computed rate of return on fixed capital of 15 percent (and even more on equity capital) for manufacturing is likely to represent a minimum. Of course, a high average return for the entire sector implies neither a high marginal return nor similarly high rates for individual branches. However, the same calculation for 1958 shows even higher returns in that year, so that it appears that the marginal rates were even greater than the average returns.

Supporting this finding of high profitability even in years of low investment is a study of a large sample of firms at a more disaggregated level, conducted by the Bank of Israel for 1957, which found that declared profits as a percentage of equity capital were 9.6 percent.[20] Declared profits were later found to be underestimated by 80 percent, thus yielding profitability figures similar to the aggregate ones. Moreover, parallel to the global figures, the sample data indicate increasing profitability over time, the declared ratio of profits to equity capital rising to 11.8 percent by 1958.[21]

Thus direct estimates of profitability, considerably higher than the real rate of interest, suggest an unsatisfied demand for greater investment in manufacturing in the post-1955 period.[22] The implication of this for monetary policy is considered below.

Since 1955, industrial investment has increased rapidly,[23] presumably reflecting continued high profitability on the demand side[24] and increased availability of funds, especially from public sources, on the supply side; the greater availability of public funds reflected the decreasing importance of agricultural and dwelling financing.

19. Meir Tamari, "Changes in the Financial Structure of Israel's Industrial Companies, 1956/57 to 1961/62," Bank of Israel, *Bulletin,* no. 19.

20. Ibid., p. 34.

21. Ibid.

22. Halevi and Klinov-Malul, *Economic Development of Israel,* p. 213, however, doubt that even such rates of return were sufficient to propel high investment without the added inducement of low interest rates.

23. The decline in 1957 was probably attributable to the continuing impact of the Sinai War in late 1956.

24. Nonwage returns are not available for recent years, so that no direct estimates of profitability are possible.

Public expenditures

Public consumption has usually accounted for about 20 percent of current price GNP. Of this about 40 percent is attributable to defense and special budgets, which are presumably also for defense expenditures.[25] Thus about eight percent of GNP is explicitly devoted to defense spending. Moreover, part of the costs associated with the construction of social overhead capital, and expenditures on some agricultural settlements and in some branches of industry undoubtedly should be included in defense. On the other hand, some defense outlays are probably substitutes for civilian activities, for example, education.[26] In any case defense imposed a large burden on the economy, which when added to the public consumption on health and education as well as the essential private consumption growth required for the successful absorption of immigrants, substantially reduced the scope for significant national saving.[27]

MACROECONOMIC POLICIES

Having considered the disposition of total resources among its various uses and the determinants of the major sources of domestic absorption, we shall now consider the use of major macroeconomic instruments.

Taxation

The overall level of restriction of private spending may be measured by the ratio of total current tax receipts[28] to national income at factor cost. A calculation of this ratio for other countries, as well as Israel, is provided in Table 7.4.[29] Israel's tax ratio is seen

25. *Statistical Abstracts,* various issues. Similar figures are given by Patinkin, *Israel Economy: The First Decade,* pp. 55–60; Halevi and Klinov-Malul, *Economic Development of Israel,* pp. 193–94.
26. Ibid.
27. Public sector saving was negative in almost all years.
28. This excludes capital levies such as estate taxes.
29. Income at factor cost rather than GNP is used, as the latter includes indirect taxes; thus, even if two countries have the same tax receipts and national income, the one with the higher level of indirect taxes will seem to perform more poorly.

Table 7.4: General Government Tax Revenue As a Percentage
of National Income at Factor Cost, 1964–66

France	50.2	Mauritius	23.9
West Germany	45.6	Malaysia	23.0
Austria	45.0	Portugal	20.6
Norway	44.7	Ecuador	20.5
Netherlands	41.2	Costa Rica	20.5
Luxembourg	39.0	Malta	20.1
Italy	37.3	Peru	20.0
Finland	36.0	South Africa	20.0
Belgium	36.0	Venezuela	19.9
Canada	35.9	Barbados	19.5
Denmark	35.9	Jamaica	19.4
Israel	35.5	Trinidad and Tobago	16.9
		Panama	16.8
United Kingdom	35.4	Burma	16.1
United States	33.4	Taiwan	15.6
Uruguay	31.0	Sierra Leone	14.6
New Zealand	30.2	Philippines	14.4
Ireland	29.9	Spain	13.9
Australia	28.2	Togo	13 8
Tunisia	27.2	Colombia	13.8
Zambia	26.5	Bolivia	13.7
Switzerland	25.6	India	11.8
Greece	24.6	Honduras	11.1
Chile	24.6	Guatemala	9.5
Japan	23.9	Republic of Korea	8.4

Source: U.N. Yearbook of National Accounts Statistics 1966.

to be roughly as high as that in many West European countries, an impressive achievement given the almost complete lack of experienced tax administrators at the beginning of independence.

Indirect taxes have been the major revenue source. This is consistent with the experience of most underdeveloped countries in which administrative bottlenecks limit the possible reliance on more sophisticated forms of direct taxation. However, rapidly growing administrative competence has permitted a major transformation of the tax system from one relying primarily on commodity taxation to one in which income taxation has become increasingly important; indeed the increase in the aggregate tax rate has been almost entirely attributable to the growth in direct taxes. This transformation was of great importance, as it provided the government with flexibility in adjusting its revenue policies to the necessary structural changes in the economy, particularly the increasing importance of the manufacturing sector. Typically, most governments have difficulty in taxing domestically produced goods as successfully as those imported, a problem primarily attributable to the dispersion of domestic production *vis-à-vis* the number of ports of entry, as well as the existence of better records in international, than in internal, trade.[30] A government desiring to maintain a given growth rate of expenditures without resorting to inflationary financing may have to limit the rate of import substitution or engage in a series of ad hoc tax-raising devices, which are as likely as not to conflict with other societal goals, such as equity and efficiency. The ability of the Israeli government to generate increasing revenues from direct taxes, as well as commodity taxes on domestic production, constituted an important permissive factor in the rapid import substitution program.

The major source of direct tax receipts, accounting for over 80 percent, has been the personal income tax. An analysis of the evolution of the personal income tax structure, particularly in the early years of statehood, indicates the considerable influence of taxation principles based on the experience of western nations. The restructuring of the system was guided by a series of United Nations Missions[31] and was mainly concerned with the equity and incentive features of the structure, particularly the amelioration of the impact of inflation. After independence the country continued to use the tax rates, the exemption structure, and the width of tax brackets that had been in force since the mandatory period of the early 1940s. The rapid inflation between 1948 and 1951, however, had shrunk the real value of basic exemptions, so that even low income families had become subject to positive tax rates by 1951. In addition, inflation had diminished the real width of the existing tax brackets; thus progressive tax rates applied initially

---

30. For estimates of the importance of imports in determining tax revenue shares, see Harley Hinrichs, "Determinants of Government Revenue Shares among Less Developed Countries," *Economic Journal* 75 (Sept. 1965): 546–56. See also the comment by Vito Tanzi and Clayton McCuistion, *Economic Journal* 77 (June 1967): 403–05.

31. For the reports of these missions, see United Nations Technical Assistance Programme, *Revenue Administration and Policy in Israel* (New York, 1953); Second Report (New York, 1955); and Third Report (New York, 1958).

in 1941 to increments of I£1,000 were now applied to the same increments, despite the greatly reduced real income corresponding to each such increment. As a result of these developments a considerable number of tax-paying units were subject to marginal rates of 80 percent.[32] Not only was the general structure steeply progressive, but, in addition, specific features were likely to discourage work on the part of people whose skills were in short supply. Many women in the population were highly educated and of potential importance in performing services needed in the immigrant absorption program. Yet the law provided only a small additional exemption for working wives (as compared to nonworking wives), despite large additional household costs imposed by such work.[33] Similarly, there was little incentive for overtime work, given the steep tax rate, thus reducing the utilization, particularly of professionals and self-employed businessmen.

The tax structure was not an elastic source of revenue as the tax accruals generated were often not paid for a year or more, at least for those most likely to have substantial liabilities. Although most wage earners were subject to withholding taxes, current payments of the self-employed were based upon tax accruals of the three preceding years.[34] Thus postponement of liabilities resulted in a decrease in the real value of tax payments, compared to their original purchasing power.[35]

By 1953 all the above flaws in the law were corrected, except for the absence of pay-as-you-earn taxation; exemptions had been increased, rate brackets widened, the steepness of progression reduced, and special allowances made for working wives.[36] Inflation continued after these revisions; therefore almost all subsequent personal income tax legislation provisions were designed

32. See United Nations, *Revenue Administration and Policy in Israel* (1953), p. 12.

33. Shortages of most basic goods led to the development of queuing as one rationing method. Households in which wives worked thus either had to hire domestic help or acquire goods in the "gray" market, both alternatives implying higher costs.

34. United Nations, *Revenue Administration and Policy in Israel* (1953), p. 14.

35. This delay feature may well have been at least partially intended to alleviate some of the disincentive effect of the high progressivity.

36. United Nations, *Revenue Administration and Policy in Israel*, Third Report (1958), p. 29.

to prevent a return to the problems embodied in the 1951 structure. Thus there were frequent rate reductions and changes in the exemptions and bracket structure. For example, Table 7.5 shows

Table 7.5: Ratio of Net Income to Gross Income
Based on Tax Rates in Effect in Different Years

Net income as a percentage of gross income

Basic wage per month	At 1957/58 rates	At 1959/60 rates	At 1961/62 rates	At 1963/64 rates
200	97.6	98.6	98.3	98.3
400	86.4	88.4	88.4	87.3
600	78.8	81.7	82.0	80.0
800	70.5	74.6	75.8	73.1
1,000	64.0	68.7	71.3	68.1

Note: Net income equals gross income minus tax and other compulsory payments.

Source: Bank of Israel, *Annual Report, 1963,* pp. 188–89.

the ratio of net to gross income for several years, given the tax rates in effect in each year. The basic wage is exclusive of the cost-of-living allowance,[37] although for the bulk of income recipients (those below I£500 per month) the basic wage was fully tied to the cost-of-living index. As a result of the revisions, disposable incomes were increased for all groups, the percentage increase being greater for high income recipients. One interpretation of the motives underlying this pattern of changes is that it represented an effort to maintain the real incomes of those whose incomes were not fully tied to the cost-of-living index (incomes over I£500 per month) and political necessities led to across-the-board revisions. Had tax rates remained fixed in money terms, the aggregate personal tax-income ratio would have grown, although, in fact, it remained constant from 1957 to 1961 (Table 7.6), though rising somewhat thereafter.

Direct tax receipts are, of course, not the only means of restricting personal consumption; indeed, indirect consumption taxes may

37. See pp. 203–05 below.

Table 7.6: Ratio of Taxes to National Income, 1952–66

	Indirect taxes:		*Direct taxes:*		
	On domestic products	*On imports*	*On corporations*	*On households and private nonprofit institutions*	*Total*
1952	11.7		0.4	5.9	18.0
1953	13.9		1.1	5.7	20.7
1954	15.2		1.4	7.8	24.4
1955	10.1	7.0	2.2	8.6	27.9
1956	9.7	7.2	1.9	9.2	28.0
1957	11.9	8.0	1.8	10.7	32.4
1958	13.8	6.5	1.9	10.3	32.5
1959	13.7	7.9	1.8	9.8	33.2
1960	14.4	7.8	1.8	10.4	34.4
1961	15.7	8.4	1.9	10.3	36.3
1962	15.0	7.6	2.0	10.8	35.4
1963	14.3	6.3	2.5	11.0	34.1
1964	14.1	6.7	3.0	11.5	35.3
1965	12.9	6.4	2.9	12.3	34.5
1966	13.7	5.6	2.5	13.5	35.3

Source: Statistical Abstract of Israel, 1968, pp. 154, 155, 160, 161.

be a more potent means of reducing consumption,[38] assuming that they are passed forward to consumers. Throughout the period considered, receipts from indirect taxes have been greater than, or equal to, those from direct taxes, although the ratio of the former to the latter has been declining (Table 7.6). The erratic movement of import taxes has mainly reflected the changing degree of the overvaluation of the official exchange rate and the attempt to offset this via tariffs. Thus, between 1955 and 1961, the ratio of import

38. If a proportional income tax and an equal yield consumption tax are compared in terms of their efficiency in reducing private consumption, the latter can be shown to be superior if the marginal propensity to save is positive. For an analysis of the relative effectiveness, see E. Cary Brown, "Analysis of Consumption Taxes in Terms of the Theory of Income Determination," *American Economic Review* 40 (Mar. 1950) 74–89; Richard A. Musgrave, *The Theory of Public Finance* (New York: McGraw-Hill, 1959), pp. 447–52. For a critical view, see Amotz Morag, *Taxes and Inflation* (New York: Random House, 1965).

taxes to national income rose erratically and then, after the devaluation of 1962, fell rapidly.

The maintenance of a relatively constant share of indirect taxes to national income does not represent the result of a fixed rate structure applied to an expanding base.[39] Rather, it is the outcome of ongoing revisions in both the structure of rates and their base. The three major sources of indirect tax revenue are customs duties, purchase tax and excise taxes (on tobacco, alcohol, cement, tires, and fuel). All have been subject to changes in rates, increases being designed to augment revenues and to increase the protection of domestic products, decreased rates being utilized to offset the price effects of devaluation.

Although taxes on imported final consumption goods have often been raised to high levels,[40] there is little evidence to suggest that the excise tax structure was used in a selective manner to discourage the consumption of domestically produced goods having a high import content. Using the 1958 input-output table, taxes on intermediate inputs destined for final consumption were added to the final taxes on domestically produced consumption goods.[41] The rank correlation coefficient between the tax component and the import component was insignificant. Thus the level of indirect taxes, rather than their composition, was the main instrument of control. This finding underlies the focusing of attention on the aggregate ratio of taxes (including direct taxes) to national income. Earlier we have seen that this overall level was comparatively high by international standards. However, its height relative to other countries is not a sufficient indicator of the adequacy of tax policy in restricting domestic demand, as in no other country is the import surplus as great a percentage of GNP.

A simple numerical illustration highlights the problem faced by the government. In 1963 the trade deficit was I£1,156 million. To have eliminated this deficit by restricting consumption and ex-

---

39. However, all taxes were levied on ad valorem bases, so that receipts automatically expanded as either the volume or the price of output increased.
40. In 1958 imported final consumption goods accounted for less than 4 percent of total private consumption.
41. The total tax burden per dollar of consumption of good j can be obtained as the sum of intermediate taxes, $T_j = \sum_i t_i r_{ij}$ plus final taxes per unit on good j.

panding exports by an equal amount[42] would have necessitated an increase in personal income taxes of roughly I£1,300 million, assuming an unchanged marginal propensity to consume of .9. This additional taxation represents 22 percent of national income at factor cost, which, when added to the existing 34 percent tax rate, implies an overall tax burden of about 56 percent of national income or 45 percent of GNP. The same type of calculation shows that reducing the trade deficit to $200 million (I£600 million) would have required additional taxation equal to 10 percent of national income or an overall rate of 44 percent.

Although these tax rates appear to be prohibitive, had the latter tax level been achieved, it would still have permitted aggregate consumption to increase at a rate of over 8 percent per annum (compounded) or about 4 percent per capita during the years 1954–63. The absence of any such action by the government indicates the political dilemma it faced in suggesting an increase in tax burdens, when existing levels were already relatively high; there was genuine perplexity on the part of most of the populace who could not easily understand the rather abstract notion that the country's current use of resources far exceeded its production, while the immediate fact of very high taxes was felt. Apart from this important problem in communication, there are a number of more fundamental political and social reasons for the failure to restrict consumption.

Throughout the statehood period an increasing percentage of the population has consisted of immigrants and their children. They have had lower family incomes (considerably lower on a per capita basis), consumption levels, and presumably stocks of durable goods.[43] Moreover, during at least part of the 1950s, differences in pretax income were widening; as might be expected the immigration lowered the level of unskilled wages relative to skilled.[44] The intervention of the Histadrut, which reflected their strongly egalitarian philosophy, prevented actual differences in income from reaching levels that would have occurred solely through market

42. We assume for convenience that consumption and exports have the same import component. In fact, the latter is higher.
43. See, e.g., *Family Expenditure Surveys* (CBS, Jerusalem, 1963) and Hanoch, "Income Differentials in Israel."
44. Uri Baharal, *The Effect of Mass Immigration on Wages in Israel* (Jerusalem: Falk Project, 1965).

forces. Nevertheless, there were growing differences between incomes of veteran (pre-1948) residents and new immigrants.[45] In the face of initial differences in standard of living, policies designed to restrict the growth of immigrants' consumption might well have resulted in substantial social tension. The problem would have been particularly acute in the case of immigrants from Asia and Africa. Many had emigrated to Israel not out of choice but as a result of the deterioration of political conditions in their countries of origin.

In the countries from which they came not a few of the Easterners enjoyed relatively high social status. As a community they had been more literate and better educated than their compatriots . . . Expecting a dramatic rise in living standards they have found instead inadequate housing and low wage employment.[46]

If these factors limited the government's ability to constrain the growth of immigrants' consumption, austerity would have had to fall on pre-1948 residents or the few relatively successful new immigrants. Although some of this latter group shared the ascetic ideology of Zionism, inevitably they were in a minority.[47]

Among the veteran residents were two subgroups crucial for continued development: the first consisted of those, mainly university-trained, whose skills were in international demand; the second was composed of members who might broadly be termed the managerial elite, particularly in the private sector, but also included some members of the government and Histadrut bureaucracy. The absolute income of the former group was about one-third or one-quarter of U.S. income (although a higher percentage compared to Europe) for similar qualifications. Both professional training (which utilizes western, particularly American, materials and methods) and cultural background, led to familiarity with western standards of living and, of considerable importance, the western employment environment. The lure of a private car was supplemented by that of well-equipped work facilities and large numbers of professional colleagues. That such attractions were decisive in

45. Cf. Hanoch, "Income Differentials in Israel."
46. Leonard Fein, *Israel: Politics and People,* 2nd ed. (Boston: Little, Brown, 1968), p. 58.
47. Cf. Eisenstadt, *Israeli Society,* chap. 3.

emigration decisions is difficult to prove, but it is worth noting that emigration has always been substantial; the emigration rate usually being well over 3 percent of the population.[48] While some of this simply represented the exodus of recent immigrants using Israel as a way station, there was undoubtedly among them, particularly in the 1960s, a substantial skilled group of Israeli-born or long-time residents.[49] If the highly educated are viewed as a crucial resource once the growth possibilities of simple industries such as food processing and textiles are exhausted, emigration of this type could not be viewed with equanimity. Even heavier taxation of their low (by international standards) incomes would have increased the likelihood of emigration.

The second group whose consumption growth could not be cut was the managerial group. Once the decision was made to pursue development along the private enterprise path (albeit often with large loans), continued motivation required that the business elite be allowed to reap at least some of the benefits of success in the form of increasing consumption levels. This is not inconsistent with the fact that the government was an important factor in identifying and financing industrial activity; for once companies were started, successful operation required high motivation. This, of course, was true not only for the members of the industrial managerial class but also in other branches such as private services.

From these two groups, whose high consumption was an integral part of the development process, there was a spillover to high level civil service personnel who had similar training. Had their incomes not been maintained roughly in parity with that of those with opportunities abroad and the upper level businessmen, larger numbers probably would have switched to the private sector. As it was, there were considerable losses from the upper strata of the

48. See, e.g., *Statistical Abstract, 1968,* p. 99. There are a number of problems of definition, particularly difficult in the case of residents who remain abroad but do not declare emigration. The 3 percent figure includes an estimate of those who have not formally indicated an emigration decision.

49. In 1966 the government had begun an intensive campaign of "moral suasion" to convince students studying abroad to return to Israel. Of course, not only students were to be attracted, but also those already working in their fields or who were visiting other countries to study the latest developments.

civil service. In the 1956–60 period over 8 percent of administrative and professional civil servants left their jobs each year.[50] Soon after, a rapid increase of public sector wages began, often implemented not through changes in the wage paid for a given grade but via upgrading of employees to higher levels.

The rapid growth in income of the university-trained and the managerial elite was one of the causes of the widening in income inequality during the 1950s.[51] Since this growth served an economic objective (again assuming a major role for the private sector), it would have been contradictory to redress it by increasing the tax burden on the upper income group. On the other hand, given the need to integrate the new immigrants, the lower income households could not be heavily taxed, especially in view of the rapid increase in high incomes; thus the scope for achieving a decrease in private consumption through taxation was limited. With these limits in tax receipts and the large, relatively fixed defense, education, and health components of public expenditure, potential public saving was low. It was here that the role of foreign aid became crucial. It allowed the country to escape the difficult choice between a high investment ratio necessary for full employment and a rapid consumption growth rate important for social integration.[52]

This in no way implies that the course followed by the government was optimal or that the consumption growth rate could not have been slowed, say from 5 to 3 percent per capita in the years of steady growth from 1954 to 1965. Undoubtedly, such growth in excess of that required for motivation arose in both the private and public sectors.[53] Continuing wage gains of public employees which provided part of the wherewithal for this excess were often gained not so much as a result of potential quitting due to continued differentials between private and public salaries, but through the bargaining strength of individual units within the Histadrut and

50. Bank of Israel, *Annual Report, 1960,* Table 9-4.

51. See Hanoch, *Income Differentials in Israel,* chap. 1 for details. A good discussion of the welfare implications is provided by Halevi and Klinov-Malul, *Economic Development of Israel,* pp. 115–23.

52. See Chap. 8.

53. Compare Eisenstadt, *Israeli Society,* p. 214.

the threat, occasionally carried out, of strikes.[54] One might have been able to design tax structures that were finely enough honed to prevent excess consumption by particular groups, while allowing the required amount of income incentives. However, it is extremely difficult to implement such policies.[55] Moreover, defining the "correct" amount of required consumption growth is far from simple. Thus excess consumption may be viewed as part of the cost of social cohesion and rapid growth relying on the private sector. Although excess consumption is not a deadweight loss in the usual sense, the high consumption growth policy may have contained the seeds of a future recession insofar as the recession engineered by the government in 1966–67 and the enormous amount of foregone national income was a response to the continued growth of the import surplus.[56]

Despite past difficulties in moving toward tax levels that are sufficiently high to begin the reduction of the import surplus, a move in this direction must begin at some point, unless a stop-go policy is followed.[57] The social and economic reasons that may have justified the past high consumption policy have lost much of their force. Many of the new immigrants have attained a reasonably high standard of living, albeit one still below that of veteran residents. In turn, the managerial group among the latter has accumulated substantial stocks of durables, large living quarters, and other accoutrements of western living style.[58] The major difficulty would now seem to be one of political opposition to slower consumption growth, rather than adverse consequences in terms of social cohesion and continued growth. Indeed, some would argue

54. It has been suggested that one reason for the reduction of personal tax rates in 1964 may have been the intention to increase the net income of government employees without raising their gross wages. The latter might have been the signal for greater wage demands in other sectors; cf. Bank of Israel, *Annual Report, 1964,* pp. 219–20.

55. Essentially, a form of schedular taxation would be needed, with income from different sources taxed at different rates. For a discussion of the problems presented by such a system, see Richard Bird and Oliver Oldman, eds., *Readings on Taxation in Developing Countries* (Baltimore: Johns Hopkins Press, 1964), pp. 80–86.

56. See pp. 216–17 below.

57. See pp. 217–18 below.

58. See, for example, the chapters on consumption in the Bank of Israel, *Annual Reports,* particularly the indices on the possession of consumer durables.

that such a point was reached in the early 1960s and that a considerable amount of unnecessary consumption was taking place even at that point. Regardless of the correct dating of the time when constraint became both propitious and feasible, there can be little doubt that it has become an objective that must now be pursued with diligence.

Savings incentives

Despite the failure to restrict consumption by increasing the overall level of taxation, other approaches to reducing the consumption rate were tried, particularly schemes to encourage saving.[59] In 1956 the Saving Encouragement Law allowed a tax credit (not to exceed 20 percent of the amount saved) for long term deposits in savings accounts.[60] This, in effect, raised the interest rate by a maximum of 25 percent, which, though not negligible, still left the real rate of interest quite low, as we shall see below. Other devices to induce saving, which were adopted later, were the exemption from tax liability of the interest received on savings deposits and an upper limit of 25 percent tax on interest from selected bonds. Finally, recipients of restitution payments were allowed to keep these funds in foreign currency accounts, which served as a hedge against devaluation.

All of the various saving-encouragement devices had one factor in common: they offered a low real rate of return on saving. Between 1956 and 1961 deposits benefiting from tax incentives were linked neither to the dollar nor to the domestic price level, and the interest paid was a maximum annual rate of 6 percent plus a one-time bonus of up to 10 percent on deposits held for over four years.[61] In these years the implicit price deflator for consumption rose by well over 5 percent per annum (on the average), so that the real rate of return was close to zero. Even in "linked" savings accounts, only the principal was protected, while the interest payments were unlinked and calculated at only 4 percent per annum. Thus

59. For details, see United Nations, *Revenue Administration and Policy in Israel*, pp. 38, 39, and various issues of Bank of Israel, *Annual Report*.
60. It is to be noted that this is a credit and not a deduction, i.e., after the determination of tax liability, the credit for saving is deducted, so that the value of the credit did not depend upon the marginal tax rate of the saver, as it would if the deduction were used.
61. See Bank of Israel, *Annual Report, 1962,* pp. 318, 319.

favorable tax treatment could not really make these rates attractive for saving. Even complete exemption of interest income from taxes provides a yield of only 6 percent when the existing interest rate is 4 percent (assuming a 50 percent marginal tax rate) or barely enough to cover the usual rate of price increase. Since the public seemed to respond to saving opportunities providing even low positive yields, the offer of higher yields might have elicited a substantial increase in savings accounts.[62] Whether this would merely have led to a shift in asset choice out of a fixed level of saving or to an increase in the actual level of saving is, of course, unknown, but an effort in this direction was surely warranted.

Monetary policy

Between 1954 and 1965, a period of uninterrupted growth in real output at the rate of 11 percent per annum, the money supply grew by about 17 percent per annum. The disproportion in these growth rates was undoubtedly one of the factors contributing to the more rapid growth in money demand than in real output.[63] Bank credit was an important source of business financing,[64] although not of consumer financing. The growth of the money supply may, however, have exerted some direct expansionary influence on consumption through the real balance effect, but the magnitude of this was probably small.

Although the direct expansionary effect of the growing money supply may have been important, its indirect effect in inducing additional investment via a reduced interest rate was negligible. The government established an arbitrary ceiling on interest rates, considerably below the rate that would have occurred in a free market. Because of the continuing pressures of excess demand that resulted, there was no decline in interest rates as monetary expansion occurred and hence no induced investment.

The unwillingness of the government to permit an equilibrium interest rate increased the difficulty of attaining its goals. The

62. For details, see Bank of Israel, *Bulletin,* no. 16.
63. This does not mean that we view the source of rising prices to be simply excess demand.
64. On its importance for industrial corporations see Tamari, "Changes in the Financial Structure of Israel's Industrial Companies," p. 16; "Allocation of Short Term Bank Credit to Israel's Industrial Companies, 1956/57–1963/64," Bank of Israel, *Bulletin,* no. 26.

adverse allocation effect of this policy has been discussed in previous chapters. However, the Interest Law may also have precluded an increase in the private saving rate. Although some effort was given to raising the yield on specific financial assets, such as savings accounts, the general level of yields on nonsaving-account financial assets was quite low. An alternate policy would have been one that freed the interest rate. Had the real rate been higher, say in the range of 7 to 10 percent, it is quite possible that the saving response would have been substantial. While most of the available econometric evidence on the interest responsiveness of personal savings suggests low or zero elasticities, these estimates have almost always been obtained from data in which the variation in the real interest rate has been quite small and around historical levels to which households had pretty much adapted their behavior. There is no a priori basis for assuming that low interest responsiveness will hold in countries undergoing rapid inflation and in which the real interest rate has for the most part been negative. Recent experience in South Korea—a country with macroeconomic problems similar to those in Israel—with a large increase in real interest rates indicates the great potential of such a freeing of the interest rate.[65] The response of the Israeli public to higher rates on savings accounts cited earlier shows that the public was quite sensitive to differential returns among various types of financial assets. Moreover, the often-made statement of persons buying new flats that they offered the only inflation-proof asset in the economy, along with the fact that investment in real property constituted the largest single item of household saving, also supports the assumption that a substantial increase in the level of all interest rates would have led to a considerable increase in saving rates.

While the limits imposed on interest levels were continued with a view toward encouraging investment, there is little evidence to suggest that investment would have been reduced had a higher interest regime prevailed. We have seen that in manufacturing, the sector most important to the eventual elimination of the import surplus and the main sector in which investment was subject to market forces, the average rate of return on equity capital for the entire

65. For a description of the Korean experience see, Robert F. Emery, "The Korean Interest Rate Reform of September, 1965" (Board of Governors, Federal Reserve System, Oct. 1966). (Mimeo.)

sector was well above 15 percent in the post-1955 years.[66] Although some firms may have had rates below this, there is little doubt that most firms could, and would, have paid much higher interest rates, in turn permitting financial intermediaries to pay higher rates on their assets sold to the public. With high profitability ensured through trade restrictions and tariffs, there was little need for further encouragement of investment via a low interest policy.[67] A higher interest rate could have provided the dual benefits of better allocation of investment resources and increased levels of saving; such a reform is still warranted.

INFLATION

Benefits and costs

During the entire period from 1950 to 1965 Israel experienced a substantial amount of inflation. Within this interval, there were two distinct subperiods: 1950–53 and 1954–65; during the first there was essentially a hyperinflation, while in the latter a more "normal" price increase of 5 to 10 percent per year occurred (in the GNP implicit price deflator; see Table 7.7).

Before considering quantitative details of the inflation, we briefly survey the usual reasons for concern about inflation,[68] and then indicate those effects that we believe to be crucial to an economy such as Israel's.

A sudden increase in the rate of price increase or a sustained high rate of inflation is often believed to discourage saving if neither principal nor interest is linked to the price level. People are assumed to change their spending patterns and purchase durable goods and

66. See above, pp. 179–80.

67. Evidence of the willingness of borrowers to pay higher than "official" rates can be found in the growing importance of *bill brokerage,* a device through which banks guaranteed the loan made my one of its customers to another one. The nominal interest rate in this market often exceeded 15 and sometimes 20 percent. While most loans were short-term, presumably to provide working capital, many borrowers kept renewing these loans and used them for the financing of fixed investment. A detailed description and analysis of this practice is presented in Avigdor Steinberg, "Bill Brokerage in Israel, 1963–67," Bank of Israel, *Bulletin,* no. 30.

68. Cf. Graeme S. Dorrance, "The Effect of Inflation on Economic Development," in Werner Baer and Isaac Kerstenetzky, eds. *Conference on Inflation and Economic Growth in Latin America* (Homewood, Ill.: Richard D. Irwin, 1964), pp. 37–89.

Table 7.7: GNP Implicit Price Deflator, 1950–67

	Price deflator 1964 = 100	Percentage increase[a]
1950	22	–
1951	26	11.8
1952	37	43.6
1953	47	27.9
1954	52	10.2
1955	55	6.0
1956	60	9.3
1957	64	6.8
1958	70	8.4
1959	71	1.6
1960	75	5.2
1961	81	9.3
1962	88	7.5
1963	95	8.3
1964	100	5.5
1965	110	9.6
1966	119	8.9
1967	122	2.0

[a] Calculated from unrounded price deflator.

Source: Statistical Abstract of Israel, 1968, pp. 138–41.

other inflation hedges, or, if they do save, they choose "nonproductive" assets such as real estate, jewels, and so forth, or send capital abroad to acquire stable currencies as a protection against devaluation. The above must implicitly assume that potential savers can invest neither directly in their own businesses nor in equity shares, although these may prove to be inflation proof. It is further argued that, even if business investment occurs, it is likely to be in the form of inventories, rather than fixed capital, as profits are likely to be higher (or more certain) with the former type of investment. Finally, if devaluation does not accompany the inflation, a disequilibrium system of overvaluation and import restrictions will be adopted, leading to misallocation of resources, as well as diversion of entrepreneurial abilities from productive activities toward efforts to obtain favorable government attention.

The primary potential benefit to be derived from an inflationary process is alleged to be a temporary increase in the share of investment (based on the assumption of a Robertsonian consumption lag). The possibility of a permanent rise in the investment rate resulting from a change in the income distribution toward savers is unlikely, since this would require a permanent decline in the consumption share of some group, implying consistent money illusion or market power weakness.

In Israel it is our impression that, although some deleterious effects of inflation have occurred, there have been no discernible benefits. Although the marginal propensity of individuals to save does rise with income and is somewhat higher for proprietors than employees,[69] redistribution toward the higher savers through inflation was unlikely in view of the existence of escalator wage arrangements.[70] Even if inflation were to increase corporate profits, this would not be significant insofar as private saving (household plus corporation), as recorded in the national accounts, remained at a low level throughout the period, despite the positive saving of the household sector. This suggests that corporate net saving in the form of retained earnings was quite low. Moreover, if it is assumed that household saving would have exhibited a positive elasticity with respect to the real rate of interest, then, given the fixed nominal interest policy, potential saving from this source was lowered by rising prices. Thus it seems unlikely that inflation led to an increase in the aggregate saving rate.

The effect of inflation on the composition of saving suggests at most limited distortions. There is no evidence of any capital flight. However, it is true that of the household saving rate of 5 percent observed in the surveys, the purchase of real estate constitutes the largest single component.[71] This is not sufficient to prove an undesirable distortion, unless it can be shown that the availability of these funds induced greater resources into construction than would otherwise have been the case. The regression equations for housing presented earlier did not indicate a significant response of housing investment to price changes. Even if some housing investment was motivated by inflation, it did not constitute a total waste

69. CBS, *Saving Survey, 1963/64,* p. x.
70. See below.
71. This includes the acquisition of houses, land, apartments, key money, additions, and alterations, CBS, *Saving Survey, 1963/64,* p. xlvii.

of resources because those who moved into new housing vacated existing housing, thus reducing the need for new construction. Therefore there is little reason to believe that any substantial misallocation of resources solely attributable to inflation occurred because of investment in housing. Thus, if there was any significant adverse impact of inflation on households, it may have been a reduction in their overall rate of saving, changes in composition being of limited significance.

Can any misallocation of investment, particularly in inventories, be shown? Excessive accumulation of inventories is difficult to measure, unless a specification of normal inventory behavior is possible. The results of operations research suggest that firms following optimal behavior would increase their inventories by roughly the square root of the increase in their sales. Such optimizing behavior is hardly to be expected for all firms in developed countries; for a relatively underdeveloped country one would certainly not expect this behavior, although a declining ratio of inventories[72] to GDP would be normal as managers gain experience in ordering and as domestic transport facilities become more adequate so that deliveries may be received in a short time. However, during years of rapid industrialization and general development, there may be a period of building up inventories toward desired levels, for example, as more working capital becomes available, which offsets at least some of the reduced requirements. Moreover, in Israel, military considerations have undoubtedly tended to lead to a stocking of greater inventories than might normally be desired. From the early 1950s until 1956, the ratio of inventories to GDP rose gradually, probably reflecting a lower than optimal initial ratio due to foreign exchange shortages. However, since 1957, despite continued inflation, there has been only a slight rise in their ratio (Table 7.8); these are roughly similar to those in the United States during the same period.

Perhaps the main cost of inflation came as a result of the misallocation of resources, encouraged by the various import restrictions and ad hoc export-incentive schemes introduced as a result of the increasing domestic price level and the difficulty of offsetting this

72. Inventories, not inventory investment, is meant here.

Table 7.8: Inventories and GDP, 1950–66
(1955 prices)

	Inventories (beginning of year)	GDP	Inv_t/GDP_{t-1}
1950	155.6	1,148	–
1951	167.9	1,489	14.5
1952	179.6	1,584	11.3
1953	226.6	1,551	14.3
1954	257.3	1,858	16.5
1955	295.7	2,117	15.9
1956	366.5	2,312	17.4
1957	401.9	2,508	17.4
1958	435.2	2,695	17.4
1959	488.4	3,019	18.0
1960	550.2	3,269	18.2
1961	617.9	3,648	18.9
1962	686.4	4,052	18.9
1963	773.5	4,488	19.0
1964	841.0	4,934	18.8
1965	957.8	5,279	19.3
1966	987.2		18.7

Sources: Inventories: A. L. Gaathon, unpublished data.
GDP: *Statistical Abstract of Israel, 1966*, pp. 158–59.

via devaluation. As these measures and their impact were discussed in detail in Chapter 4, we shall not consider them here.

The propagation mechanism

Although it is virtually impossible to identify the original source of inflation,[73] an analysis of the propagation mechanism is of some interest. Before considering the period of relatively slow inflation from 1953 onward, we shall briefly summarize Patinkin's analysis of the hyperinflation that preceded this year.[74]

Between 1950 and 1953 the GNP implicit price deflator rose from .22 to .47 (1964 = 100) or by roughly 125 percent. Even this figure probably understates the true rate of inflation, as price controls led to a significant black market whose prices are not reflected

73. Paul A. Samuelson and Robert M. Solow, "Analytical Aspects of Anti-Inflation Policy," *American Economic Review* 50 (May 1962): 177–94.
74. Patinkin, *Israeli Economy: The First Decade.*

in the index. Despite the difficulties of differentiating between demand-pull and cost-push, especially in relatively mild inflation, it does not require a powerfully discriminating model to arrive at the conclusion that, during this period of hyperinflation, the main determinant of the price rise was excess demand, stimulated by the large government deficits that resulted from the problems associated with the absorption of immigrants.

Patinkin's argument, that the inflation of this period may be explained by the naïve quantity theory of money, is quite persuasive. During the pre-1952 period most of the credit expansion in the banking system went to the government (Table 7.9) to finance

Table 7.9: Causes of the Increase in the Quantity of Money, 1949–52

Percentage of change due to changes in:

| | *(1)* Net foreign balances of banking system | Credit of banking system to: | | | |
		(2) Government	*(3)* Public	*(4)* Other factors	*(5)* Total (1)–(4)
1949	−13.7	78.4	47.2	−11.9	100
1950	−33.5	104.0	57.9	−28.4	100
1951	−17.0	86.8	54.0	−23.8	100
1952	−17.2	26.1	186.0	−34.9	100
Dec. 1948–Dec. 1951	−21.9	90.6	53.4	−22.1	100

Source: Patinkin, *Israel Economy: The First Decade*, p. 112.

continued deficits. As a result of price controls, real money balances doubled during the period from 1949 through early 1951. Even if allowance is made for black market prices, it is probable that the increase was quite large. The excess demand that resulted was eventually dissipated by the price increases permitted by a new economic policy, which along with a devaluation were implemented in February of 1952.

Since 1953, inflation has proceeded at a rate of 5 to 10 percent per annum. Although most observers have acknowledged that it is difficult to pinpoint the original inflationary impetus, there is a tendency to focus on the cost-of-living allowance (COLA) as a primary agent transmitting any stimuli that do arise, as well as to assume that it may lead to self-sustaining inflation. This assertion seems dubious and can be shown to depend on a particular set of assumptions that do not appear to be empirically justified in the case of Israel.

Assume that after a period of wage-price stability, some exogenous shock (such as an increase in import prices) leads to an increase in the price level and that, according to the COLA formula, wages are raised after one period by a fixed proportion of the percentage price increase, or algebraically:

$$\dot{w}_t = \alpha P_{t-1} \qquad (7.1)$$

where $\dot{w}_t = w_t/w_{t-1} - 1$ and $\dot{P}_{t-1} = P_{t-1}/P_{t-2} - 1$. If businesses immediately pass on the entire wage increase (but no more than this) in the form of higher prices, then the price increase in period t will be

$$P_t = \alpha P_{t-1} B \qquad (7.2)$$

where B is the share of wages in national income. The solution to Equation 7.2 is

$$P_t = P_0(\alpha B)^t \qquad (7.3)$$

Thus, if $\alpha B < 1$, $\dot{P}$ eventually approaches 0. The price formation equation (7.2) assumes that businesses are willing to allow an attrition of the profit share in value added. A more realistic model would assume an attempt to maintain profits, although some decline may be acceptable,[75] for example, by assuming a markup on each increase in wage costs, so as to maintain the initial rate of profit per dollar of wages. In this situation, assuming a markup on wages of m percent, the price equation becomes

$$P_t = \alpha B \bar{m} P_{t-1} \qquad \bar{m} = 1 + m \qquad (7.4)$$

whose solution is

$$P_t = P_0(\alpha B \bar{m})^t \qquad (7.5)$$

Thus, even in an "escalated" economy, an initial inflationary impulse may die out if $(\alpha B \bar{m}) \leq 1$.[76] Assuming a policy which

75. We are abstracting here from the distribution of real productivity changes.
76. If $\alpha B \bar{m} \geq 1$, this is simply another way of saying that no group is willing to take a reduction in real income.

roughly succeeds in maintaining profits, $B\bar{m}$ will be very close to 1, so that the crucial magnitude will be the degree of escalation, that is, how much of any price increase is translated into a wage increase, or alternatively, how carefully real wages are protected.[77] If α is equal to 1, the rate of price increase may not slow down. However, this formulation overstates the possibility of instability, as it assumes that wages are *fully* adjusted within one period and that the markup on this wage increase is also fully realized within one period. If these adjustments occur with a lag,[78] it increases the likelihood that the COLA mechanism would not *by itself* lead to a continuing inflation. Thus the usual assertion that escalated economies have self-perpetuating inflations depends upon crucial assumptions about behavioral parameters.

In Israel it does not seem to be true that the COLA mechanism by itself was a major factor in propagating inflation. The agreement in effect from 1952 to 1954 provided for an increase in wages proportional to that in prices for those with a gross wage of 1 £ 80 per month or less, those above this income level receiving an allowance based upon a wage of I£ 80. Thus not all wages were tied to the price index, nor were all workers covered by the agreement (although a majority were). As a result it would appear that, in this period, the escalator coefficient, α, was less than one.[79]

Between 1954 and 1956 a new agreement was introduced that probably led to α being greater than 1.[80] Within this period then, the COLA could have led to a self-perpetuating inflation, as perhaps 80 percent of all workers were covered by these agreements,[81] the exact value of α depending on the percentage of workers with incomes over I£ 80 per month. Nevertheless, even $\alpha > 1$ is not

77. It should be emphasized that we are ignoring changes in real wages brought about by productivity gains.

78. In Equation 7.5 a reaction coefficient, $k < 1$ could be introduced, along with a more complicated lag structure.

79. The following discussion of the details of the cost-of-living allowance draws mainly upon Appendix A in Baharal, *Effect of Mass Immigration on Wages in Israel*.

80. Ibid.

81. Until 1959, the COLA agreements were enforced only in those enterprises having formal labor contracts, an estimated 80 percent of all workers. After 1959 it was supposed to be enforced in all firms but apparently has not been. See Bank of Israel, *Annual Report, 1959,* p. 99; Bank of Israel, *Annual Report, 1963,* p. 186.

sufficient for generating continued inflation because the speed of reaction must be considered. The actual mechanics of the adjustment process in most years worked against destabilization of the system, since wages were not adjusted until the index had risen by some minimum percentage. Thus at least slow price rises could occur for a substantial period (usually six months) without any adjustment in wages. However, under the 1954 agreement, the allowance was increased if the index had moved three points (less than $1\frac{1}{2}$ percent) within three months.[82] Thus, between 1954 and 1956, not only was α quite high but the adjustment was rapid and the COLA may well have been destabilizing.

However, from 1956 onward, the COLA mechanism undoubtedly worked against a self-sustaining, inflationary process. Typically, the COLA agreements were fashioned in a manner that contained the following basic features:[83] (1) the COLA was revised on a semiannual basis, and adjustments depended on whether the consumer price index had risen by a given percentage (minimally 3 percent) rather than a given number of points; (2) the COLA only applied to the first I£500 of wages (until 1964) and was proportional to the rise in the consumer price index.

Thus, not only was a relatively long lag introduced into the adjustment mechanism, but the upper limit of I£500, although covering most workers at the time of introduction, was exceeded by an increasing proportion of the labor force, as time passed. Thus a diminishing percentage of wages was tied to prices. Further reducing the self-perpetuating impact of the COLA were the attempts of the government to delay these adjustments for some time, or to limit the proportion of wages covered, even when they were justified under the formula,[84] although such attempts were often subverted by employers in the increasingly competitive labor market following 1959.

In view of these considerations it appears unlikely that the COLA was a major independent determinant of the continuing inflation, although, of course, this does not rule out the possible contribu-

82. Bank of Israel, *Annual Report, 1956,* p. 112.
83. Ibid.; Bank of Israel, *Annual Report, 1961,* p. 147.
84. Bank of Israel, *Annual Report, 1960,* p. 93; Bank of Israel, *Annual Report, 1964,* p. 221.

tion of other components of wage increases.[85] Table 7.10 shows
the percentage increase in nominal wages and the rate of unemploy-

Table 7.10: Nominal Wage Changes and Unemployment Rates, 1956–67

	Wages *(percentage change* *from previous year)*	*Unemployment* *(percentage of* *labor force)*
1956	11.0	7.8
1957	8.5	6.9
1958	11.4	5.7
1959	7.2	5.5
1960	6.3	4.6
1961	11.0	3.6
1962	13.0	3.7
1963	12.0	3.6
1964	12.0	3.3
1965	20.0	3.6
1966	19.0	7.4
1967	0	10.4

Source: Column 1: Halevi and Klinov-Malul, *Economic Development of Israel*,
Table 84 for 1956–64; Bank of Israel, *Annual Report, 1967*, p. 247, for 1965–67.
  Column 2: Halevi and Klinov-Malul, Table 17 for 1956–64; Bank of Israel,
Annual Report, 1967, pp. 224, 247, for 1965–67.

ment since 1955. In the period until 1960 there is little suggestion
that increases in nominal wages were systematically connected
with the level of unemployment; this independence of wages from
the state of the labor market may be evidence of cost-push inflation. After 1961 the rate of wage increase was higher than any
experienced before 1961, while the unemployment rate remained
at historical low levels. This might suggest demand-pull inflation.
However, as Samuelson and Solow have pointed out, such simple
tests on ex post data are unlikely to be able to discriminate in a
powerful way between alternate ex ante hypotheses of demand-pull
or cost-push inflation.[86] For example, the post-1961 wage rise may
have resulted from an attempt to return to an earlier, higher ratio
of wage to nonwage income.

85. Halevi and Klinov-Malul, *Economic Development of Israel*, p. 277,
make the stronger statement that inflation in the post-1956 period was not
induced by either the cost-of-living allowance or other wage increases.
  86. Samuelson and Solow, "Analytical Aspects of Anti-Inflation Policy."

Whatever the source of inflation, a balance of payments consistent with anticipated inflows of capital has been maintained by a number of restrictive practices that periodically culminate in formal devaluations. Quantitative restrictions and high tariffs were used to restrict imports, while a variety of export subsidies were implemented to improve the profitability of exports.[87] Formal devaluations took place in 1949, 1955, 1962, and 1967, the first and last in connection with the devaluation of the British pound. The 1955 devaluation which established a rate of I£1.8 per dollar simply gave official recognition to the fact that most transactions under the existing multiple exchange rate system were already occurring at this rate. Similarly, the 1962 devaluation from I£1.8 to I£3.0 per dollar achieved a much smaller effective devaluation as tariffs and export subsidies had by 1961 resulted in an effective exchange rate of around I£2.4 per dollar for commodity imports and I£2.3 per dollar for commodity exports.[88]

The formal devaluations seem to have had little impact on the balance of payments on current account. Only in the year following the 1962 devaluation did the balance of payments improve and it severely deteriorated in 1964. Moreover, there was only a limited amount of import liberalization connected with them, so that an important potential secondary benefit was not derived. However, following the 1962 devaluation, there was some unification of export subsidies, although they soon became diverse again.

While we cannot enter into an analysis here of the relative merits of frequent devaluation versus extended periods of differential tariffs and export subsidies,[89] it is important to reemphasize that, in the past, the failure to have uniform exchange rates and the considerable variation in the granting of protection and subsidies has

87. Details are provided in Chap. 4. A thorough history of the various measures and the series of devaluations is provided in Halevi and Klinov-Malul, *Economic Development of Israel,* Chap. 10. For the period until 1960, Rubner, *Economy of Israel,* provides an extremely useful, if occasionally polemic, detailed study of the same matters.

88. Baruh, "Import Taxes and Export Subsidies in Israel."

89. A very useful discussion of this general question is given by Charles P. Kindleberger, "Liberal Policies Versus Controls in the Foreign Trade of Developing Countries," AID Discussion Paper no. 14, Agency for International Development, Department of State, Washington, D.C. (Apr. 1967).

diverted substantial effort away from usual efficiency questions.[90] Despite some liberalization, this might still prove to be an important factor retarding the growth of efficiency if inflation continues and devaluation or floating exchange rates (both of which have considerable drawbacks in the Israeli institutional framework) are avoided.

THE FINANCING OF EXCESS DEMAND AND THE NATIONAL SAVING RATE

The continuing import surplus implies that, in total, the major real sectors of the economy, households, business, and the government have spent more than they have received in domestic income. Data on the extent of the deficit spending and the sources of finance are available within a flow of funds format for the years since 1958. Tables 7.11 and 7.12 show flows between eight sectors,

Table 7.11: Percentage of Demand Surplus Accounted for by Real Sectors

	Private business enterprises and households	Public sector	Public sector companies	Nonprofit institutions
1958	35	32	17	16
1959	42	28	14	16
1960	32	26	25	17
1961	40	21	26	13
1962	39	30	22	9
1963	43	29	18	10
1964	48	26	17	9
1965	26	41	20	13
1966	7	63	16	14
1967	−66	135	19	12

Sources: 1958: Bank of Israel, *Annual Report, 1960*, p. 269.
1959: Bank of Israel, *Annual Report, 1961*, p. 321.
1960: Bank of Israel, *Annual Report, 1962*, p. 351.
1961: Bank of Israel, *Annual Report, 1963*, p. 339.
1962: Bank of Israel, *Annual Report, 1964*, p. 360.
1963: Bank of Israel, *Annual Report, 1965*, p. 352.
1964–66: Bank of Israel, *Annual Report, 1966*, p. 405.
1967: Bank of Israel, *Annual Report, 1967*, p. 430.

90. See Chap. 4.

Table 7.12: The Financing of Sectoral Demand Surpluses, 1958-66

	(1) Net credit to (−) or from (+) real domestic sectors	(2) Net credit to (+) or from (−) financial sector	(3) Net credit from abroad	(4) Net transfer from abroad	(5) Omission and rounding	(6) (1) − (2) + (3) + (4) + (5) Demand surplus
Private households and business enterprises						
1958	22	⎫	41	184	−24	223
1959	155	⎬	34	179	−15	353
1960	−23	⎭	60	252	−95	194
1961	177	153	17	280	23	336
1962	0	284	233	575	23	547
1963	79	403	202	682	13	573
1964	108	143	198	686	−21	828
1965	99	445	269	601	−94	430
1966	−31	288	−85	577	−102	71
1967	−42	994	−119	588	−402	−919
Public sector						
1958	−211	⎫	153	259	0	201
1959	−209	⎬	148	239	−	178
1960	−254	⎭	180	228	0	157
1961	−353	−74	205	249	3	175
1962	−225	−31	390	233	0	429
1963	−266	−248	147	253	−1	381
1964	−253	−196	298	217	−1	457
1965	−406	−241	546	287	0	668
1966	−225	−466	492	183	−6	910
1967	−314	−827	463	899	19	1894
Public sector companies						
1958	102		8	0	−5	105

Year						
1959	—[a]		—	0	—	50
1960	155		—3	0	0	152
1961	167	—8	39	0	0	214
1962	205	—46	63	0	1	315
1963	173	—46	13	0	2	234
1964	142	—29	126	0	0	297
1965	262	—77	2	0	—5	336
1966	219	—46	—66	0	0	199
1967	335	—18	—85	0	—3	265

Nonprofit institutions

Year						
1958	—⎫		0	78	—	95
1959	—⎬		0	85	—	101
1960	14⎭		0	86	3	103
1961	9	—8	0	92	0	109
1962	20	16	0	114	3	121
1963	14	7	0	128	—1	134
1964	3	—5	0	151	—1	151
1965	45	—14	0	156	2	217
1966	37	—36	0	146	2	221
1967	21	—5	0	136	12	164

[a] Dash indicates data not available.

Source: 1958: Bank of Israel, Annual Report, 1960, pp. 269, 272.
    1959: Bank of Israel, Annual Report, 1961, p. 321.
    1960: Bank of Israel, Annual Report, 1962, pp. 351, 357, 363.
    1961: Bank of Israel, Annual Report, 1963, pp. 339, 341.
    1962: Bank of Israel, Annual Report, 1964, pp. 357, 366.
    1963: Bank of Israel, Annual Report, 1965, pp. 352, 360.
    1964–65: Bank of Israel, Annual Report, 1966, pp. 405, 413.
    1966–67: Bank of Israel, Annual Report, 1967, pp. 433, 438.

four real and three financial, and the rest of the world. Real transactions include purchases and sales on both current and capital account and transfer payments (including taxes). The demand surplus for each sector (Table 7.11) is equal to its expenditures (current and capital) minus receipts from sales and net transfers to it (or plus net transfers to other sectors). The demand surplus is financed by net long-term and short-term borrowing both domestic and foreign and transfers (unrequited receipts) from abroad. While the aggregate demand surplus for the entire economy is covered in toto by credits and transfers from the rest of the world, any individual sector may be a net borrower or lender to the other domestic sectors, depending on the relation between its own transfers and credit from abroad compared with its demand surplus. Thus a given sector may not only have its own demand surplus but may also, directly or indirectly, help to finance another sector.

The data in Table 7.11 show that every real sector exhibited a demand surplus between 1958 and 1965. Throughout this period private businesses and households were the major source of demand surplus, their share of the total surplus varying between 26 and 48 percent. Unfortunately, the data do not permit a separation in the accounts between these two groups. However, in view of the positive saving recorded in the household savings surveys, it may be assumed that a major share of the demand surplus originated in the business sector.

The public sector has been the second largest source of excess demand, which is simply an alternative way of indicating its failure to balance the budget. Public sector companies have also been a net excess demand group, presumably as a result of the bunched, large investment programs that have been undertaken and have not begun to yield receipts sufficient to cover further investment costs. Insofar as public sector companies are an instrument, albeit indirect, for fostering general economic development, their policies and hence demand surpluses cannot be considered as independent of general government policy. When both public sector and public sector companies are combined, their demand surplus is greater than that of the household-business sector.

Finally, the private nonprofit institutions such as hospitals have had the smallest demand surplus of any sector. In an important sense these institutions have a built-in demand surplus insofar as their structure relies mainly on overseas income and little effort is made to cover the value of services through charging high fees for them.

Both the real resources and the financing needed to satisfy excess sectoral demands came, of course, from abroad. As seen in Table 7.12, a considerable amount came in the form of transfers both to private and public recipients. Increasing reliance has been placed on commercial or government credit from the rest of the world, with the public sector a major recipient. In most years its receipts from transfers and credit were greater than its demand surplus; the public sector was thus able to provide finance to the private sector, acting as an intermediary between the rest of the world and the private sector, primarily by providing funds through the Development Budget.

It must be emphasized in examining the sectoral pattern of excess demands that *all* real sectors spent more than their disposable income, or alternatively, domestic demand exceeded supply, necessitating an import surplus. The public and private sectors both contributed to the realized demand surplus, although in an important sense it may be argued that the responsibility ultimately lay with the failure of the government to restrain private spending. However, as these data are *ex post* they are not capable of providing a way of differentiating among the sectoral sources of inflation, since it is not possible to ascertain the ex ante demand surpluses of the various sectors. Hence there is no basis for singling out particular sectors as initiators of the inflation.

In considering the economy's demand surplus, it is interesting to compare the rough orders of magnitude of the excess demand generated by the immigration into Israel, since one might assume that the costs of absorbing immigrants constituted a major part of the demand surplus. Patinkin has made a rough estimate of these costs for the years 1950–58, those of heaviest immigration relative to population.[91] He assumes the following: (1) an average lag of one year before immigrants were absorbed into the labor force; (2) in the years of immigration the per capita consumption expenditure per immigrant was two-thirds of the rest of the populace (which included immigrants of previous years); (3) as an

91. Patinkin, *Israel Economy: The First Decade,* pp. 101–03.

upper limit, immigrants in the year of immigration consumed 50 percent more government nondefense expenditures per capita than other members of the population; (4) immigrants are charged with their share of total depreciation. Based on these assumptions, the calculated costs of immigration for the entire 1950–58 period were equal to the total amount of domestic dissaving, 3 percent of GNP. Patinkin's estimate is on the conservative side, as it omits the additional housing expenditures necessitated by immigration, equal to, say, 50 percent of investment in dwellings during this period.[92] The latter constituted 12 percent of GNP during the period,[93] so that the immigration cost in housing was 6 percent of GNP. Adding this to the 3 percent of recorded dissaving, we find that the maximum cost attributable to immigration was 9 percent of GNP in this period. The import surplus, 32 percent of GNP in this period, far exceeds the revised cost. Thus the direct costs of immigration accounted for only a limited part of the import surplus during the pre-1958 period and presumably for a much smaller proportion since then. However, as immigrants began producing it was, for reasons suggested earlier, difficult to tax them (as well as upper-income groups) heavily enough to prevent their consumption from rising. Thus the financing of investment to permit the employment of those still unemployed, as well as new immigrants, had to come from foreign sources. In this sense, by failing to provide a source of saving comparable to that which might be expected in a resident group, immigrants were a continuing cause of the need for foreign capital inflow.[94]

We have yet explicitly to consider net saving, and for this the national accounts data are helpful. The financing of gross capital formation is shown in Table 7.13. Until 1958 net national saving was negative in every year but one (1951), while since 1959 it has usually been positive. In most years, even if "errors and omissions" had stemmed from an overestimate of consumption, but not other expenditures, so that private saving is underestimated by the

92. The migration balance accounted for about two-thirds of total population increase between 1950 and 1958. However, some of the added housing expenditure was due to upgrading of nonimmigrant housing standards, and we thus assume that 50 percent of total housing investment was a result of immigration.
93. Calculated in constant (1955) prices.
94. See Chap. 8, pp. 230–31.

full amount appearing in line 4, net national saving would rarely have been positive.[95] Further, the data reflect imports evaluated at the official exchange rate, although it has been suggested that valuation at a more realistic rate would reduce the saving estimate.[96]

Table 7.13: The Financing of Gross Domestic Capital Formation, 1950–67
(millions of I£—current prices)

	1950	1951	1952	1953	1954	1955	1956	1957	1958
1 Gross domestic capital formation	143	231	356	401	515	707	735	905	1000
2 Depreciation allowances	18	28	69	110	147	174	214	253	283
3 Net national saving	−21	27	−53	−57	−32	−67	−227	−45	−35
a. General government	−38	−43	−63	−83	−34	−74	−234	−41	−17
b. Private sector	17	70	10	26	2	7	7	−4	52
4 Errors and omissions	41	46	87	52	57	111	122	119	106
5 Import surplus	105	130	253	296	343	489	626	578	576
Net unilateral transfers as a percentage of import surplus	31.9	38.2	62.2	65.8	109.7	74.2	67.5	73.1	79.0

Note: In calculating import surplus, imports exclude taxes on imported commodities and exports exclude export subsidies.

95. Cf. Patinkin, *Israel Economy: The First Decade*, p. 95.
96. The impact of different exchange rates on the estimate of national saving has been a much discussed topic in Israel, both because of the size of the import surplus and the existence throughout most years of a multiple exchange rate system. The use of the official, overvalued exchange rate is alleged to yield an overestimate of national saving. Thus Patinkin, and Halevi and Klinov-Malul following him, have reestimated saving, using a rate above the official one for valuing the import surplus. (See Patinkin, *Israeli Economy: The First Decade*, pp. 92–94; Halevi and Klinov-Malul, *Economic Development of Israel*, pp. 96–97).

There are difficulties here: first, had imports actually entered at some higher rate, estimated investment would have been greater, as the import component would have had a higher value attached to it. (Patinkin mentions this problem, ibid., p. 93.) Thus, domestic saving would not decline by the full amount of the revaluation of the import surplus. Second, had a higher exchange rate been in force, and assuming some price responsiveness in the domestic economy, realized imports and exports would have

214 Structural Change and Economic Policy in Israel

Table 7.13: (continued)

	1959	1960	1961	1962	1963	1964	1965	1966	1967
1 Gross domestic capital formation	1109	1187	1532	2067	2284	2940	3012	2504	1868
2 Depreciation allowances	316	364	438	631	765	878	1022	1144	1240
3 Net national saving	113	84	144	−69	139	333	335	102	−647
a. General government	3	−11	8	−168	−211	−66	−203	−431	−1605
b. Private sector	110	95	152	99	350	399	538	543	958
4 Errors and omissions	155	175	209	183	83	89	181	46	124
5 Import surplus	525	564	725	1262	1297	1640	1474	1202	1151
Net unilateral transfers as a percentage of import surplus	79.7	92.3	77.6	70.9	77.2	58.5	62.9	65.6	119.4

Sources: Lines 1, 2, 4, 5: *Statistical Abstract of Israel, 1968*, pp. 138–39 except for 1950, 1951. 1950–51: CBS, *Israel's National Income and Expenditure (1950–1962)*, Tables 7, 9.

Line 3a: *Statistical Abstract of Israel, 1968*, p. 155, except for 1950, 1950: *Israel's National Income and Expenditure*, p. 20.

Line 3b: Calculated as a residual.

Net unilateral transfers 1950–60: Halevi and Klinov-Malul, *Economic Development of Israel*, p. 155. 1961–67: Bank of Israel, *Annual Report, 1967*, p. 47.

Table 7.13 also shows the importance of unilateral transfers, which were the main source of financing the import surplus, in most years after 1955, accounting for at least 75 percent of the surplus, the remainder being financed by normal credit.[97] Assume for the moment that unilateral transfers were viewed by both private and public recipients as discretionary income, providing a choice of spending patterns identical to that of income originating

been different than the observed; presumably the realized import surplus would have been smaller. Thus, unless the entire adjustment process is specified, an arbitrary change in the accounting rate used to evaluate the import surplus may provide a misleading impression of the extent of dissaving.

97. A detailed discussion of the financing of the import surplus and an analysis of its implications is given in Halevi and Klinov-Malul, *Economic Development of Israel*, chap. 8.

in the domestic economy.[98] If the aggregate (public and private) consumption levels reflect the impact of transfers on expenditure, then the saving estimate for the entire economy should be raised by the amount of transfers, as this represented additional disposable income that is not taken into account in the conventional national accounting framework. This approach may provide the best behavioral interpretation of the low national saving rate.

It has been argued by some that, when viewed as a conscious result of government policy, the low saving rate was not harmful insofar as the flow of unilateral transfers was sufficient to finance most of the import surplus; hence investment could be maintained at a high level without reducing the rate of growth of consumption. In discussing the limits on taxation we have suggested that this position can be put on firm ground, when the social absorption of immigrants and motivational problems are considered. As long as the government assumed that these transfers would continue, or at least not decline precipitously, a gradual reduction in their level could be met by a slow introduction of measures to reduce domestic absorption and, if need be, by some allotment of foreign exchange reserves to meet any unanticipated decline in the availability of financing.[99] The government's confidence in its policy was buttressed by a number of forecasts of declines in the level of unilateral transfers that failed to materialize. Rather than view the appearance of a new source of transfers as a reprieve, it was implicitly assumed that all such forecasts were too pessimistic.[100] Even during the early 1960s, a period of considerable prosperity, there was no movement toward restraint of private demand (Table 7.6).

The "wait-and-see" policy, however, had a built-in flaw; it assumed an unrealistically high potential for rapid implementation and realization of restrictive policies if it became necessary to adopt them. Any type of restrictive policy in which rapid impact was

98. This point, in more detail, is made by Patinkin, *Israel Economy: The First Decade*, pp. 99–100.

99. In the early 1960s the value of foreign exchange reserves were often in excess of half a year of imports.

100. Most elected members of the government were quite skeptical about the forecasts of economists. The origins of this attitude lay partly in the reports of a number of British commissions during the mandatory period that Palestine could support only a few hundred thousand people, the reports being used as one justification for limiting immigration into the country in the period preceding World War II.

needed would face difficulties. On the one hand, an income tax increase designed to counter an anticipated fall-off in transfers could have little short-run impact because consumers would attempt to maintain recently achieved consumption levels, this effect being reinforced by the assumption, in view of earlier experience, that higher tax levels were likely to be temporary. On the other hand, a sudden decrease in expenditures that would have an immediate impact on the level of demand would inevitably lead to a slower growth of GNP, as a simultaneous increase in exports could not be expected. Labor immobility, changes in specifications for foreign purchasers, the development of marketing and financial arrangements inevitably introduce substantial delays in realizing exports.[101]

In 1964 these became the options to be faced. The continued growth of private consumption, along with continued high investment and public expenditure levels, led to a situation in which the government felt it necessary to take some measures to limit the size of the import surplus, which threatened to exceed anticipated capital inflows. The reason for concern about the future of the balance of payments, which became acute in both the government and the press in late 1964, can be gleaned from a brief consideration of the development of the trade deficit. Between 1956 and 1960 the import surplus had leveled off at an annual rate below $350 million, with some year-to-year fluctuations that reduced the level to as low as $314 million.[102] In 1960 the surplus was $337 million. However, in 1961, it rose to $432 million. Partly as a result of this rapid increase in the deficit, there was an official devaluation in 1962, reducing the exchange rate from $.56 per I£ to $.33 per I£. While this move temporarily stemmed the increasing discrepancy between imports and exports (the deficit falling to $404 million in 1963), the year 1964 saw an enormous widening of the deficit to $528 million; an increase of 57 percent had occurred in only four years. This rise in the import surplus, combined with an anticipated falling off of capital inflows, led to a decision to decrease the government deficit by reducing both direct

---

101. Of course, even if an income tax increase had been implemented earlier, it would have faced similar difficulties, but these could have been met over a longer time span.

102. Halevi and Klinov-Malul, *Economic Development of Israel*, Table 50.

investment expenditures, particularly housing, and the financing of private investment, and by raising taxes early in 1966. These policies began to have an effect in late 1965 and 1966, with aggregate demand growth slowing considerably.[103] The planned slowdown turned into a standstill, as private nondwelling investment also declined substantially.

The recession profile of major GNP components conformed to what might have been expected on an a priori basis. Real GNP in 1966 increased by only 0.3 percent, yet real private consumption grew by 3.7 percent and total public consumption by 5.5 percent. The continued growth of private consumption was not surprising in view of the often observed insensitivity of current consumption to current income. Actual leveling off of consumption would presumably have required the maintenance of the depressed level of overall demand. The brunt of the decrease in domestic absorption occurred in all categories of fixed investment. Finally, the import surplus decreased substantially, by over 16 percent, the decrease being accounted for by the slight decline in imports, combined with a 15 percent increase in exports, of which one-third was attributable to an increase in export prices. The income foregone in this period may be viewed as a cost of earlier stable growth, to the extent that the previous rapid rise in consumption is viewed as integral to the absorption of immigrants, as well as providing incentives important for continued growth. However, as suggested earlier, further rapid growth in living standards does not seem to be a necessary ingredient of future growth. The task policy makers now face is to restrict consumption growth and increase the ratio of exports to GNP.

The evidence of the recession indicates that this will not be an easy or quick matter. Simply restricting domestic demand without altering the profitability of exporting is inadequate. Thus, in the 1966–67 recession, industrial exports excluding polished diamonds increased only slightly faster than in earlier years, despite considerable excess capacity. Although part of this failure to increase more rapidly may be attributable to slower growth in world demand, other factors were also probably operative. For example,

103. The decline in demand engineered by the government reinforced and accelerated a slowdown that would have occurred in any case as a result of the accumulation of excess capacity in privately financed dwelling and office buildings, a development that became quite evident during 1965.

as a result of prolonged protection of the domestic market, many producers may have had variable costs that exceeded international prices, and devaluation or export subsidies were required. However, an alternative view of the failure to increase exports is that domestic producers could have been competitive on the international market (though preferring the higher profitability of the protected domestic market), but the large initial cost for entering these markets resulted in decisions not to export. Mathematically, let $\pi = \int_o^t (P - V)e^{-rt}$ represent the present value of profits from foreign markets over the t periods of the anticipated recession, where P is the unit export price (in domestic currency) and V the variable cost. Although exports are produced with unutilized capacity it pays to begin them only if $\pi > F$, where F equals the initial entry costs. Here π depends on the length of time during which excess capacity is expected to continue; the shorter the expected length of the recession, the smaller π would be relative to F. If entry cost is an important obstacle to increased exports, several measures apart from devaluation could be used: reducing F by pooling arrangements, government-financed trade fairs, and so forth.

If, on the other hand, exports would not be profitable at current exchange rates even if initial costs were subsidized, other measures would be necessary. In 1966, direct subsidies in fact became a major policy instrument, amounting to 1 to 8.5 percent of the f.o.b. price, the rate depending upon the percentage of value added in foreign exchange: subsidies were again raised in early 1967. In addition, rebates were offered on domestic indirect taxes and shipping costs.[104] In 1966 most of the increase in exports was in products whose production has traditionally been oriented toward exports and in which domestic absorption had been of little significance. However, in 1967, domestically oriented branches began to increase their exports.[105] Although this movement is as yet too brief to indicate a definite trend, it is preliminary evidence of the potential of a combined reduction in domestic demand and the restructuring of relative profitability in the home and foreign markets.

104. For a detailed description of the subsidy system, see Bank of Israel, *Annual Report, 1966*.
105. Bank of Israel, *Annual Report, 1967*, pp. 66–68.

8

Social Factors
in the Development Process

The preceding chapters have focused essentially on two themes: (1) a description of the growth process and the major determinants of its evolution, and (2) an analysis of how the process could have been improved, given the country's objectives. In Chapter 2 it was seen that factor growth, particularly capital, was an important source of growth, and in the previous chapter we saw that most of capital formation was financed by capital inflow. It is tempting to draw the conclusion that foreign aid was the sufficient condition for growth and that without it much slower growth would have been realized. As this notion has intuitive appeal, it is necessary to consider its basis in some detail.

Using the "two-gap" terminology developed by Chenery and a number of collaborators,[1] it appears that, in Israel during the period following 1954, the growth of GNP would have been constrained by a shortage of saving rather than of foreign exchange; given the range of products produced, foreign exchange earnings could have been increased had domestic absorption been reduced.[2] If this is correct, then the major effect of capital inflow in Israel has been the augmentation of domestic saving, permitting higher investment levels than would have been achieved in its absence. However, it is not accurate to assume that smaller capital inflows

1. Hollis B. Chenery and Michael Bruno, "Development Alternatives in an Open Economy: The Case of Israel," *Economic Journal* 62 (Mar. 1962) 79–103; Hollis B. Chenery and Alan Strout, "Foreign Assistance and Economic Development," *American Economic Review* 56 (Sept. 1966): 679–733.

2. However, it is true that foreign exchange would have become more expensive in terms of domestic inputs, had it become necessary to begin to export products whose production had high costs in Israel.

would have been reflected in a commensurate decline in investment levels, for it is inconceivable that, had no aid been available, the actual national saving rate would have been as low as the recorded rate. Given the value system and the growth orientation of both the political leaders and the major economic institutions, it is probable that substantial saving would have been generated via government surpluses, although not at a level permitting an investment-GNP ratio of 30 percent.

If this ratio had been 20 percent, the rate of growth of capital would have been two-thirds of its recorded value of 10.7 percent; and the growth rate of GNP for the total private economy would have been 9.3, rather than 11.4 for the years 1954–64, and the per capita rate 4.3 percent.[3] To assume any lower rate of saving in the absence of aid in the post-1954 years would constitute a serious misreading of the ideological and political climate within which Israel's leaders functioned.[4] However, it does seem unlikely that significant saving could have been generated in the pre-1954 period, given the magnitude of the immigration absorption and defense burdens. Had there been no capital inflows during this period, growth would inevitably have been adversely affected, during succeeding years, because a disproportionate part of saving in the post-1954 period would then, of necessity, have been devoted to social overhead capital such as housing and electricity generation, which are not immediately productive in terms of increased output of goods and services.

High investment levels are not, however, the major source of high growth rates. This may be inferred from international comparisons. For this purpose we compare cumulative investment

3. It should be noted that these estimates depend on the accuracy of the specification of the production function; the one underlying the calculation in the text is the Cobb Douglas function estimated for the entire private economy (Table 2.9, Equation 1). The specification of technical change as being disembodied is obviously of importance for the calculation in the text. If some of the technical change calculated as disembodied were in fact embodied, the effect of the decreased capital accumulation would have been more than indicated in the text. However, the omission in the original production function of many factors of importance in the growth process leads us to believe that the disembodied assumption is probably not too far from the mark. See Chap. 2, n. 30.
4. On related matters, especially the pioneering and ascetic motivations of the various elites, see S. N. Eisenstadt, *Israeli Society*, chap. 2.

ratios[5] and rates of GNP growth for the years 1955–64. (See Fig. 8.1.) There is little systematic association discernible between investment ratios and growth rates. Several countries with high levels of investment are matched in growth by lower investment countries. For example, in Latin America, Argentina, Colombia, and Peru were matched in GNP performance by Paraguay, Ecuador, and Brazil, respectively despite the considerably lower investment rates in the later group. Figure 8.1 suggests that, even had Israel's investment rate been considerably lower (as a result of reduced aid), it would have performed well as compared with other countries. The same relatively good performance is found in GNP per capita comparisons, which partially eliminate the effect on total growth of the rapid increase in Israel's labor force during this period.

These results are not surprising. Many other factors play an important role in the development process and may act as constraints on growth; labor force quality, market size, and government policy all play crucial roles. Even concentrating on investment, its distribution between construction and equipment may be crucial.[6] In explaining the Israeli performance, particular emphasis is often placed upon the high educational achievements of a substantial part of the population and the fact that the initial stock of education was costless to the country.[7] While it was certainly true that, at the beginning of statehood, Israel's manpower resources in terms of both average education and the percentage of college graduates in the total population were extraordinary, two qualifying factors must be kept in mind, namely, the skill composition of those who were highly educated in 1948 and the education and skill levels of new immigrants.

First, despite the high percentage of college graduates in 1948,

5. The sum of investment for the years 1955–64 divided by the sum of GNP for these years, both being in constant prices where available. The GNP growth rate is a fitted one, rather than the compound rate between endpoints.

6. See, for example, Carlos Diaz-Alejandro, *Essays on the Economic History of the Argentine Republic* (forthcoming) and T. P. Hill, "Growth and Investment According to International Comparisons," *Economic Journal* 74 (June 1964): 287–304.

7. For a good statement of this view, see Richard E. Easterlin, "Israel's Development: Past Accomplishments and Future Problems," *Quarterly Journal of Economics* 75 (Feb. 1961): 63–86.

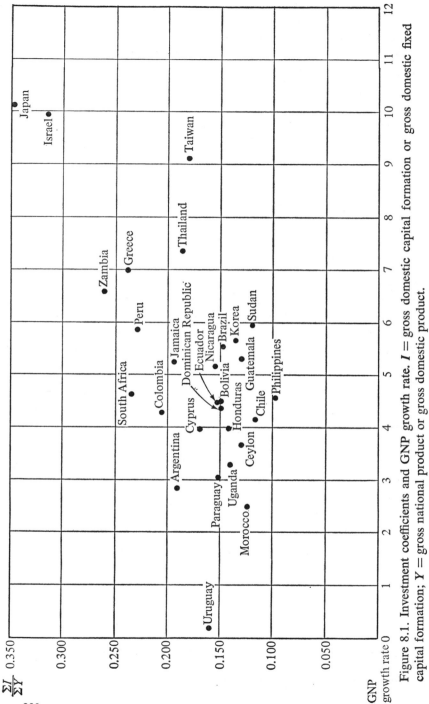

Figure 8.1. Investment coefficients and GNP growth rate. I = gross domestic capital formation or gross domestic fixed capital formation; Y = gross national product or gross domestic product.

222

it appears that relatively few, aside from physicians, had technical education.[8] There were relatively few engineers or scientists who are usually considered necessary for the adoption of technology and the expansion of local industry. Many of those most highly educated had been trained in the liberal arts and law.[9] There were few labor force members with previous administrative experience abroad in government or business, although in this category it is true that many of those in such positions in Israel in 1948 had gained considerable experience in Mandatory Palestine. Finally, although the presence of a relatively large supply of teachers was an important factor in reducing illiteracy and providing future sources of educated manpower, the immediate productive contribution of education was limited. However, by the mid-1950s students who had undergone training in the Israeli school system were entering the labor force and presumably their productivity was augmented by their education.

The percentage of high school graduates was also quite high. Moreover, in some sectors such as manufacturing a considerable amount of experience had been accumulated, albeit more in workshops than in factories. A group of managers and workers existed who were familiar with industrial methods, upon whom future growth could be built. A substantial skill base also existed in agriculture, which was probably the most advanced branch in relation to existing technology.

Thus, during the first years of the state, the country probably had

8. These statements are based upon data from the 1961 Census on occupation abroad of immigrants who arrived in Israel before independence. While the age coverage of the data is somewhat limited, and the correspondence between education and occupation may not be exact, we believe they provide a reasonable basis for inferring the type of education embodied in the 1948 labor force. The data are to be found in Population and Housing Census, 1961 (Israel) Publication no. 27, *Labor Force, Part IV*.

9. This finding does not contradict the hypothesis suggested in Chap. 2 that part of the rapid rate of aggregate growth may be explainable in terms of a high elasticity of substitution, which in turn depends on a considerable number of technically trained men. Although many of the 1948 college graduates were not technically trained, after statehood a substantial percentage of degree recipients were in technical fields. For example, in 1956–57, about 45 percent of all university degrees were awarded by the Technion, the Israel Institute of Technology. It was primarily in the period after 1953 that the ability to assimilate more capital intensive techniques would have assumed major importance.

a shortage of some types of appropriate high level manpower directly useful in assimilating the technology necessary for development but was endowed with a considerable supply of manpower that possessed skills important for other aspects of development. There can be little doubt that the entire labor force, despite some high level scarcities, was well endowed to accelerate development. However, the country was immediately faced with an influx of immigrants who, by and large, lacked either appropriate education or occupation.

Immigrants arriving after 1948 were poorly equipped for participation in a modern society. Many were illiterate and had received limited education;[10] moreover, their occupation structure before immigration did not have much correspondence with the requirements of the new state: 50 to 70 percent of post-1948 immigrants had to change occupation before finding employment.[11] Any surplus of educated, professional manpower that may have existed was quickly exhausted, and shortages soon became a constraining factor.[12] However, as a result of the ongoing internal education process, the percentage of highly educated manpower began to return to its 1948 levels by the 1960s. Thus, by 1961, 7.3 percent of the population over twenty-five years of age had completed fifteen or more years of education, a percentage similar to that in 1948.[13] This extraordinary achievement was the result of the substantial resources devoted to the educational system.

To summarize, then, the initial population in 1948 was well educated, although its education may not always have corresponded to the skills required in the development process. However, the vastly different educational and occupational backgrounds of new immigrants had little relation to the country's requirements and

10. See the data on changes in education levels, Chap. 2.
11. These figures are based upon the 1954 labor force survey and the 1961 census. For the former results, see Moshe Sicron, *Immigration to Israel: 1948–1953* and for the 1961 census results, *Labor Force, IV*, Table 5.
12. On these questions see Ofer, *Service Industries in a Developing Economy*, chap. 5, and the sources cited therein, particularly Hanoch, "Income Differentials in Israel"; Moshe Sicron, *Immigration to Israel: 1948–1953*.
13. These figures were calculated from unpublished data of the 1961 census.

necessitated extensive switching of occupation, as well as reeducation. Moreover, a large part of existing skilled manpower was used in a widening process, to bring new immigrants up to modern educational and health standards. Thus, while the quality of human resources played an important role in explaining Israel's development, it is easy to overstate its role. Undoubtedly, in comparison with a number of less developed countries in both Asia and Africa, the differential investment and educational levels explain a considerable part of the difference in growth. However, in attempting to explain the difference in performance of Israel and some Latin American countries, particularly Argentina, neither investment nor educational differentials seem to constitute a sufficient explanation.

Argentina provides a useful comparative framework for analyzing the conditions that led to large disparities in growth rates between two countries with a number of similar characteristics. Without entering into a detailed study, it may be noted that Argentina has extremely good agricultural and other natural resources; a skilled labor force,[14] much of it of European origin and presumably thoroughly inculcated with modern economic values; and a high investment ratio, about 20 percent of GNP. Nevertheless, since the mid-1940s the Argentine experience has been one of low growth.[15] From our viewpoint a useful point of departure is the consideration of the (implicit) welfare function that is being maximized by public policy makers.

Economic models usually assume that the government is attempting to maximize the rate of growth of per capita GNP or per capita consumption. Although distribution is recognized as one possible objective to be reconciled with income growth, it is rarely given formal attention in theoretical models of how development proceeds, although to be sure many development programs at least suggest some measures relating to distribution. The omission of distribution questions not only limits the explanatory power of development models, but also focuses attention on issues whose

14. See, e.g., Frederick Harbison and Charles Myers, *Education, Manpower and Economic Growth* (New York: McGraw-Hill, 1966), chap. 3.
15. Our discussion of Argentina follows closely the interesting study by Carlos Diaz-Alejandro, "The Argentine State and Economic Growth: A Historical Review" (forthcoming) and his *Essays on the Economic History of the Argentine Republic*.

impact is likely to be small relative to those generated by an attempt to meet the distribution goals.

To be more explicit, in many countries the government is controlled by a dominant group whose specific interests are often reflected in economic policy.[16] The welfare of this group may not depend on the maximization of national income growth but on its distribution. For this group it may be optimal to slow the aggregate rate of growth if, out of a smaller product, they receive a larger absolute income than they would have obtained had more rapid growth occurred but their share been smaller. For example, in Argentina, the Peron government, representing industrial workers, maintained an overvalued exchange rate and a high rate of protection. The price of industrial products to the agricultural sector was raised, and at the same time agricultural exports were discouraged by the overvalued exchange rate. As both the static and dynamic comparative advantage of the country lay in agricultural exports, the real growth of the economy was slowed. Nevertheless, in terms of the welfare of industrial workers, the distorted situation may well have been preferable to the maximum growth configuration. In any case the government acted as if this were so. The sectoral conflict was also manifested in an inappropriate distribution of government expenditure, particularly inadequate agricultural extension services and poor transport facilities, which also retarded aggregate growth.

Similar divergences between national and group interests may also be based upon conflicts on the size distribution of income or on the functional distribution (which will often overlap the question of size). Thus Hirschman and others have interpreted the rapid inflation in some Latin American countries as simply a battle over the functional distribution of income. If one takes the view that rapid inflation has often been deleterious to growth, it becomes obvious that the distribution and growth problems are closely related. Or to cite another example, economic discrimination among regions, for example, the coastal and hill areas in Colombia or capital cities versus rural areas, may have led to realized output falling short of the potential output which could have been gener-

16. The dominant group may cut across conventional classes, e.g., include labor and management in the industrial sector.

ated if a more equitable policy had been pursued.[17] While such conflicts need not necessarily result in a deceleration of growth, empirically they are often resolved by decisions that do, in fact, lead to this outcome.

In Israel, conflict about the division of income among sectors, factors of production, or size of income groups has been relatively unimportant. The absence of such conflict can be explained in terms of the backgrounds of the leaders of both the government and the major economic institutions, particularly the Histadrut. Almost all of these leaders had emigrated to Palestine from Eastern Europe in the early years of the twentieth century. Most came with strong social democratic views. Initially, many sought and remained in jobs as farm laborers or semiskilled industrial workers, even when middle-class job opportunities existed. Being strongly imbued with the concept of strengthening both the economic and social structure of Palestine, they eventually formed the administrative nucleus of the key institutions, both economic and political. They thus entered positions of power not as representatives of particular group interests, but with a perception of themselves as the embodiment of national interests.

Consistent with their earlier work experience and ideological commitments, the members of the Second *Aliyah*,[18] as they were known, attempted to foster development within a collective framework. Thus both the agricultural sector, consisting mainly of kibbutzim and moshavim, and the industrial sector, in which many of the large firms were owned by the Histadrut itself, were organized on a collective basis.[19] One result was the relative absence, for a considerable period, of distributional conflict along lines of either the equality of income distribution or its functional breakdown. Moreover, there was relatively little sectoral conflict

17. See, for example, the discussion of the concentration of investment in Caracas rather than the countryside during the Jimenez regime in Charles W. Anderson, *Politics and Economic Change in Latin America* (Princeton, N.J.: Van Nostrand, 1967), chap. 10.

18. Literally, second immigration, i.e., those who immigrated to Israel between 1905 and 1914.

19. Including construction and transport, as well as mining and manufacturing. Even large parts of the service sector such as insurance and marketing were Histadrut enterprises.

between agriculture and industry, as there was a strong sense of interdependence, based upon a mutual recognition of the need for economic cooperation if a Jewish state were to be forged.

The increasing importance of private ownership of industrial and service firms that followed the middle-class immigration of the 1930s and the availability of investment capital after the formation of the state have inevitably reduced the consensus on the desirability of collective principles as the dominant strain in economic life. Nevertheless, those in power in most major economic and political institutions continue to be members of the Second *Aliyah,* and they have maintained a consensus that has remained relatively free from serious conflict over questions of distribution.[20]

One important result of the dominant social democratic outlook of the leaders is the relatively low (by international standards) inequality of the size distribution of income,[21] which is partly the outcome of arrangements that tie wages of each industrial or occupational group to all others. Although differential wage and salary movements contravening these official agreements have occurred, for example, during periods of tight labor markets when workers are "promoted" to higher job classifications to justify wage increases, by and large there has been no substantial change in the degree of inequality, although some widening has occurred. One impact of this is the perception by most income classes that continued gains in their living standards will depend upon the growth of national income, rather than the diversion of an increasing share toward themselves.[22]

It seems to us that the absence, throughout most of the period, of serious sectoral or income group conflict constituted one of the important preconditions for growth. We have suggested that this was in large measure attributable to the characteristics of the

20. It will be suggested below that at least some of this cohesion was due to the rapidly rising absolute standard of living, which undoubtedly helped to assuage a number of potential conflicts.

21. See Hanoch, "Income Differentials in Israel"; Halevi and Klinov-Malul, *Economic Development of Israel,* pp. 115–23. It is important to note that government tax and expenditure policies were quite progressive, altering the pretax distribution considerably.

22. One undesirable effect of the egalitarian policy, along with fairly rigid rules preventing the firing of workers, may have been the diminution in work incentives. Despite the often voiced complaints on this count, it is difficult to gauge its importance.

leadership group. One more observation is worth making, namely, the absence of corruption. Despite the fact that several billion dollars were channeled into the country, much of it through government institutions and the extensive use of controls, particularly in international trade, there has been a marked absence of any corruption. Given the recent experiences of a number of developing countries, this was not an insignificant accomplishment.[23]

The distribution question has a number of other important dimensions. As seen in the previous chapter, the tax level in Israel was quite high relative to most less developed countries; it is high even if the ratio of taxes to total resources rather than GNP is used. The lower tax ratios in many countries cannot simply be ascribed to difficulty in raising revenue; rather it is often a result of the adamant opposition to such increases by important power groups within the country.[24] Limited budgets usually result in small expenditures on directly productive economic services such as agricultural extension and rural road systems, as well as more indirect inputs such as education and health. These expenditures were undoubtedly of considerable importance in Israel. Although it is not possible to quantify its impact, agricultural research, particularly on arid zone problems, and extension services were quite important sources of agricultural productivity gains. Similarly, it is difficult to envision the current and planned economic structure of the economy had extensive education and health expenditures not been made to raise the standards of new immigrants. Although meaningful functional breakdowns of government expenditures are difficult to obtain for most less developed countries, available data suggest that Israel's public expenditures on education have been relatively high.[25] These must be kept in mind in understanding

23. Cf. Anderson, *Politics and Economic Change in Latin America,* chap. 6.

24. While it is often suggested that the lack of literacy and accurate record-keeping limit the achievable levels of tax revenue, there is considerable evidence that, where the political will exists, suitable tax devices can be arranged. An early statement of the difficulties involved in administering income taxes is found in Richard Goode, "Reconstruction of Foreign Tax Systems," *Proceedings of the 44th Annual Conference on Taxation, 1951* (Sacramento, Calif.: National Tax Association, 1951). A skeptical evaluation of this thesis is provided by Vito Tanzi in "Personal Income Taxation in Latin America: Obstacles and Possibilities," *National Tax Journal* 19 (June 1966): 156–62.

25. See Tables 5 to 8 in Harbison and Myers, *Education, Manpower and*

Israel's economic performance; a considerable part of the current labor force has been educated within the country. Its high educational level was not a gift that the economy received but represents a substantial investment. The current returns from these expenditures on education are thus in the nature of a return to investment rather than a rent to the system.[26]

So far we have argued that the main role of foreign aid was to replace the need for domestic saving. Had aid not been available, the orientation of national leaders leads us to believe that a government surplus on current account, engineered by higher taxation, would have provided financing for a high level of investment, though perhaps not quite equal to realized levels. The crucial point for our argument is that, regardless of the source of investment, it would have been productive because of the nature of the leadership group.

What then was the real impact of foreign aid? In the last chapter we suggested that an important function of aid was to allow the growth of consumption, which in turn was important for successful integration of the immigrants, and to provide incentives to the managerial and technical groups. In a sense the availability of transfers allowed Israel to avoid a development process that might have followed the labor surplus model in essential aspects.[27] If we view the economy that existed in 1948 as the advanced sector, the entry of a huge number of immigrants and the resulting high level of unemployment could have led to increasing employment at a constant wage. As expansion occurred, with real wages constant, the resulting high profits could have provided domestic saving to stimulate continued expansion, so that the need for foreign trans-

---

Economic Growth, for data. The Bank of Israel, *Annual Report, 1966,* Table 2-1, indicates that Israel was devoting roughly 6 percent of GNP to education. This considerably exceeds the UNESCO estimate used by Harbison and Myers and is based on much more careful analysis. Of course, it is possible that there are underestimates in other countries as well, so that the conclusions based on these data are necessarily tentative.

26. Interestingly, under Peron, Argentina did devote considerable resources to education, but the adverse impact on efficiency of other policy measures apparently offset the positive effects of education.

27. Cf. W. Arthur Lewis, "Economic Development with Unlimited Supplies of Labor," *Manchester School* (May 1954); John Fei and Gustav Ranis, *The Development of the Labor Surplus Economy* (Homewood, Ill.: Richard D. Irwin, 1964).

fers would have diminished. In Israel, in fact, real wages did not remain constant nor did profit recipients save a very high percentage of their income. The government and the Histadrut, committed to nation building in a broad sense, did not allow market forces full latitude, an important institutional feature of the labor surplus model. Real wages increased and thus the consumption of immigrants rose. Upper income groups, in which profits were concentrated, did not have a high saving propensity; their tax rates were not raised to levels that would have permitted a government surplus on current account. The impact of aid in this framework was to replace the saving that failed to be generated because of the specific circumstances of Israel's history, particularly the need to absorb immigrants in a social, as well as an economic sense, and the switch to greater reliance on private enterprise with a consequent need to provide incentives to the managerial group.

Had market forces been allowed to work and/or taxes raised to provide a government surplus, saving could have been generated and the import surplus reduced, a case of success within the labor surplus paradigm. Although diminished incentives and increased social tension, perhaps reflected in lower productivity, might have occurred, the general consensus on national goals of the leadership group and their control of the major political parties and the Histadrut would almost certainly have prevented open distributional conflict of a type adversely affecting growth. What does seem likely is that by 1965, post-1948 immigrants, or at least a high percentage of them, would have felt less an integral part of the nation; the same relative discrepancy in living standards between this group and veteran residents as existed in 1965 would have been accompanied by a failure of many immigrants to have achieved the absolute standard that the veteran population had in 1950. Success according to a purely economic criterion would not have been synonomous with any meaningful measure of social integration.

The preceding may leave the impression that all that is needed for successful development is a government of outstanding virtue; replacing the Schumpeterian innovator and the Weberian accumulator is the selfless bureaucrat. This is far from our intention. The frame of reference in which a development-oriented government assumes strategic importance is one of a high saving rate, (or potential high saving if aid is currently available), a fairly skilled labor force, and a stock of highly educated manpower. This implies that many of the most basic problems of achieving sustained development have already been overcome. The validity of our tentative identification of government motivation as a sufficient condition for growth is relevant only to countries at a similar stage of development; these are to be found mainly in Latin America, rather than in Asia or Africa. Previous chapters have discussed the extent of specific development problems and the ways in which they were approached. Many of these policies could potentially be duplicated in Latin American countries, since their requirements do not exceed the availability of education endowment, capital, and so on. To understand Israel's success fully requires a comparative approach that examines the failure of particular policies to be adopted elsewhere, and thus requires an excursion into a type of political economy whose outline has been sketched here.

Statistical Appendix

The following tables provide data which have not, for the most part, been utilized in the body of the study, but which may be of interest to others engaged in research. They have been prepared according to a comprehensive data plan suggested by Nancy and Richard Ruggles. This plan has also been used in the other studies in the Economic Growth Center country-study series. Some of the tables present time series, others data for selected dates in line with the standard format. This appendix is less inclusive than those presented in the other country studies, particularly in the areas of agricultural and foreign trade data. Omissions are made in the former area on the grounds that cross section work done on the agriculture sector of less developed countries is likely to concentrate on countries in which the sector is of major importance and in which the technology is non-modern. International trade data have been omitted because of the ready availability of the book by Halevi and Klinov-Malul (cited in the bibliography), which has extensive tables on Israel's international trade. A more comprehensive, mimeographed appendix, fully comparable to the other country-study statistical appendixes may be obtained by request to the Executive Secretary of the Economic Growth Center, Yale University.

Very detailed explanations of the method of generating the reported data are provided in all the publications of the Central Bureau of Statistics (see the bibliography, below). In particular, the reader interested in the details of the estimation of the national account data should consult the introduction to *Israel's National Income and Expenditure (1950–1962)*.

Table 1: Expenditure on Gross National Product
(Current prices; I£ million)

	1950	1951	1952	1953	1954	1955	1956	1957	1958
A. Private consumption expenditure[a]	342.6	484.0	791.0	1,023.8	1,326.0	1,575.9	1,869.9	2,156.4	2,462.7
1. Food	128.9	170.1	321.8	423.9	571.8	612.4	724.6	823.1	940.5
2. Clothing	38.9	55.5	68.8	106.4	167.9	202.2	227.2	242.6	280.1
3. Rent	36.9	49.6	76.7	98.2	128.6	171.7	227.0	253.6	281.3
4. Durables	24.6	40.7	62.3	66.3	86.0	91.3	109.4	143.9	164.3
5. Other	113.6	169.0	264.3	333.7	432.0	498.3	581.7	693.2	796.5
B. Government current expenditures[b]	92.0	131.0	197.0	250.0	320.0	428.0	675.0	620.0	672.0
1. General expenditures	—[c]	—	—	—	—	—	—	—	—
2. Development expenditures	—	—	—	—	—	—	—	—	—
C. Gross fixed domestic capital formation	139.7	226.3	326.7	375.6	479.5	636.5	695.5	865.4	936.3
1. Government fixed capital formation	—	—	42.7[d]	52.8[d]	59.6[d]	—	—	—	—
2. Residential construction	62.7	105.2	127.3	133.4	179.4	241.1	235.0	299.4	300.2
3. Enterprise fixed capital formation	—	—	156.7	189.4	240.5	—	—	—	—
D. Changes in stocks	4.3	4.7	29.2	24.9	35.9	70.8	39.3	39.6	63.4
E. Exports of goods and services[e]	15.0	22.0	74.0	128.0	234.0	257.0	315.0	412.0	451.0
F. Less: Imports of goods and services[f]	131.0	164.0	345.0	452.0	617.0	831.0	1,055.0	1,140.0	1,154.0
G. Gross Domestic Product	460.0	702.0	1,073.0	1,351.0	1,778.0	2,139.0	2,547.0	2,958.0	3,437.0
H. Less: Net factor payments abroad	2.0	4.0	11.0	17.0	16.0	15.0	13.0	19.0	24.0
I. Gross National Product	458.0	698.0	1,062.0	1,334.0	1,762.0	2,124.0	2,534.0	2,939.0	3,413.0

(Continued)

Table 1—*Continued*

	1959	1960	1961	1962	1963	1964	1965	1966	1967
A. Private consumption expenditure[a]	2,766.6	3,093.9	3,646.9	4,407.7	5,245.2	6,086.7	7,136.3	7,908.6	8,166.4
1. Food	1,034.1	1,147.3	1,312.8	1,528.9	1,761.5	1,945.5	2,174.0	2,398.8	2,552.8
2. Clothing	287.9	320.3	374.9	432.6	493.7	560.4	659.0	739.4	709.4
3. Rent	324.0	374.8	448.8	570.0	742.8	891.6	1,078.6	1,177.6	1,220.8
4. Durables	193.0	221.8	263.9	354.5	415.9	518.5	586.4	571.8	479.6
5. Other	927.6	1,029.7	1,246.5	1,521.7	1,831.3	2,170.7	2,638.3	3,021.0	3,203.8
B. Government current expenditures[b]	748.0	828.6	1,038.2	1,393.1	1,654.4	1,805.2	2,206.7	2,643.4	3,411.2
1. General expenditures	–	–	–	–	–	–	–	–	–
2. Development expenditures	–	–	–	–	–	–	–	–	–
C. Gross fixed domestic capital formation	1,031.2	1,101.7	1,440.5	1,942.1	2,181.1	2,757.7	2,926.2	2,394.1	1,934.2
1. Government fixed capital formation	–	125.5	135.2	156.0	–	–	–	–	–
2. Residential construction	337.1	346.9	472.1	686.7	725.7	865.6	974.3	781.3	528.5
3. Enterprise fixed capital formation	–	630.0	813.5	1,099.4	–	–	–	–	–
D. Changes in stocks	77.9	85.7	91.8	124.9	103.0	181.8	85.6	109.7	−66.3
E. Exports of goods and services[e]	569.0	731.0	880.0	1,395.0	1,719.0	1,864.0	2,113.0	2,513.0	2,909.0
F. Less: Imports of goods and services[f]	1,264.0	1,453.0	1,796.0	2,949.0	3,339.0	3,895.0	4,033.0	4,104.0	4,297.0
G. Gross Domestic Product	3,935.0	4,395.0	5,301.0	6,314.0	7,563.0	8,801.0	10,435.0	11,465.0	12,057.0
H. Less: Net factor payments abroad	26.0	26.0	54.0	84.0	39.0	50.0	56.0	81.0	123.0
I. Gross National Product	3,909.0	4,369.0	5,247.0	6,230.0	7,524.0	8,751.0	10,379.0	11,384.0	11,934.0

(*Continued*)

Table 1—*Continued*

[a] Including net consumption of foreigners in Israel.
[b] Excluding interest of the public sector.
[c] Dash indicates data not available.
[d] Including government enterprises (post office, railways, airports, municipal enterprises, ports) which are normally entered under Enterprise fixed capital formation.
[e] Exports f.o.b. excluding factor payments from abroad and including export subsidies.
[f] Imports c.i.f. excluding factor payments to abroad and including net taxes on imports.

Sources: Statistical Abstract of Israel, 1966, pp. 156, 157, 160, 161, 167–71; *Statistical Bulletin of Israel, Supplements,* XVIII, 1 (1967), pp. 18, 19, 21; *Israel's National Income and Expenditure (1950–1962),* Special series no. 153 (1964), pp. 32, 84, 85, 94, 95, 100. *Statistical Abstract of Israel, 1968,* pp. 138–45.

Table 2: Gross National Product
(1955 prices; I£ million)

	1950	1951	1952	1953	1954	1955	1956	1957	1958
Private consumption expenditure	935	1,140	1,225	1,268	1,458	1,576	1,720	1,841	2,028
Government current expenditure	275	326	308	322	376	432	622	528	541
Gross domestic capital formation	606	716	615	515	574	707	664	779	837
Exports of goods and services[a]	72	101	142	176	250	257	292	350	391
Total Use of Resources	1,888	2,283	2,290	2,281	2,658	2,972	3,298	3,498	3,797
Less: Imports of goods and services[b]	723	769	692	704	774	831	968	964	1,078
Gross Domestic Product	1,165	1,514	1,598	1,577	1,884	2,141	2,330	2,534	2,719
Less: Net factor payments abroad	17	19	13	20	17	15	12	17	23
Gross National Product	1,148	1,495	1,585	1,557	1,867	2,126	2,318	2,517	2,696

	1959	1960	1961	1962	1963	1964	1965	1966	1967
Private consumption expenditure	2,227	2,382	2,642	2,918	3,209	3,553	3,844	3,949	4,025
Government current expenditure	561	598	706	787	879	899	976	1,048	1,382
Gross domestic capital formation	915	947	1,126	1,252	1,302	1,594	1,565	1,290	953
Exports of goods and services[a]	516	653	757	887	1,019	1,083	1,171	1,314	1,457
Total Use of Resources	4,219	4,580	5,231	5,844	6,409	7,129	7,556	7,601	7,817
Less: Imports of goods and services[b]	1,153	1,324	1,642	1,893	2,028	2,302	2,320	2,300	2,372
Gross Domestic Product	3,066	3,256	3,589	3,951	4,381	4,827	5,236	5,301	5,445
Less: Net factor payments abroad	26	26	54	52	25	28	28	41	62
Gross National Product	3,040	3,230	3,535	3,899	4,356	4,799	5,208	5,260	5,383

[a] Including subsidies on exports.
[b] Including net taxes on imports.

Source: Statistical Abstract of Israel, 1964, p. 138; 1968, pp. 140, 141.

Table 3: General Government Current Receipts and Expenditures
(Current prices, I£ Million)

	1950	1951	1952	1953	1954	1955	1956	1957	1958
A. Income from property and entrepreneurship	2	7	11	11	15	26	34	51	58
B. Less: Interest on the public debt	3	3	10	16	26	35	40	49	59
C. Indirect taxes	52	79	97	150	212	289	345	467	553
1. On domestic production	–[a]	–	–	–	–	171	198	279	376
2. On imports	–	–	–	–	–	118	147	188	177
D. Direct taxes on corporations	3	4	3	12	20	37	38	43	51
E. Direct taxes on households and private nonprofit institutions	14	25	49	61	109	146	186	252	280
1. Contributions to national insurance	...[b]	...	2	3	21	39	52	65	72
2. Other[c]	14	25	47	58	88	107	134	187	208
F. Current transfers from households and private nonprofit institutions	5	5	7	9	12	17	21	25	29
G. Total current receipts	73	117	157	227	342	480	584	789	912
H. Consumption expenditure	92	131	197	250	320	432	682	625	677
I. Subsidies	–	7	...	27	11	63	66	105	124
1. On domestic production	–	–	...	–	–	30	33	67	74
2. On exports	–	–	...	...	...	3	8	26	41
3. On imports	–	–	...	–	–	30	25	12	9
J. Current transfers to households and private nonprofit institutions	19	22	23	33	45	59	70	100	128
K. Total current expenditure	111	160	220	310	376	554	818	830	929
L. Current surplus	–38	–43	–63	–83	–34	–74	–234	–41	–17

(*Continued*)

Table 3—*Continued*

	1959	1960	1961	1962	1963	1964	1965	1966
A. Income from property and entrepreneurship	81	89	101	122	152	178	216	265
B. Less: Interest on the public debt	78	97	121	191	269	330	358	384
C. Indirect taxes	668	760	975	1,087	1,223	1,446	1,599	1,767
1. On domestic production	424	493	634	721	850	980	1,071	1,256
2. On imports	244	267	341	366	373	466	528	511
D. Direct taxes on corporations	54	63	77	97	150	208	242	224
E. Direct taxes on households and private nonprofit institutions	304	355	416	517	654	801	1,020	1,233
1. Contributions to national insurance	82	105	127	145	162	180	251	321
2. Other[c]	222	250	289	372	492	621	769	912
F. Current transfers from households and private nonprofit institutions	38	46	56	69	80	93	113	150
G. Total current receipts	1,067	1,216	1,504	1,701	1,990	2,396	2,832	3,255
H. Consumption expenditure	754	836	1,038	1,393	1,654	1,805	2,207	2,643
I. Subsidies	152	197	223	172	183	228	258	325
1. On domestic production	78	88	73	98	133	153	176	203
2. On exports	67	105	148	44	31	34	43	95
3. On imports	7	4	2	30	19	41	39	27
J. Current transfers to households and private nonprofit institutions	158	194	235	304	364	429	570	718
K. Total current expenditure	1,064	1,227	1,496	1,869	2,201	2,462	3,035	3,686
L. Current surplus	3	−11	8	−168	−211	−66	−203	−431

(*Continued*)

Table 3—*Continued*

[a] Dash indicates data not available.

[b] Dots indicate no cases.

[c] Excluding absorption loan and compulsory saving which are defined as loans.

Sources: Central Bureau of Statistics, *Israel's National Income and Expenditure (1950–1962)*, Special series no. 153 (Jerusalem: Central Bureau of Statistics, 1964), pp. 20, 21; *Statistical Abstract, 1968*, pp. 154–55.

Table 4: Birth and Death Rates Per 1,000 Population

	Live Births			Deaths		
	Total	*Jews*	*Non-Jews*	*Total*	*Jews*	*Non-Jews*
1923–25		35.8			14.1	
1926–30		34.3			11.6	
1931–35		30.3			9.3	
1936–40		25.7			8.0	
1941–45		26.3			7.5	
1946		28.6			6.2	
1947		30.1			6.2	
1948		26.3			6.7[a]	
1949		30.0			6.8[a]	
1950	34.3	33.0	43.2	6.9	6.5	9.5
1951	33.8	32.7	46.5	6.6	6.4	8.8
1952	33.0	31.6	45.6	7.3	6.8	11.5
1953	32.1	30.2	48.4	6.7	6.3	9.7
1954	29.2	27.4	45.1	6.8	6.4	9.7
1955	29.2	27.2	46.0	6.1	5.8	8.6
1956	28.8	26.7	47.1	6.6	6.3	9.3
1957	28.1	26.0	46.7	6.5	6.2	9.4
1958	26.5	24.1	48.0	5.9	5.6	7.9
1959	26.7	24.3	47.4	5.9	5.8	6.9
1960	26.6	23.9	50.3	5.7	5.5	7.5
1961	25.1	22.5	49.3	5.8	5.7	7.3
1962	24.6	21.8	50.6	6.0	5.9	6.9
1963	25.0	22.0	48.8	6.1	6.0	6.3
1964	25.7	22.4	51.4	6.3	6.2	6.4
1965	25.8	22.6	50.7	6.3	6.4	6.1
1966	25.5	22.4	49.5	6.3	6.3	5.9
1967	24.2	21.5	44.9	6.6	6.6[a]	6.2

[a] Excluding wars.

Source: Statistical Abstract of Israel, 1963, p. 65; *1968,* pp. 53–55.

Table 5: Jewish Population by Age and Sex

	1948 Total	1948 Male	1954 Total	1954 Male	1959 Total	1959 Male	1964 Total	1964 Male
0-4	86,933	44,845	211,442	108,759	219,604	113,140	238,645	122,495
5-14	118,026	60,664	289,206	148,833	430,309	221,316	501,855	258,077
15-24	125,487	63,735	238,954	123,154	265,642	136,955	378,050	195,153
25-34	119,060	61,396	234,822	117,183	254,886	126,342	276,085	135,915
35-44	129,799	67,731	209,993	102,850	228,243	113,384	275,346	133,087
45-54	71,083	39,231	176,904	92,627	232,189	117,639	245,840	121,487
55-64	35,992	18,126	96,354	49,940	138,790	71,672	193,822	101,702
65-74	20,338	9,760	50,097	23,058	63,480	30,513	91,939	46,180
75+	7,887	3,730	18,237	8,417	25,698	11,571	37,595	17,107
Unknown	2,073	1,055	—	—	—	—	—	—
Total	716,678	370,273	1,526,009	774,821	1,858,841	942,532	2,239,177	1,131,203

Source: Statistical Abstract of Israel, 1962, p. 46, for the years 1948, 1954 and 1959; 1965, p. 40, for the year 1964.

Table 6: Non-Jewish Population by Age and Sex

	1955 Total	1955 Male	1959 Total	1959 Male	1964 Total	1964 Male
0–4	37,225	19,485	42,989	22,551	61,206	31,488
5–14	53,504	28,061	61,586	32,246	81,315	42,411
15–24	36,674	19,355	44,661	23,669	49,496	26,072
25–34	23,884	11,936	27,844	14,006	34,943	17,910
35–44	14,803	6,972	17,269	8,045	21,860	10,630
45–54	12,971	6,353	14,148	6,606	13,961	6,470
55–64	8,752	4,422	10,621	5,368	11,968	5,825
65–74	6,203	3,097	6,003	3,013	6,787	3,420
75+	4,540	1,990	4,723	2,197	4,849	2,386
Total	198,556	101,671	229,844	117,701	286,385	146,612

Source: Statistical Abstract of Israel, 1962, p. 49, for the years 1955 and 1959; *1966*, p. 39, for the year 1964.

Table 7: Regional Distribution of Population
(Thousands)

	Nov. 8, 1948		Dec. 31, 1954		Dec. 31, 1957		Dec. 31, 1964	
	Absolute	Percentage	Absolute	Percentage	Absolute	Percentage	Absolute	Percentage
Total	872.7	100.0	1,717.8	100.0	2,088.7	100.0	2,525.6	100.0
Northern District	144.0	16.8	285.7	16.6	303.3	15.8	397.0	15.7
Haifa District	175.1	20.5	285.4	16.6	359.2	17.2	418.1	16.6
Central District	122.3	14.3	358.5	20.9	400.1	19.1	459.9	18.2
Tel Aviv District	305.7	35.7	549.2	32.0	659.2	31.6	775.8	30.7
Jerusalem District	87.1	10.2	157.4	9.2	183.1	8.8	216.3	8.6
Southern District	21.4	2.5	81.7	4.7	156.8	7.5	258.5	10.2
Unknown[a]	17.1	—	—		—		—	

[a] Excluded in the calculation of percentages.

Source: Statistical Abstract, 1964, p. 17, for the year 1948; 1959/60, p. 12, for the year 1954; 1962, p. 37, for the year 1959; 1966, p. 23, for the year 1964.

Table 8: Distribution of Population by Size of Settlement

	Nov. 8, 1948	1954	1959	1964
Total	834,317	1,717,814	2,088,685	2,525,600
0–1,000	101,395	216,246	234,865	247,800
1,000–20,000	256,633	545,509	569,770	653,800
20,000–50,000	21,580	227,700	412,350	402,300
50,000+	421,665	707,927	849,000	1,185,900
Bedouin	15,912	20,432	22,700	31,700
Unknown	17,132	—	—	4,100

Source: Statistical Abstract of Israel, 1959/60, p. 20, for the years 1948, 1954, and 1959; *1965*, p. 28, for the year 1964.

Table 9: Illiteracy Level: 1961
(Percentage of population)

	Total	Jews	Non-Jews
14–24	12.1	8.3	35.6
25–34	15.7	12.1	51.9
35–44		12.1	
45–54	18.3	12.9	70.8
55–64		18.4	
65+	31.4	26.8	77.0
Total	15.7	12.0	51.0

Source: Central Bureau of Statistics, *Languages, Literacy and Educational Attainment*, Part I, Population and Housing Census, 1961, Publication no. 15 (Jerusalem, 1963), pp. 29, 49.

Table 10: Percentage of Given Age Groups
Enrolled in Schools: 1961

Age groups	
Jews	
14–19	53.1
20–24	9.0
24–29	3.0
Total	28.7
Non-Jews	
14–19	17.5
20–24	1.8
25–29	0.7
Total	8.3

Source: Central Bureau of Statistics, *Languages, Literacy and Educational Attainment*, Part I, Population and Housing Census, 1961, Publication no. 15 (Jerusalem, 1963), pp. 54, 81.

Table 11: Enrollments in Educational Institutions by Type of Institution

	1948–49		1954–55[a]		1958–59		1963–64	
	Total	Jewish	Total	Jewish	Total	Jewish	Total	Jewish
Educational System	134,887	127,470	364,739	339,332	517,153	483,493	635,831	584,246
Kindergartens	26,043	25,406[b]	56,315	54,543	78,499	73,746	87,385	80,652
Primary schools	97,899	91,133	257,186	234,333	370,356	342,445	436,199	393,159
Schools for handicapped children	...[c]	—[d]	3,897	3,897	6,393	6,393	10,604	10,597
Schools for working youth	...	–	11,350	11,350	11,138	11,070	5,221	5,116
Secondary schools	6,425	6,411	15,179	14,469	21,234	20,350	43,636	42,296
Secondary evening schools	...	–	2,393	2,393	3,255	3,255	5,066	5,066
Continuation classes	1,048	1,048	4,617	4,545	6,313	6,313	9,423	9,423
Vocational schools	2,002	2,002	5,839	5,839	8,668	8,668	21,028	20,862
Agricultural schools	...	–	4,535	4,535	5,220	5,220	7,390	7,336
Other postprimary schools	...	...	...	...	...	...	1,601[e]	1,565[e]
Preparatory classes to teachers training colleges	757	757	...	...	...	...	3,817	3,817
Teachers training colleges	713	713	3,428	3,428	6,077	6,034	4,461	4,357
Academic Institutions	1,635	1,635	7,171	7,171	11,050	11,050	15,309	15,309
Other Institutions	4,295	583	9,099	–	23,059	13,158	34,812	23,008
Total Education	140,817	129,688	381,009	346,503	551,262	507,702	685,952	622,563

[a] The period 1954–55 was used in lieu of 1953–54, since much of the data for the latter was not available.
[b] Mainly public kindergartens.
[c] Dots indicate no cases.
[d] Dash indicates data not available.
[e] Including only postprimary schools for part-time evening courses.

Source: Statistical Abstract of Israel, 1966, p. 587, for the periods 1948–49 and 1963–64; *1963,* p. 634, for the periods 1954–55 and 1958–59.

Table 12: Infant Mortality
(Percentage per 1,000 births)

	1926–30[a]	1936–40[a]	1949[a]	1954[a]	1959[a]	1964[a]
Total				38.8	30.6	28.2
Jews	95.0	59.5	51.7[b]	34.1	27.7	23.9
Non-Jews				61.2	43.8	42.6

[a] Excluding Bedouins.
[b] Excluding war casualties.

Source: Statistical Abstract of Israel, 1965, pp. 55–57.

Table 13: Per Capita Caloric Intake

	1949–50	1953–54	1958–59	1963–64
Cereals and cereal products	1,260	1,463	1,193	1,058
Potatoes and starches	98	78	82	77
Sugar and honey	184	231	319	359
Pulses, oilseeds, and nuts	62	73	83	98
Vegetables	65	69	69	64
Fruit	105	117	139	165
Meat	95	50	137	206
Eggs	61	51	74	89
Fish	58	25	19	16
Milk and milk products	197	236	225	209
Oils and fats	343	377	400	418
Miscellaneous	82	79	71	84
Total	2,610	2,849	2,811	2,843

Source: Statistical Abstract of Israel, 1966, p. 198, for the periods 1949–50, 1958–59 and 1963–64; 1963, p. 195, for the period 1953–54.

Table 14: Labor Force Behavior of the Male Population—Percentage
of Persons in Each Group in Labor Force

	1956	1960	1963	1965
Total for entire population	78.5	78.1	77.0	76.1
Jews	78.5	78.4	76.5	75.6
Immigrants from Europe-America	85.9	84.4	82.7	82.5
Ages 14–17	(38.5)	(16.5)	27.0	34.1
18–34	80.3	75.9	78.5	73.2
35–54	97.1	98.0	98.3	98.0
55–64	86.9	90.8	93.2	94.0
65 and over	41.3	43.5	40.3	48.0
Immigrants from Asia-Africa	74.9	77.2	76.0	77.2
Ages 14–17	53.7	36.6	41.6	46.3
18–34	82.1	83.3	81.3	80.5
35–54	92.8	94.5	94.6	94.5
55–64	57.8	71.0	78.1	84.0
65 and over	(15.9)	(26.5)	24.6	28.6
Native born	61.5	62.5	62.7	58.5
Ages 14–17	26.7	26.5	29.7	30.0
18–34	68.7	70.5	71.9	66.4
35–54	95.4	96.0	96.8	96.9
55 and over	n.a.	n.a.	n.a.	n.a.

Notes: Data for 1955 are as of November, while for later years it is the average of four surveys. Among native born 55 and over there are too few people for meaningful percentage. Numbers in ( ) have large sampling errors.

Sources: 1956, 1960: *Labour Force Surveys (1955–1961)*, Table 1 for total figures, Table 2 for Jews, Table 22 for all other data.
1963: *Labour Force Surveys (1963)*, Table 10.
1965: *Statistical Abstract of Israel, 1966*, pp. 291–99.

Table 15: Labor Force Behavior of the Female Population—Percentage
of Persons in Each Group in Labor Force

	1956	1960	1963	1965
Total for entire population	24.1	27.3	28.6	29.4
Jews	25.3	29.5	30.2	31.3
Immigrants from Europe-America	27.6	32.5	31.9	32.7
Ages 14–17	17.5	13.7	20.0	(27.5)
18–34	33.4	38.0	40.2	43.9
35–54	30.4	37.4	37.3	36.3
55–64	19.0	25.8	26.8	27.5
65 and over	5.9	10.9	9.1	(6.9)
Immigrants from Asia-Africa	18.5	21.8	24.0	25.7
Ages 14–17	41.3	32.2	36.1	38.1
18–34	21.5	28.1	30.7	33.6
35–54	14.4	18.1	20.8	21.2
55–64	5.9	7.6	6.5	(10.1)
65 and over	0.7	3.4	1.4	(1.3)
Native born	32.6	26.8	38.0	38.9
Ages 14–17	22.1	19.4	24.2	22.1
18–34	42.9	48.3	49.2	52.4
35–54	21.4	34.6	37.0	38.2
55 and over	n.a.	n.a.	n.a.	n.a.

Notes: See Table 14.

Sources: See Table 14.

Table 16: Total Employment of Labor Force by Industry Group

	November, 1955[a]		1959[b]		1964[b]	
	Number	Percentage	Number	Percentage	Number	Percentage
Agriculture, forestry, and fishing	102,200	17.4	110,400	16.3	109,900	12.9
Manufacture, mines, and quarrying	124,700	21.3	157,100	23.3	216,300	25.3
Construction and public works	54,300	9.3	63,600	9.4	87,000	10.2
Electricity, water, and sanitary services	11,900	2.0	15,900	2.4	16,200	1.9
Commerce, banking, and insurance	78,600	13.4	80,800	12.0	107,600	12.6
Transportation, storage, and communication	38,300	6.5	47,000	6.9	61,700	7.2
Services	171,400	29.3	197,900	29.3	253,600	29.7
Government and public administration	⎱ 123,300	21.1	54,100	8.0	64,000	7.5
Health, education, welfare, judiciary, etc.	⎰		93,300	13.8	122,600	14.4
Personal services and entertainment	48,100	8.2	50,500	7.5	67,000	7.8
Unknown	4,300	0.7	2,700	0.4	1,800	0.2
Total	585,700	100.0	675,400	100.0	854,100	100.0

[a] Figures are for the month of November only.
[b] Figures represent the average for the entire year. Those for 1964 represent a slightly different classification than that used in previous years.

Source: Statistical Abstract of Israel, 1964, pp. 260, 261, for the year 1955; *1959/1960*, p. 302, for the year 1959; *1966*, pp. 302, 303, for the year 1964.

Table 17: Employment of Labor Force by Occupation[a]

	November, 1955		1959		1964	
	Number	Percentage	Number	Percentage	Number	Percentage
Professional and technical workers	61,200	10.4	75,645	11.2	103,300	12.1
Administrative, managerial, and clerical workers	92,100	15.7	93,205	13.8	135,600	15.9
Merchants and salesmen	66,200	11.3	60,111	8.9	71,600	8.4
Agricultural workers	99,900	17.1	108,739	16.1	105,400	12.3
Transport and communication workers	34,600	5.9	30,393	4.5	42,800	5.0
Industrial and construction workers, craftsmen, and miners[b]	168,900	29.0	222,882	33.0	284,800	33.3
Service workers	61,200	10.4	84,425	12.5	103,000	12.1
Unknown	1,600	0.3	…	…	7,600	0.9
Total	585,700	100.0	675,400	100.0	854,100	100.0

[a] Figures for 1955 and 1959 have been compiled according to a classification which differs slightly from that for 1964.
[b] Includes unskilled.

Source: Statistical Abstract of Israel, 1965, pp. 316–17, for the year 1955; 1959/60, p. 304, for the year 1959; 1966, pp. 312–13, for the year 1964.

Table 18: Wages, Salaries, and Fringe Benefits
by Major Industrial Branch

	Average per man-day worked (I£)		Total (I£ million)	
	1959–60	*1964–65*[a]	*1959–60*	*1964–65*
Food (including beverages and tobacco)[b]	13.0	21.0	58.3	145.3
Textiles	12.7	19.2	45.0	124.4
Clothing	9.1	13.2	9.9	27.1
Wood, wood products, and furniture	11.6	19.6	25.3	67.4
Paper and paper products	13.0	24.1	8.6	18.8
Printing and publishing	14.6	24.7	23.1	54.0
Leather and leather products	12.5	17.4	9.1	17.6
Rubber and plastic products	14.5	22.9	11.9	34.2
Chemical and petroleum products[b]	17.6	29.6	34.4	67.2
Non-metallic mineral products	16.1	26.5	35.7	74.4
Diamond industry[c]	12.0	20.9	12.2	37.6
Basic metal industries	16.0	28.6	13.5	31.6
Metal products	12.3	21.0	33.0	73.2
Machinery	12.3	23.7	13.2	50.6
Electrical machinery and equipment	13.1	22.0	14.4	41.6
Transport equipment	13.8	25.1	43.5	124.9
Miscellaneous manufacturing	9.9	16.8	5.5	13.5
Mining and quarrying	18.8	36.1	14.0	37.3
Manufacturing	...	21.8	...	1,003.4
Total	13.4	22.1	410.6	1,040.7

[a] Provisional figures.
[b] Establishments engaged in production and distilling of edible oils were included in "chemical and petroleum products" in 1959–60 and in "food" in 1964–65.
[c] The coverage of this branch is incomplete because of its singular state of organization; estimates are therefore biased downwards.

Source: Statistical Abstract of Israel, 1963, p. 278, for the period 1959–60; 1966, p. 422, for the period 1964–65.

Table 19: Average Work Hours per Week by Economic Branch

	1960	1964
Agriculture, forestry, fishing	39.2	38.1
Manufacturing (industry, crafts, mining, quarrying)	41.9	42.7
Construction (including public works)	40.4	41.8
Electricity, water, and sanitary services	39.7	42.2
Commerce, banking, and insurance	45.3	44.7
Transport, storage, and communications	43.0	43.7
Services: Total	36.7	37.1
Public and business services	36.5	37.2
Personal services	37.4	36.7
All Employed Persons	40.2	40.7

Source: Statistical Abstract of Israel, 1966, p. 309.

Table 20: Industrial Production Indexes
(Base: 1958 = 100)

Year	Total	Manufacturing	Mining and Quarrying
1955	81	85	36
1956	81	84	52
1957	91	92	79
1958	100	100	100
1959	114	113	132
1960	129	128	156
1961	149	148	172
1962	169	168	184
1963	193	192	220
1964	220	218	253
1965	242	239	314
1966	245	242	331
1967	237	234	313

Source: Statistical Abstract of Israel, 1963, p. 284, for the years 1955–62; 1964,
p. 370, for the year 1963; *1968*, p. 374, for the years, 1964–67.

Table 21: Volume of Production of Major Industrial Products

	Unit[a]	1949	1954	1959	1964
Mining and quarrying					
Salt (marketing)	tons	9,300	20,636	33,988	42,555
Quartz sand (marketing)	tons		11,541	19,991	41,739
Ball and fire clay	tons		8,381	19,841	34,554
Food					
Flour[b]	1,000 tons	96.8	252.0	247	245
Natural citrus juice[c]	1,000 L		2,491	13,654	40,175
Citrus fruit drinks	1,000 L		9,632	13,321	39,939
Pasteurized milk	1,000 L		–[d]	80,618	107,848
Refined sugar	tons[e]		...[f]	24,334	36,940
Refined oils	1,000 L		14,219	25,393	31,578
Tobacco Products					
Tombac	kg		37,188	30,841	47,225
Snuff	kg		28,219	38,238	43,472
Textiles					
Cotton yarn	tons		–	9,171	23,313
Cotton fabrics	tons		–	6,476	10,748
Wood					
Plywood	m³		15,689	35,206	88,323
Paper and cardboard					
Writing and printing paper	tons		–	11,992	18,796
Other paper	tons		–	3,499	13,401
Rubber Products					
Tires	tons		3,778	8,018	13,740
Chemical and petroleum products					
Ammonia	tons		...	19,041	31,126
Ammonium sulphate	tons		...	64,712	77,750
Sulphuric acid (100 percent)	1,000 tons		44	119	156
Superphosphates (16 percent)	1,000 tons	6[g]	71	94	107
Fuel oil	1,000 tons		–	523	1,261
Gas oil	1,000 tons		–	305	804
Non-metallic mineral products					
Cement	1,000 tons	241	566	781	1,260

[a] Metric tons.
[b] Including flour used for baking matzot.
[c] Pasteurized juice (with or without sugar) and preserved natural juice included.
[d] Dash indicates data not available.
[e] For 1959; 1,000 L for 1964.
[f] Dots indicate no cases.
[g] 1949–50.

Sources: United Nations, *Statistical Yearbook, 1956,* 8th issue (Statistical Office of the U.N., Department of Economic and Social Affairs: New York, 1956), pp. 174, 197, 218, 236, 242, 253, for the year 1949; *Statistical Abstract of Israel, 1963,* pp. 294–99, for the years 1954 and 1959; *1965,* p. 439, and *1966,* pp. 442–46, for the year 1964.

Table 22: Electric Power Production and Consumption
(Millions of kilowatt-hours)

	1949	*1954*	*1959*	*1963*
Production	. . .	1,076	1,968	3,153
Consumption	329	896	1,665	2,692
Industry	97	201	365	1,037
Irrigation	65	270	630⎫	
Other uses	167	425	670⎭	1,655

Source: Statistical Abstract of Israel, 1958/59, p. 160, for the year 1949; *1961*, p. 229, for the years 1954 and 1959; *1964*, p. 380, for the year 1963.

Table 23: Consumer Price Indexes

	Jan.	Feb.	March	April	May	June	July	Aug.	Sept.	Oct.	Nov.	Dec.	Average
							September 1951 = 100						
1948	77	79	82	86	89	91	93	94	94	93	96	96	89
1949	97	97	97	98	94	92	90	89	87	85	85	84	91
1950	84	84	84	84	84	83	83	84	85	85	86	89	85
1951	90	92	93	94	96	95	96	98	100	103	105	107	97
1952	113	120	132	144	150	157	162	165	169	173	175	178	153
1953	181	182	184	187	191	197	200	201	205	207	208	212	196
1954	214	216	217	217	218	214	217	222	227	227	228	228	220
1955	228	228	229	230	230	232	233	231	239	238	236	239	233
1956	238	239	244	246	249	249	244	247	260	259	248	250	248
1957	254	259	261	265	270	258	264	269	268	268	267	263	264
1958	267	269	268	272	276	267	274	274	280	280	273	274	273
							January 1959 = 100						
1959	100.0	100.8	100.9	100.4	104.3	99.3	98.0	97.9	100.1	101.9	102.1	101.6	100.6
1960	101.2	101.4	102.4	101.2	103.2	100.8	101.3	101.5	104.1	106.2	105.8	105.1	102.9
1961	107.5	106.6	106.8	106.7	114.3	110.4	108.0	107.1	110.7	112.2	113.1	114.6	109.8
1962	115.0	115.6	118.2	120.3	119.1	117.5	118.5	119.9	122.7	124.0	124.9	126.3	120.2
1963	126.3	126.3	126.3	124.9	129.0	127.9	128.0	125.9	128.4	129.4	131.9	132.6	128.1
1964	133.6	133.6	133.4	132.2	136.7	132.9	134.7	133.4	134.4	135.9	137.1	138.5	134.7
							1964 = 100						
1965	103.7	104.2	106.3	107.2	109.4	108.9	108.1	106.9	108.3	109.4	110.0	110.1	107.7
1966	111.5	112.7	114.6	116.7	117.2	116.8	117.1	115.8	117.5	118.5	117.9	118.7	116.3
1967	118.6	117.5	118.0	119.8	120.1	118.8	117.9	116.8	116.7	117.6	118.1	118.9	118.2

Note: The Index for January 1959 based on the September 1951 base was 275.3.

Source: Statistical Abstract of Israel, 1968, p. 231.

Table 24: Consumer's Price Index by Economic Branches

	Agricultural produce	Industrial production	Electricity and water	Communication, transport, and posts	Services
1967	149.4	135.8	137.9	198.1	212.3
1966	144.1	133.4	128.6	193.5ª	207.3
1965	139.5	125.4	119.4	174.8ª	188.3
1964	124.8	119.7	113.5	152.7	171.3
1963	123.4	118.2	113.5	150.7	149.3
1962	118.2	114.1	107.2	137.9	131.8
1961	111.6	106.6	102.7	123.8	113.3
1960	104.6	100.6	100.6	110.5	105.3
1959	103.9	99.2	99.0	100.1	101.6

ª Only transport and posts.

Source: Statistical Abstract of Israel, 1964, p. 234; 1965, p. 280; 1967, p. 242, 1968, p. 234.

Table 25: Size of Manufacturing Establishments

Number of employees	1959		1963–64	
	Number	Percentage	Number	Percentage
1–4	4,483	49.1	4,604	44.1
5–9	2,366	25.9	2,789	26.7
10–14	748	8.2	846	8.1
15–24	608	6.7	844	8.1
25–49	516	5.6	750	7.2
50–99	247	2.7	326	3.1
100–299	123	1.3	198	2.0
300 and over	45	0.5	73	0.7
Total	9,136	100.0	10,430	100.0

Source: Statistical Abstract of Israel, 1961, p. 218, for the year 1959; 1965, p. 415, for the period 1963–64.

Table 26: The Supply of Money
(I£ million)

	Currency in circulation	Demand deposits of the public and other credit balances	Total money supply
1949	38	86	123
1950	56	113	170
1951	82	143	224
1952	102	146	247
1953	120	170	290
1954[a]	141	221	362
1954[b]	141	188	328
1955	165	231	395
1956	201	264	465
1957	230	328	558
1958	249	393	642
1959	267	457	724
1960	287	532	820
1961	340	631	970
1962	380	746	1,126
1963	491	983	1,474
1964	582	1,097	1,679
1965	644	1,181	1,826
1966	712	1,250	1,963
1967	912	1,432	2,344

Note: For the year 1954, *a* and *b* indicate different definitions for the various monetary series before and after that year.

Source: Statistical Abstract of Israel, 1964, pp. 438, 439; *1968,* p. 461.

Table 27: Time Deposits
(I£ million)

Year	Yearly average
Old Series	
1949	5.8
1950	8.5
1951	11.3
1952	11.7
1953	13.7
1954	17.1
New Series	
1954	51.3
1955	63.1
1956	80.8
1957	101.3
1958	123.8
1959	139.6
1960	162.1
1961	189.6
1962	176.2
1963	197.3
1964	217.2
1965	241.2
1966	293.4

Note: The old series grouped deposits in foreign currency with deposits in Israeli currency; the new series does not. In the old series, deposits held as security for liabilities were grouped with demand deposits; in the new series, with time deposits. Finally, the old series included only those fixed time deposits maturing within one year.

Source: Statistical Abstract of Israel, 1967, p. 461.

Table 28: The Import Surplus and Its Financing, 1950–67
(Millions of dollars)

	Imports	Exports	Import surplus	Net unilateral transfers	Net capital transfers Total	Net capital transfers Long term	Net capital transfers Short term	Errors and omissions
1950	328	46	282	90	119	68	51	73
1951	426	67	359	137	165	133	32	57
1952	393	86	307	191	116	115	1	0
1953	365	102	263	173	75	69	6	15
1954	373	105	238	261	1	71	−70	−24
1955	427	144	283	210	76	76	0	−3
1956	535	178	357	241	100	78	22	16
1957	557	222	335	245	79	70	9	11
1958	569	235	334	264	66	67	−1	4
1959	602	287	315	251	55	80	−25	9
1960	696	359	337	311	41	101	−60	−15
1961	857	425	432	346	104	176	−72	−18
1962	958	503	455	331	98	203	−105	26
1963	1,011	607	404	347	73	171	−98	−16
1964	1,225	656	569	351	227	275	−48	−9
1965	1,271	750	521	341	219	248	−29	−39
1966	1,277	832	445	291	180	185	−5	−26
1967	1,356	919	437	522	29	256	−227	−114

Sources: 1950–65, Halevi and Klinov-Malul, pp. 141, 155.
1966–67, *Statistical Abstract of Israel*, 1968, pp. 186–88.

Bibliography

ARTICLES AND ESSAYS

Ablin, Richard. "Household Saving in Israel." *Bulletin of the Oxford University Institute of Economics and Statistics* 28 (May 1966): 131–43.

Arrow, Kenneth, Hollis B. Chenery, Bagicha Minhas, and Robert M. Solow. "Capital-Labor Substitution and Economic Efficiency." *Review of Economics and Statistics* 43 (Aug. 1961): 225–50.

Bachi, R. "Immigration to Israel." In *Economics of International Migration*, ed. B. Thomas, pp. 313–44. London: Macmillan, 1958.

Baer, Werner, and Michel Herve. "Employment and Industrialization in Developing Countries." *Quarterly Journal of Economics* 80 (Feb. 1966): 88–107.

Balassa, Bela. "Tariff Protection in Industrial Countries: An Evaluation." *Journal of Political Economy* 73 (Dec. 1965): 573–94.

Barkai, Haim. "The Public, Histadrut and Private Sectors in the Israel Economy." *Sixth Report, 1961–63*. Jerusalem: Falk Project for Economic Research in Israel, 1964.

Berglas, Eitan. "Investment and Technological Change." *Journal of Political Economy* 73 (Apr. 1965): 173–80.

Black, Albert G. "Reflections upon Israel's Recent Agricultural Development and Its Relationship to General Development." *Symposium on the Challenge of Development,* Hebrew University, 1957 (Jerusalem: 1958), pp. 199–212.

Bowen, William G. "Assessing the Economic Contribution of Education: An Appraisal of Alternative Approaches." *Higher Education,* Report of the Committee under the Chairmanship of Lord Robbins, 1961–1963. London: HMSO, 1963

Brown, E. Cary. "Analysis of Consumption Taxes in Terms of the 40 (Mar. 1950): 74–89.

Theory of Income Determination." *American Economic Review*

Bruno, Michael. "A Programming Model for Israel." In *The Theory and Design of Economic Development,* ed. I. Adelman and E. Thorbecke, pp. 327–54. Baltimore: The Johns Hopkins Press, 1966.

———. "Optimal Patterns of Trade and Development." *Review of Economics and Statistics* 49 (Nov. 1967): 545–54.

———. "Estimation of Factor Contribution to Growth under Structural Disequilibrium." *International Economic Review* 9 (Feb. 1968): 49–62.

Bruton, Henry. "Productivity Growth in Latin America." *American Economic Review* 57 (Dec. 1967): 1099–1116.

Chenery, Hollis. "Patterns of Industrial Growth." *American Economic Review* 50 (Sept. 1960): 624–54.

Chenery, Hollis B., and M. Bruno. "Development Alternatives in an Open Economy: The Case of Israel." *Economic Journal* 62 (Mar. 1962): 79–103.

Chenery, Hollis B., Shuntaro Shishido, and Tsunehiko Watanabe. "The Pattern of Japanese Economic Growth. 1914–1954." *Econometrica* 30 (Jan. 1962): 98–139.

Chenery, Hollis B., and A. Strout. "Foreign Assistance and Economic Development." *American Economic Review* 56 (Sept. 1966): 679–733.

David, Paul A. "Measuring Real Net Output: A Proposed Index." *Review of Economics and Statistics* 48 (Nov. 1966): 419–23.

Domar, Evsey D. "On Measurement of Technological Change." *Economic Journal* 71 (Dec. 1961): 709–29.

Domar, Evsey D., et al. "Economic Growth and Productivity in the U.S., Canada, United Kingdom, Germany and Japan in the Post-War Period." *Review of Economics and Statistics* 46 (Feb. 1964): 33–40.

Dorrance, Graeme S. "The Effect of Inflation on Economic Development." In *Conference on Inflation and Economic Growth in Latin America,* ed. Werner Baer and Isaac Kerstenetzky, pp. 37–89. Homewood, Ill.: Richard D. Irwin, 1964.

Easterlin, Richard E. "Israel's Development: Past Accomplishments and Future Problems." *Quarterly Journal of Economics* 75 (Feb. 1961): 63–86.

Eckaus, Richard. "The Factor Proportions Problem in Underdeveloped Countries." *American Economic Review* 45 (Sept. 1955): 539–65.

Emery, Robert F. "The Korean Interest Rate Reform of September, 1965." Mimeographed, Board of Governors, Federal Reserve System, October, 1966.

Geary, R. "The Concept of Net Volume of Output, with Special Reference to Irish Data." *Journal of the Royal Statistical Society* 107, pts. 2–4 (1944): 251–59.

Ginor, Fanny. "The Impact of Capital Imports on the Structure of Developing Countries." *Kyklos* 22, fasc. 1 (1969): 104–23.

Goode, R. "Reconstruction of Foreign Tax Systems." *Proceedings of the 44th Annual Conference on Taxation, 1951.* Sacramento, Calif.: National Tax Association, 1951.

Griliches, Zvi. "Research Expenditures, Education and the Aggregate Agricultural Production Function." *American Economic Review* 54 (Dec. 1964): 961–74.

————. "The Sources of Measured Productivity Growth: U.S. Agriculture 1940–1960." *Journal of Political Economy* 71 (Aug. 1963): 331–46.

Haldi, John, and David Whitcomb. "Economies of Scale in Industrial Plants." *Journal of Political Economy* 75 (Aug. 1967): 373–85.

Hanoch, Giora. "Income Differentials in Israel." *Fifth Report, 1959–1961.* Jerusalem: Falk Project for Economic Research in Israel, 1961.

Harberger, Arnold. "Using the Resources at Hand More Effectively." *American Economic Review* 49 (May 1959): 134–46.

Hill, T. P. "Growth and Investment According to International Comparisons." *Economic Journal* 74 (June 1964): 287–304.

Hinrichs, Harley. "Determinants of Government Revenue Shares among Less Developed Countries." *Economic Journal* 75 (Sept. 1965): 546–56.

Houthakker, Hendrik. "On Some Determinants of Saving in Developed and Underdeveloped Countries." In *Problems in Economic Development,* ed. E. A. G. Robinson, pp. 212–24. London: Macmillan, 1965.

Jorgenson, Dale. "The Embodiment Hypothesis." *Journal of Political Economy* 74 (Feb. 1966): 1–17.

Keesing, Donald. "Labor Skills and Comparative Advantage." *American Economic Review* 56 (May 1966): 249–58.

Kleiman, Ephraim. "The Place of Manufacturing in the Growth of the Israel Economy." *Journal of Development Studies* 3 (Apr. 1967): 226–48.

Kreinin, Mordecai. "Windfall Income and Consumption—Additional Evidence." *American Economic Review* 51 (June 1961): 388–90.

Lansing, John B., and Harold S. Lydall. "An Anglo-American Comparison of Personal Saving." *Bulletin of the Oxford Institute of Economics and Statistics* 22 (Aug. 1960): 225–58.

Leibenstein, Harvey. "Allocative Efficiency vs. 'X' Efficiency." *American Economic Review* 56 (June 1966): 392–415.

Lewis, Stephen R., Jr. "Effects of Trade Policy on Domestic Relative Prices: Pakistan, 1951–64." *American Economic Review* 58 (Mar. 1968): 60–78.

Lithwick, Nathan H., George Post, and T. K. Rymes. "Postwar Production Relationships in Canada." In *The Theory and Empirical Analysis of Production*, ed. M. Brown, pp. 139–257. New York: National Bureau of Economic Research, 1967.

Lutz, Vera C. "The Growth Process in a Dual Economic System." *Banca Nazionale del Lavoro, Quarterly Review*, no. 46 (Sept. 1958): 279–324.

Massell, Benton. "A Disaggregated View of Technical Change." *Journal of Political Economy* 69 (Dec. 1961): 547–57.

Merrill, William C., and Norman Schneider. "Government Firms in Oligopoly Industries: A Short Run Analysis." *Quarterly Journal of Economics* 80 (Aug. 1966): 400–12.

Nelson, Richard R. "A 'Diffusion' Model of International Productivity Differences in Manufacturing Industry." *American Economic Review* 58 (Dec. 1968): 1219–48.

———, Richard R. "Aggregate Production Functions and Medium Range Growth Projections." *American Economic Review* 54 (Sept. 1964): 575–606.

———. "Full Employment Policy and Economic Growth." *American Economic Review* 56 (Dec. 1966): 1178–92.

Patinkin, Don. "Multiple Plant Firms, Cartels, and Imperfect Competition." *Quarterly Journal of Economics* 61 (Feb. 1947): 173–205.

Rosen, S. "The Kibbutz Movement." *Hedim* (July 1958).

Samuelson, Paul A., and Robert M. Solow. "Analytical Aspects of Anti-inflation Policy." *American Economic Review* 50 (May 1962): 177–94.

Soligo, Ronald, and Joseph Stern. "Tariff Protection, Import Substitution and Investment Efficiency." *Pakistan Development Review* 5, no. 2 (1965): 249–70.

Solow, Robert M. "Technical Progress, Capital Formation and Economic Growth." *American Economic Review* 52 (May 1962): 76–86.

Tanzi, Vito. "Personal Income Taxation in Latin America: Obstacles and Possibilities." *National Tax Journal* (June 1966): 156–62.

BOOKS

Anderson, Charles W. *Politics and Economic Change in Latin America*. Princeton, N.J.: Van Nostrand, 1967.

Baharal, U. *The Effect of Mass Immigration on Wages in Israel.* Jerusalem: Falk Project for Economic Research in Israel, 1965.

Barclay, George W. *Techniques of Population Analysis.* New York: Wiley, 1958.

Bruno, Michael. *Interdependence, Resource Use and Structural Change in Israel.* Jerusalem: Bank of Israel, 1962.

Darin-Drabkin, Haim. *Paterns of Cooperative Agriculture in Israel.* Tel-Aviv: Israel Institute for Books, 1962.

Denison, Edward. *The Sources of Economic Growth in the United States and the Alternatives Before Us.* New York: Committee for Economic Development, 1962.

Díaz Alejandro, Carlos F. *Essays on the Economic History of the Argentine Republic.* New Haven: Yale University Press, 1970.

Eisenstadt, S. N. *Israeli Society.* New York: Basic Books, 1968.

Fei, John, and Gustav Ranis. *The Development of the Labor Surplus Economy: Theory and Policy.* Homewood, Ill.: Richard D. Irwin, 1964.

Gaathon, A. L. *Capital Stock, Employment and Output in Israel, 1950–1959.* Jerusalem: Bank of Israel, Research Department, 1961.

———. *Economic Productivity in Israel, 1950–65.* New York: Praeger, 1970.

———. *Survey of Israel's Economy, 1951.* Jerusalem: Central Bureau of Statistics and Falk Project for Economic Research in Israel, 1959.

Garfunkel, R., ed. *The Role of Cooperation in Rural Development.* Papers presented to the International Symposium. Tel-Aviv: Gvil-Press, 1966.

Halevi, Nadav, and Ruth Klinov-Malul. *The Economic Development of Israel.* New York: Praeger, 1968.

Harbison, F., and C. Myers. *Education, Manpower and Economic Growth.* New York: McGraw-Hill, 1966.

Hovne, Avner. *The Labour Force in Israel.* Jerusalem: Falk Project for Economic Research in Israel, 1961.

Johansen, Leif. *A Multisectoral Model of Economic Growth.* Amsterdam: North Holland, 1960.

Kanovsky, Eliyahu. *The Economy of the Israeli Kibbutz.* (Cambridge: Harvard University Press, 1966.

Kleiman, Ephraim. "The Structure of Israel Manufacturing Industries." Mimeographed. Jerusalem: Falk Project for Economic Research in Israel, 1969.

Klinov-Malul, Ruth. *The Profitability of Investment in Education in Israel.* Jerusalem: Falk Institute for Economic Research in Israel, 1966.

Kuznets, Simon. *Six Lectures on Economic Growth.* New York: Free Press of Glencoe, 1959.

Lubell, Harold. *Israel's National Expenditure, 1950–1954.* Jerusalem: Falk Project for Economic Research in Israel, 1958.

Mandelbaum, Moshe, and Haim Roet. "Minutes of the Knessett, 1953." Unpublished manuscript. (In Hebrew.)

Morag, Amotz. *Taxes and Inflation.* New York: Random House, 1965.

Mundlak, Yair. *Long-Term Projections of Supply and Demand for Agricultural Products in Israel.* Jerusalem: Falk Project for Economic Research in Israel, 1964.

Musgrave, Richard A. *The Theory of Public Finance.* New York: McGraw-Hill, 1959.

Ofer, Gus. *The Service Industries in a Developing Economy: Israel as a Case Study.* New York: Praeger, 1967.

Patinkin, Don. *The Israel Economy: The First Decade.* Jerusalem: Falk Project for Economic Research in Israel, 1960.

Rubner, Alex. *The Economy of Israel.* London: Frank Cass, 1960.

Safran, Nadav. *The United States and Israel.* Cambridge: Harvard University Press, 1963.

Shahar, H. Ben. *Interest Rates and the Cost of Capital in Israel, 1950–1962.* Basel: Kyklos-Verlag, 1965.

Sicron, Moshe. *Immigration to Israel: 1948–1953.* Jerusalem: Falk Project for Economic Research in Israel, 1957.

Szereszewski, Robert. *Essays on the Structure of the Jewish Economy in Palestine and Israel.* Jerusalem: Falk Institute for Economic Research in Israel, 1968.

PUBLICATIONS OF CENTRAL BUREAU OF STATISTICS

Central Bureau of Statistics. *Statistical Abstract of Israel.* Jerusalem: Government Press. Annual issues.

———. *Demographic Characteristics of the Population.* Part III: *First Results from Stage "B" of the Census.* Census Publication no. 13. Jerusalem, 1963.

———. *Families' Expenditure Surveys (1950/51; 1956/57; 1959/60).* Special Publication Series no. 148. Jerusalem, 1963.

———. *Industry and Crafts Surveys (1955–1960).* Special Series no. 156. Jerusalem, 1964.

———. *Industry and Crafts Survey (1964).* Special Series no. 219. Jerusalem, 1967.

———. *Labour Force.* Part I: *Labour Force Characteristics and Employed Persons, by Economic Branch, Occupation, and Employment*

Status—Data from Stage "B" of the Census. Census Publication no. 9. Jerusalem, 1963.

———. *Labour Force.* Part II: *Labour Force Characteristics and Employed Persons by Educational Attainment and Literacy—Data from Stage "B" of the Census.* Publication no. 21. Jerusalem, 1964.

———. *Labour Force.* Part IV: *Occupation Abroad.* Census Publication no. 27. Jerusalem, 1965.

———. *Israel's National Income and Expenditure (1950–1962).* Special Series no. 153. Jerusalem, 1964.

———. *Labour Force Survey (June 1956).* Special Series no. 68. Jerusalem, March 1958.

———. *Labour Force Surveys (1955–1961).* Special Series no. 162. Jerusalem, 1964.

———. *Labour Force Surveys (1962).* Special Series no. 162. Jerusalem, 1964.

———. *Labour Force Surveys (1963).* Special Series no. 176. Jerusalem, 1965.

———. *Saving Survey, 1963/64.* Special Series no. 239. Jerusalem, 1967.

OTHER GOVERNMENTAL PUBLICATIONS

Bank of Israel. *Annual Reports* and *Bulletins.*

Berger, L., ed. *The Israel Yearbook.* Various issues. Israel: Israel Yearbook Publications.

Bruno, Michael. "The Optimal Selection of Export Promoting and Import Substituting Projects." *Planning the External Sector: Techniques, Problems and Policies.* New York: United Nations, 1967.

Economic Appraisal of a Project for Citric Acid Plant in Israel. Jerusalem: Industrial Advisory Group, 1959.

Industrialization of the Development Areas. Jerusalem: Ministry of Commerce and Industry, 1965. (In Hebrew.)

Israel Economic Bulletin. Various issues. Jerusalem: Ministry of Commerce and Industry.

Israel's Industrial Future. Outlook, 1960–1965. Jerusalem: Ministry of Commerce and Industry, 1961.

Memorandum on Economic Evaluation of Industrial Projects. Jerusalem: Ministry of Commerce and Industry, 1960.

Programme for Israel's Industrial Development. Second Outlook, 1965–1970. Jerusalem: Ministry of Commerce and Industry, n.d.

United Nations Technical Assistance Programme. *Revenue Administration and Policy in Israel.* New York, 1953. *Second Report,* New

York, 1955. *Third Report,* New York, 1958. (UNTAA/ST/TAA/K/Israel/1, 4, 5.)

————. *Yearbook of National Account Statistics, 1966.* Department of Economic and Social Affairs. New York: United Nations, 1967.

U.S. Department of Commerce. Bureau of the Census. *United States Census of Population: 1950,* vol. 2, *Population,* pt. 1.

Index

Economic Growth Center Book Publications

*Werner Baer, *Industrialization and Economic Development in Brazil* (1965).

Werner Baer and Isaac Kerstenetzky, eds., *Inflation and Growth in Latin America* (1964).

*Bela A. Balassa, *Trade Prospects for Developing Countries* (1964).

Carlos F. Díaz Alejandro, *Essays on the Economic History of the Argentine Republic* (1970).

*John C. H. Fei and Gustav Ranis, *Development of Labor Surplus Economy: Theory and Policy* (1964).

*Gerald K. Helleiner, *Peasant Agriculture, Government, and Economic Growth in Nigeria* (1966).

*Lawrence R. Klein and Kazushi Ohkawa, eds., *Economic Growth: The Japanese Experience since the Meiji Era* (1968).

*A. Lamfalussy, *The United Kingdom and the Six* (1963).

*Markos J. Mamalakis and Clark W. Reynolds, *Essays on the Chilean Economy* (1965).

*Donald C. Mead, *Growth and Structural Change in the Egyptian Economy* (1967).

*Richard Moorsteen and Raymond P. Powell, *The Soviet Capital Stock* (1966).

Howard Pack, *Structural Change and Economic Policy in Israel* (1971).

*Frederic L. Pryor, *Public Expenditures in Communist and Capitalist Nations* (1968).

Gustav Ranis, ed., *Government and Economic Development* (1971).

Clark W. Reynolds, *The Mexican Economy: Twentieth-Century Structure and Growth* (1970).

*Lloyd G. Reynolds and Peter Gregory, *Wages, Productivity, and Industrialization in Puerto Rico* (1965).

*Donald R. Snodgrass, *Ceylon: An Export Economy in Transition* (1966).

* Available from Richard D. Irwin, Inc., 1818 Ridge Rd., Homewood, Ill. 60430. All others available from Yale University Press, 92A Yale Station, New Haven, Conn. 06520.